India's Scheduled Areas

This volume explores the complexities of governance, law, and politics in India's Scheduled Areas. The Scheduled Areas (SAs) are those parts of the country which have been identified by the Fifth and Sixth Schedule of the Constitution of India and are inhabited predominantly by tribal communities or Scheduled Tribes. SAs are often identified by their geographical isolation, primitive economies, and relatively egalitarian and closely knit society. Irrespective of the constitutional provision for governance and a mandate of devolution of power in terms of funds, functions, and functionaries, the backwardness of these areas have remained a challenge.

This volume attempts to explore the reasons behind the disregard for legal and institutional mechanism designed for the SAs. It examines the role of the state in the neoliberal era on fund allocation and utilisation, the governance of land and forest resources, and the ineffectiveness of the existing administrative structures and processes. It also looks into the interpretations of law by the judiciary while dealing with community rights vis-à-vis the state's prerogative of bringing development to the regions, and how development concerns are addressed in the name of 'good governance' by various stakeholders.

Comprehensive and topical, this volume will be useful for scholars and researchers of political studies, development studies, developmental economics, sociology and social anthropology, and for policy makers.

Varsha Bhagat-Ganguly is former Professor at the Centre for Rural Studies, LBSNAA, Mussorie and the Nirma University, Ahmedabad, India. As fellow of Indian Institute of Advance Study, Shimla, she researched on protest movements in Gujarat. She has worked as a researcher, an academician, and a development practitioner; her areas of interest include the land question, collective action for social justice, research methodology, and Gujarat. Of 14 publications, the recent ones are on protest movements in Gujarat (2015), land rights in India (2016, 2018), and on land titling in India (2017). Her forthcoming publications are on the land question in neoliberal India and e-waste management in India. She has also edited and contributed to various academic journals of repute.

Sujit Kumar is affiliated with St. Joseph's College, Department of Political Science, Bengaluru, India. His areas of research interest include Adivasi politics, political economy, political thought, and Indian politics. He has studied the different aspects of Adivasi society, particularly in context of land acquisition. He has published articles in journals like *Studies in Indian Politics, Studies in Humanities and Social Sciences, Economic and Political Weekly, Seminar,* and *Journal of Adivasi and Indigenous Studies*.

India's Scheduled Areas

Untangling Governance, Law and Politics

Edited by Varsha Bhagat-Ganguly and Sujit Kumar

Routledge
Taylor & Francis Group
LONDON AND NEW YORK

First published 2020 by Routledge

2 Park Square, Milton Park, Abingdon, Oxon, OX14 4RN
605 Third Avenue, New York, NY 10017

Routledge is an imprint of the Taylor & Francis Group, an informa business

First issued in paperback 2020

British Library Cataloguing-in-Publication Data
A catalogue record for this book is available from the British Library

Library of Congress Cataloging-in-Publication Data
A catalog record for this book has been requested

ISBN: 978-1-138-58372-6 (hbk)
ISBN: 978-0-367-78511-6 (pbk)

Typeset in Sabon
by Apex CoVantage, LLC

To all the inhabitants of India's Scheduled Areas and their well-being

Contents

Illustrations

Map

Figures

Tables

Box

Contributors

Chandra Bhushan Kumar is an Indian Administrative Service officer with 23 years of working in areas of public policy and governance. As a district administrator, he served in the tribal-dominated areas of Arunachal Pradesh and Andaman and Nicobar Islands wherein specific insights on administering scheduled areas were acquired. A Mathematics and Law graduate, he also has a Master's in Public Policy from Syracuse University and completed his PhD in Human Geography from Aberystwyth University, United Kingdom, wherein he examined the water governance issues of Delhi megacity. He is currently serving as Deputy Election Commissioner at Election Commission of India.

Sonali Ghosh is an Indian Forest Service officer with 18 years of work experience in the field of forest and wildlife conservation in India. As part of her job, she has worked as a field manager in country's finest Protected Areas such as Kaziranga and Manas. She has travelled extensively and written about forest and people's livelihood issues in northeast India. She holds a dual master's degree in Wildlife Science and Forestry and a PhD degree in Geography from Aberystwyth University, United Kingdom. A WWF-PATA Bagh Mitra awardee, she has also served as a Scientist (on secondment) at the UNESCO Category 2 Centre on World Natural Heritage Management and Training for Asia and the Pacific Region at Wildlife Institute of India, Dehradun. She is currently serving as the Director of the Swachh Bharat Mission at the Government of India.

Richard Hemraj Toppo is a PhD student at the International Institute of Social Studies, The Hague. His research focuses on the Adivasi groups' interaction with the state and the Maoists in Jharkhand, towards realising their (Adivasi) rights and demands. The research aims to understand the processes of social movement when situated within the context of conflict.

Emma Jane Lord is a PhD candidate at the Centre for the Study of the Sciences and the Humanities, University of Bergen, Norway. She holds a BSc in Environmental Science and an MSc in Sustainable Tropical Forestry, through the Erasmus Mundus scholarship programme 'Sutrofor,' and was formerly a visiting researcher at Universitat Autonoma de Barcelona. She has carried out inductive research in Tanzania and Colombia, and now conducts policy analysis of 'Landscape Centred REDD+; reducing emissions from deforestation and forest degradation.' She focuses on how this complex policy utilises global concerns of deforestation and food security to justify neoliberal agendas, with decontextualised economic logic and pseudo-scientific rationalities of agricultural intensification justifying the intertwining of private interests with globalised research institutes and governments.

Shomona Khanna is a lawyer practicing in the Supreme Court of India and Delhi High Court, is associated with numerous civil and democratic rights issues since 1991 and has been writing her experience and learning. She has authored and co-authored books and papers on indigenous peoples and the Indian Constitution, rights of forest dwellers and dalits, and sexual harassment at the workplace, and continues to handle several human rights cases, forest and environmental laws, rights of forest dwellers and Adivasis, and monitoring of jurisprudential developments in the courts. Having worked as Legal Adviser to the Union Ministry of Tribal Affairs between 2013 and 2017, she continues to provide a range of professional legal services to tribal and forest dwelling communities under the aegis of the newly founded 'Legal Resource Centre,' which is incubated in her law chambers.

Asoka Kumar Sen, Former Professor of History, is currently an Independent Researcher in Adivasi History based at Chaibasa, West Singhbhum, Jharkhand, India, and the Editor of the *Journal of Adivasi and Indigenous Studies* (online). He was awarded a short fellowship at the Department of Sociology, Delhi School of Economics, India, in 2004 and had the distinction of working as a Researcher for Sussex University, United Kingdom. He is the author of *The Educated Middle Class and Indian Nationalism* (1988), *Bengali Intelligentsia and Popular Uprisings 1855–73* (1992), *Representing Tribe: The Ho of Singhbhum during Colonial Rule* (2011), *From Village Elder to British Judge: Custom, Customary Law and Tribal Society* (2012), and *Indigeneity, Landscape and History: Adivasi Self-fashioning in India* (2018). His is presently engaged in the study of the Dynamics of Adivasi Rural Life.

Siddharth Sareen is a postdoctoral researcher at the Department of Geography and the Centre for Climate and Energy Transformation of the University of Bergen in Norway. He leads a project on the governance of solar energy in Portugal. Besides a research interest in the politics of energy transitions across sites and scales and an analytical focus on accountability, he has worked on issues of access and authority in resource governance in India within development studies and political ecology traditions. Besides a Double PhD at the University of Copenhagen and

Padova University, he has worked with the Regulatory Assistance Project, the University of Washington-Seattle, Erfurt University, the Institute of Economic Growth, Nordic Institute for Asian Studies, Aarhus University, and the Indian Institute of Technology Madras.

Bhanu Shree Jain is an Advocate who is currently working as an Associate at Chir Amrit Legal LLP. She has completed her Bachelor degrees in Commerce and Law from Nirma University, India and is also a Qualified Company Secretary. She has worked in areas related to financial advisory and indirect taxation. Her area of interest is constitutional law.

Anjana Singh is Assistant Professor in the Department of History in Nirmala College, Ranchi University, Jharkhand, India. She has been writing in the *Indian History Congress Proceedings*, *Journal of Adivasi and Indigenous Studies* and has contributed a chapter in the e-PG Pathshala scheme of MHRD, India, and other edited volumes. She is interested in working on regional language movements in Bihar and Jharkhand, Naxalism, oral histories, Adivasis of Jharkhand, and gender issues.

Sumarbin Umdor teaches Economics at North Eastern Hill University (NEHU) in Shillong, Meghalaya. His area of interest and research is on local economic development of the northeast region including the functioning and finances of local governments in the region, credit markets, and experiences and challenges of local economic development in the region. He is currently working on the impact of the North East industrial policy initiated by the government of India since 1997–1998 on industrialisation in the region. Besides teaching and research, he also collaborates with NGOs, multinational agencies, and the private sector on action research projects.

Foreword

Virginius Xaxa

When India became independent in 1947, tribes in general lived in geographical isolation as well as in social, educational, and economic backwardness. Where they had come in contact with non-tribes, they had been increasingly losing control over their land and other resources. Hence a special concern was shown for tribes in the post-independent India. This is reflected in the provisions enshrined for them in the Indian constitution. Besides conferment of rights to tribes as any other citizen, the post-independence India also extended certain special rights to them. They were conferred those rights on consideration of being a distinct community and marked by low level of social and economic development. The special rights were broadly of three kinds. One was the provision of reservation, which was extended in three different spheres. The provision of reservation in parliament and state legislature in proportion to the size of the tribal population was one of them. The others were the reservations (i) in jobs and appointments in state employment, and (ii) in education, especially in the institutions of higher learning. There is also the Directive Principle of the constitution that requires that the educational and economic interest of the weaker section of the society, including tribes, is especially promoted. Accordingly, planned development efforts have been made since independence for their social, educational, and economic development. Besides reservation and promotion of social and economic development, there are also provisions in the constitution that empower the state to bring the area inhabited by the tribes under special administration. In administrative parlance such areas are known as the Fifth or Sixth Scheduled areas (articles 244 and 244[a]). The Fifth Schedule has a provision for special legislative power of the Governor, Governor's report, and most importantly the tribal advisory council. The Sixth Schedule has provision for autonomous district council and hence it provides scope for self-governance. The sixth schedule in general is at work in the Northeastern region and the fifth in other regions of India where tribes in a district or a part of it form a majority. In addition to these, there were provisions for restricting the right of the ordinary citizen to move freely or settle in tribal areas (or acquire property in them) and for conserving the language, dialects, and culture etc. of tribes. The constitution thus aimed at the development of tribes but without compromising them with provisions of their protection, safeguard, and identity. In short, development and protection were supposed to be the pillars of tribal policy and development.

The lineage of this special administrative provision in the constitution is traceable to the administrative arrangement in vogue under the British. Prior to the incorporation of tribes into the British rule, tribes enjoyed autonomy of governance over the territory they occupied. They held control over the land, forest, and other resources and governed themselves in terms of their own laws, traditions, and customs. This they lost under the British as they came under laws, rules, and regulations relating to land, forest, crimes, and punishment that were alien to them. The British also opened tribal areas to traders, money lenders and land hungry peasants from the plains through extension of roads, railways, and other means of communication. This led to a massive transfer of land from tribes to non-tribes through such measures as fraud, deceit, mortgage etc. Since tribes had no practice of record keeping, as they did not have the knowledge of reading and writing, non-tribes took advantage of forging evidence and documents in their favour. The local administration, which was manned by the non-tribes, worked in glove with their ethnic kinder men to ensure the smooth transfer of land from tribes to non-tribes. The court language was alien to tribes, and they had absolutely no idea of what was happening in the court. While this process was going on, the colonial state took upon itself the right over the forest, thereby denying tribes the right to collect fuel and other daily necessities of life for which they were so heavily dependent on forest. These processes at work caused havoc in tribal society. The response of tribes to these took the form of armed struggle. In fact, a series of revolts and rebellions marked the early encounter of the British with the tribes.

In response to these resistance movements, the British administration toyed with the idea of a suitable administrative set-up for the agitated tribes. After much experimenting, it came up with 'arrangements' different from those in the non-tribal areas. This was reflected in Regulation X of 1822 which introduced the concept of a Non-Regulated System for carrying on the administration in difficult areas. There was provision in the regulation under which the executive could govern such areas as per the principles and spirits of the regulations subject to restriction and modification ordered by the Governor-General in Council. The genealogy of the Fifth and Sixth could be traced to this system in practice in various places in British India. The regions under such an administrative arrangement later came to be known by different names such as Scheduled Districts or excluded and partially excluded areas. The purpose of such an administrative arrangement was to maintain peace and good governance by minimum of interference from outside. The Indian Constitution continued with this governance structure with a view to safeguard and protect the interests of the tribes.

Notwithstanding such constitutional provisions and the state agenda for tribal development, tribal people in India are among the poorest and most marginalised section of the society. Not only do they represent disproportionately among the poorest and the most illiterate and vulnerable, they also suffer disproportionately from loss of their land, forest, and other resources. The people living below the poverty line are the highest among the tribals. And so it has been the case with health indicators such as infant mortality, under five mortality, undernourished children, maternal mortality, and so on. The sphere of education is no different whether it is primary, upper primary, high school, higher secondary school, or higher education. Enrolment is still a problem; though there has been much improvement, dropout rates are exorbitantly high.

At the same time, despite constitutional safeguards, the legislation's massive alienation of land from tribes to non-tribes through fraudulent transfers, forcible eviction, mortgages, leases, and encroachments have been going on in Scheduled Areas, especially the Fifth Scheduled Area. The state has not been able to protect them. Nor have tribes been able to take advantage of the law. Lack of knowledge and resources to fight the battles in the court of law has been one of the main reasons. Equally important has been the absence of strong grassroot organisations to prevent such occurrences. While laws aimed at restricting the alienation of land from tribes to non-tribes legally aims to restrain the volume and pace of alienation, the same cannot be said of the loss of land by tribes arising out of development related projects. The post-independence era of rapid economic and infrastructure development as a part of the national reconstruction process led to the massive expansion of development and infrastructure projects leading to large scale displacement of tribal people. Displacement has in fact turned out to be the most important factor accounting for the loss of control over land and forest by the tribals in the post-independence era. Of the total of 21.3 million people estimated to have been displaced during 1951–1990 in the states of Andhra Pradesh, Bihar, Gujarat, Maharashtra, Madhya Pradesh, Rajasthan, and Orissa, 8.54 million, that is, 40 percent are stated to be from tribes.

As to why tribes stand poorly in social development indicators has, to a great extent, to do with tampering the provisions of protection and safeguard ensured in the Constitution. This safeguard was most evident in distinct administration provided in the form of the Fifth and Sixth Schedules in the constitution.

The edited volume engages empirically with the various dimensions of constitutional and legal safeguards on the one hand and development related issues in the Scheduled Areas on the other. These include working important laws meant to safeguard the interest of the tribal people. The two such laws have been the Provisions of Panchayat Extension to Scheduled Areas and the Schedule Tribe and Other Forest Dwellers Act. Governance in the Fifth and Sixth Schedule Areas has always been a subject of much debate, but these have been done at the very general level and without much empirical data. In fact, a large number of papers in the volume address this issue in a specific regional context of the Fifth and Sixth Scheduled Areas. In the case of the Fifth Schedule Area, the focus ranges from the legislative, policy, and judicial combine and the politics of governance to the traditional system of governance, including the place of conflicting ideologies in the village governance. The governance in the Sixth Area has been examined by probing into the functioning of the tribal autonomous councils. Other aspects that the volume deals with are issues of rights and legalism in respect to minor forest produce, state allocation of funds, and politics of dispossession that are of critical important in both the Scheduled Areas. Although there has been a lot of interest and concern on tribes in the Scheduled Areas, systematic and well-worked-out research contributions have been far and few. This edited volume is an endeavour in that direction.

Virginius Xaxa

Preface

Much has been discussed and written about Scheduled Tribes (STs) or tribals/ Adivasis in India, but very little has been written about the areas in which they live. As such, the Indian Constitution, finance planners, and policy makers have thought of the Scheduled Areas as areas requiring both special attention and special arrangements for financial allocation, administrative structures, and special plans for the development of these areas as well as their inhabitants. Nonetheless, the focus of discussions and policy decisions have continued to focus on the inhabitants (i.e., STs or Adivasis and not on the geographically carved) distinct areas. Therefore, it is difficult to say whether the underdevelopment of Adivasis are due to negligence of the areas or regions they live in or vice-a-versa. This is the core idea of this volume. We wish to address issues of Scheduled Areas, shift focus to the Scheduled Areas as specially carved geographic areas – their development in structural manner and on agenda of regional planning and its spatial development – through the existing institutions, as much of the focus is on STs and their underdevelopment, marginalisation on various spheres – economic, legal, geographic, political and socio-cultural. It is important as this juncture that we initiate and expand a discourse to provide a schematic representation to the issues of closely inter-linked law, governance, and politics in the Scheduled Areas of India in the post-liberalisation phase (i.e., after 1991).

The neoliberal state in India has redefined the individual rights while at the same time attempted to discipline the 'population' according to the broader criteria of market-led development. In the formal sense, the vocabulary of rights-based legislation sounds quite empowering, but, in fact, the larger scheme of capitalist development criss-crosses the legal provisions applicable in Scheduled Areas at several levels. The challenge is that 'regional development' is seen as a singular entity in the parlance of development and financial planning while the Schedules Areas are spread across 15 States of India, as part of the Fifth Schedule and Sixth Schedule of the Indian Constitution, having separate historical routes for identity, recognition, and existence. Periodically and gradually, these areas are expanded with political initiatives, but their development needs to match up with the existing governance and legal structures.

We have attempted to present our thoughts and discussion in a nuanced manner on important aspects of regional development across India and of the Scheduled Areas through good governance and inter-twining law, rights' perspective, politics of translating policy into practice, and administrative structures and their procedures which need attention that could be activated. In this endeavour, through theoretical framework of 'governmentality,' we have covered a wide range of issues pertaining to the customary form of governance, governance of finances and forest resources, identity-based movements, politics of land dispossession, legal entanglements, left wing extremism, local autonomy, environmental rhetoric, and so on in individual chapters. We wish to present this volume as a critical reflection on the methods and mechanism of governance in the Scheduled Areas.

Varsha Bhagat-Ganguly and
Sujit Kumar

Acknowledgements

A general ignorance prevails among the lay person regarding the special laws applicable in certain parts of India which are constitutionally earmarked as Schedules Areas (SAs); also known in common parlance as tribal areas. Not much has been done in the academic world either to capture the dynamism which these diverse set of laws have brought to the governance of SAs. The idea of bringing out a volume on the SAs has appealed to us exactly for these stated reasons. We decided to walk on untrodden path with the spirit of exploration and enunciation. For us, this journey has been very enjoyable and enriching. Within a short span, we could mobilise the contributors from different disciplines – law practitioners, civil servants, academia, and research scholars. Some social activists cum academics wished to join, but due to certain constraints they couldn't join in this venture. We were supported by each of them immensely; those who contributed to this volume and those who couldn't come aboard. We would like to thank our contributors for readily agreeing to write for the proposed volume. This would not have been possible without their own zeal to understand these ignored and neglected pockets of this vast country. Dr Asoka Kumar Sen is the first to be greeted and thanked for he introduced us to many academicians and upcoming research scholars as contributors to the volume. He also helped us to approach Dr Virginius Xaxa for writing a foreword to this volume. We are thankful to Dr Xaxa for writing a foreword from his vast experience, focusing on scheduled tribe and scheduled areas. We deeply appreciate and thank Dr Siddharth Sareen for suggesting various readings and helping us conceptualise few points which are at the core of this entire volume. He also shared reading materials and sharpened academic discourse on the topic. We thank all of the contributors for their rigour, hard work, and patience. They have not only responded to our persistent editorial queries but some of them also prepared chapters within a short span without compromising the quality of this volume. Any academic publication undergoes such exercise, but this volume is special, as the topic is newer and nuanced. Though the volume seemingly overlaps with existing works on Adivasis or Scheduled Tribes, which is a much explored academic area, we are happy to have captured some very important themes existing in the Scheduled Areas. Just to name a few, the volume talks about customary institutions, finances, autonomous councils, wildlife sanctuaries, minor forest produce, land dispossession, forest rights, left-wing extremism, and notions of self-governance in their sharp relevance to Scheduled Areas. Every contributor has tried to address issues of governance, law, and politics for that being a matrix to understand the Scheduled Areas from their respective disciplines.

We are also thankful to Institute of Law, Nirma University, which could be considered as genesis of the volume, as this germination started by teaching a course on 'Law and governance in tribal areas by Varsha Bhagat-Ganguly. Last but not the least, we would like to acknowledge the perseverance shown by inhabitants of Scheduled Areas and their struggle against the onslaught of various forces, sometimes even the wilful neglect of the state.

Varsha Bhagat-Ganguly
Sujit Kumar

Abbreviations

AAGR	Average Annual Growth Rate
AAPTL	Assam Plains Tribal League
ABD	Accumulation by Dispossession
ABSU	All Bodo Students Union
ADC	Autonomous District Councils
ADR	Alternative Dispute Resolution
ATREE	Ashoka Trust of Research on Ecology and Environment
BISAG	Bhaskaracharya Institute for Space Applications and Geo-Informatics, Gujarat
BLT	Bodo Liberation Tigers
BPL	Below Poverty Line
BSA	Bihar State Archives
BTAD	Bodoland Territorial Areas District
BTC	Bodoland Territorial Council
CAA	Constitutional Amendment Acts
CAD	Constitution Assembly Debates
CADC	Chakma Autonomous District Council
CAG	Comptroller and Auditor General
CAMPA	Compensatory Afforestation Fund Management and Planning Act
CCIU	Collective Command and Individual Use
CFR	Community Forest Resource
CMAS	Chali Mulia Adivasi Sangh
CNTA	Chotanagpur Tenancy Act
CS	Craven Settlement
CSE	Centre for Science and Environment
CSR	Corporate Social Responsibilities
CSS	Centrally Sponsored Scheme
CSVAP	Craven Settlement Village Enquiry Paper
CSVN	Craven Settlement Village Note
DCOS	Deputy Commissioner's Office Singhbhum
DHAC	Dima Hasao Autonomous Council
DLC	District Level Committee

DRRC	District Record Room Chaibasa
EDR	Expenditure Decentralisation Ratio
FDI	Foreign Direct Investment
FRA	Forest rights Act/Scheduled Tribes and Other Traditional Forest Dwellers (Recognition of Forest Rights) Act
FRC	Forest Rights Committee
FSO	Forest Settlement Officer
GHADC	Garo Hills Autonomous District Council
GIS	Geographic Information System
GoI	Government of India
GPS	Ground Positioning System
GS	Gram Sabha
HDI	Human Development Index
HLC	High Level Committee
IRV	India Rhino Vision
ITDA	Integrated Tribal Development Agency
IUCN	International Union for Conservation of Nature
JFM	Joint Forest Management
JHADC	Jaintia Hills Autonomous District Council
JPRA	Jharkhand Panchayati Raj Act
KAAC	Karbi Anglong Autonomous Council
KHADC	Khasi Hills Autonomous District Council
LAA	Land Acquisition Act
LADC	Lai Autonomous District Council
LAMPS	Large Size Multi Purpose Societies
LRAR	Land Revenue Administration Report
LWE	Left-Wing Extremism
MADC	Mara Autonomous District Council
MCC	Maoist Communist Center
MWHS	Manas World Heritage Site
MFP	Minor Forest Product
MGNREGA	Mahatma Gandhi National Rural Employment Guarantee Act
MHA	Ministry of Home Affairs
MLM	Marxist-Leninist-Maoist
MNC	Multi-National Company
MoTA	Ministry of Tribal Affairs
MoU	Memorandum of Understanding
NBA	Narmada Bachao Andolan
NDC	National Development Council
NER	North Eastern Region
NGO	Non-Governmental Organisation
NTPC	National Thermal Power Station
OTFD	Other Traditional Forest Dwellers
OUV	Outstanding Universal Value
PDA	Personal Digital Assistant

PDS	Public Distribution System
PESA	Panchayat (Extension to Scheduled Areas) Act, 1996
PF	Protected Forests
POL	Petroleum, Oil, and Lubricants
PRI	Panchayatiraj Institutions
PTCA	Plains Tribal Council of Assam
PVTG	Particularly Vulnerable Tribal Groups
PW	People's War
RDR	Revenue Decentralisation Ratio
RF	Reserve Forests
RFCTLARR	Right to Fair Compensation and Transparency in Land Acquisition and Rehabilitation & Resettlement Act, 2013
SA	Scheduled Areas
SAR	Special Area Regulation
SC	Scheduled Caste
SCA	Special Central Assistance
SCC	Supreme Court Cases
SDO	Sub-Divisional Officer
SDLC	Sub-Divisional Level Committee
SGSY	Swarnajayanti Grameen Swarozgar Yojana
SHG	Self-Help Group
SIP	Sponge Iron Projects
SPTA	Santhal Parganas Tenancy Act
ST	Scheduled Tribes
SWFPDR	South West Frontier Political Dispatch Register
TA	Travelling Allowance
TAADC	Tripura Tribal Area Autonomous District Council
TAC	Tribal Advisory Council
TSKP	Tuckey Settlement Khuntkatti Papers
TSP	Tribal Sub-Plan
TSVN	Tuckey Settlement Village Note
TA	Travelling Allowances
ST	Scheduled Tribe
UNESCO	United Nations Educational, Scientific, and Cultural Organisation
UTNLF	United Tribal Nationalist Liberation Front
UT	Union Territory
VKY	Vanbandhu Kalyan Yojana
WB	World Bank
WR	Wilkinson Rules
WWF	World Wildlife Fund
XISS	Xavier Institute of Social Sciences

Glossary

Aadhar Card	Personal identification cards issued by the Government of India
Adivasi	Indigenous/Autochthonous people, designated in Indian Constitution as the Scheduled Tribe
Akhara	Meeting place in a Munda and Oraon village
Bala	Killis with which marriage relations may be formed
Bandh	An embankment made at the lower end of a depression or by embanking three sides of a slope
Bonga	Spirit
Chaukidar	Watchman of a village
Dakua	A village constable
Deuri	A village priest
Diku	Outsider
Gheraos	Siege, encircling a person
Gitiora	Village dormitory among the Adivasis
Gonong	Bride price among the Ho Adivasis
Gora	Cultivated upland
Gram Ganarajyas	Village republics
Gra Pradhan	Village Headman as elected representative
Gram Sabha	Village assembly
Ham	Village founder
Hatu	Village
Haga	Brotherhood
Jal	Water
Jameen	Land
Jangal	Forest
Kanungo	Village and district revenue officer
Khas Mohal	Districts held in the management of the government
Khatians	Record of Rights
Khuntkattidar	Original Clearer of land in a village
Khuntkatti hatu	Village of the family of original settlers
Maghe parab	Ho festival generally scheduled to be held in January-February

Manjhi	central place of a Santal village where meetings are held
Manki	Head of a pir
Marang Gomke	Supreme Leader
Mukhiya	Traditionally, a village headman
Munda	Head of a village
Non-obstante	A clause in a statute conveying a dispensation from the legislature or executive to perform an action notwithstanding any statute to the contrary
Pahan	The brotherhood of allied and associated villages of Mundas
Paragana	It refers to geographic area covered, a paragana could be made of more than one existing district. Santhal paragana is made of six districts of Jharkhand state – Godda, Deoghar, Dumka, Jamtara, Sahibganj, and Pakur
Paraganait	Chief of a pargana
Parha	The brotherhood of allied and associated villages of Mundas
Parha pir	A cluster of villages resembling a pargana
Panchayati Raj	Local governance system
Pathalgadi	Erection of stone slabs
Pattas	Record of rights
Patti	Wider organisation of Parha
Pir dakua	Constable of the pir
Pugry	A turban
Purkha Sahitya	Ancestral literature
Raiyats	Tenants
Ramnavmi	Lord Rama's birthday
Sarna	Sacred grove
Sarpanch	Head of a village Panchayat (modern governance system)
Sasandiri	A gravestone placed flat over the burial bones in Sasan (i.e., burial place)
Singbonga	Highest God of the Ho Adivasis
Tahasildar	Village accountant, appointed by the state government
Thana	Police station
ultra vires	Beyond the scope or in excess of legal power or authority
Zamindars	Big landlords

1 Introduction

Varsha Bhagat-Ganguly and Sujit Kumar

Overview of India's Scheduled Areas

India is home to many Adivasi[1] communities regarded as indigenous[2] groups elsewhere. They constitute 8.6 percent of the population (Census 2011) and a majority of them is concentrated in the Eastern, Central, and Western belt covering the nine states[3] under the Fifth Schedule while four states[4] are covered under the Sixth Schedule.[5] The Scheduled Areas[6] (SAs) were first notified in the year 1950; the criterion for the declaration of an area as a Scheduled Area was identified by the first Scheduled Areas and Scheduled Tribes Commission (Dhebar Commission) (MoTA 2014: 65). After independence the Bordoloi Sub-committee and Thakkar Committee framed the Schedules V and VI, respectively. The completely excluded areas in North Eastern Region (NER) were recognised under Schedule VI, serving greater autonomy in governance. The 'excluded and partially excluded areas' in the mainland India were recognised as Scheduled Areas under Schedule V of the Indian Constitution.[7] As of now, only Parliament is competent to enact laws that deal exclusively with SAs and STs under entry 91 of the Union List. Paragraph 5 of the Schedule V envisages the Governor as the sole legislature for SAs who can make provisions for the administration and good governance of SAs in consultation with the Tribal Advisory Council (TAC). The fifth schedule is hence eulogised as 'constitution within the constitution'.

Hardly one-third of the Adivasi population was covered under these designated spaces, the SAs in 1950 when the constitution was enacted. As per the 1951 Census, SAs existed over 99,693 sq. miles (258,203.68 sq. km) and cover a tribal population of 86 lakhs [8.6 million] (GoI 1961). The coverage of the Adivasi population under SAs increased to 70 percent only after the first *Tribal Sub-Plan* (TSP) started in 1974 (Sharma 2010). Recently, the Union Cabinet chaired by the Prime Minister has given approval to the declaration of Scheduled Areas in respect of Rajasthan (state) under the Fifth Schedule to the Constitution of India by rescinding the Constitution Order (C.O.) 114 dated 12 February 1981 and with the promulgation of a new Constitution Order (Ministry of Tribal Affairs, 25 April 2018).[8] With this addition, total land area under the Scheduled Areas will increase from 19,818.86 sq. km to 23,354.96 sq. km and the Scheduled Tribe population covered under the

Scheduled Area will thus increase from 4,188,056 to 4,551,917, while the total population covered under the Scheduled Areas will become 6,463,353.

The idea of SA is inter-twined with Scheduled Tribes (ST) in India; the features of such an area were these: the preponderance of tribal population,[9] compactness and reasonable size of the area, the under-developed nature of the area, and the marked disparity in the economic standard of the people (MoTA 2014: 65). Despite this, the smaller Adivasi groups in large states like Karnataka, Kerala, Tamil Nadu, West Bengal, and others did not receive the protection available to those in SAs.[10] While there is a provision for constituting the TAC even within states without SAs no effort has been made by the governments in such states to constitute them. In terms of the financial allocation made to the TACs between 2012–2013 and 2016–2017, the SAs largely depend upon the state governments for the funding rather than the central government even though there exists a centralised framework to govern the SAs (Wahi and Bhatia 2018: 22). Inclusion of some areas in the SA is explained by the press as 'the tribals[11] living there can avail the benefit of protective measures under its provisions' (PTI 26 April 2018) and because of 'the assembly elections due this year end' (Hindustan Times 25 April 2018). This establishes a 'tribal oriented, protection measure' as well as 'wooing of tribals for electoral politics' by the elected representative (i.e., the Prime Minister, while constitutionally, the President and the Governor of the respective state are the authorities with statutory powers for the SAs).

The shift from 'backward areas' to 'excluded areas' in the British era to 'Scheduled Areas' in independent India is a continuation of colonial arrangements or tribal-oriented thinking. However, radical change in consonance with the need to protect tribal culture and identity raises a gamut of questions regarding governance, rule of law, and volition of the state. After independence, there have been intensive discussions and debates by the members of the Constituent Assembly,[12] the respective state representatives, and members of government-appointed committee[13] on whether there is a need to continue arrangement of special areas for tribal population or not[14] (The Framing of India's Constitution, Vol. III). Different states reacted differently in identifying the criteria for inclusion of geographical areas into Schedule V. For example, states like Gujarat did not considered the 'inaccessibility of areas' and 'the distinctive way of life' of people therein as criteria. However, states like Madhya Pradesh identified 'primitive way of life and the practice of shifting cultivation' as viable criteria for notifying a Scheduled Area (GoI 1961: 61). These criteria were put down on the ground that they are community specific rather than geographical. In fact, the Scheduled Areas and Scheduled Tribes Commission under the Chairmanship of U.N. Dhebar had recommended the abrogation of Schedule V once the objectives for which the notified Scheduled Areas are fulfilled (i.e., the Scheduled Tribes start enjoying their existing rights and their economic, educational, and social progress is ensured) (GoI 1961: 39). As against this B.D. Sharma, Commissioner for Scheduled Castes and Scheduled Tribes during 1986–1991, argued for the retention of the Schedule V and went on to organise *Bharat Jan Andolan*, demanding the recognition of the customs, culture, and indigenous political system of the STs.

There is a plethora of secondary literature on the Scheduled Tribes that has focused on questions of their tribal identity, poverty, vulnerability, displacement, and alienation from the Indian State. But there doesn't exist as much literature on the Scheduled Areas, or the specialised relationship between the Scheduled Tribes and the Scheduled Areas (Wahi and Bhatia 2018). For instance, Census 1951 based data describe that SAs existed over 99,693 sq. miles (258,203.68 sq. km) and cover a tribal population of 86 lakhs (8.6 million) (GoI 1961). The updated statistics interlinking Scheduled Areas and the inhabiting Scheduled Tribe population, based on Census 2011 are not available. In this context, the existing 23,354.96 sq. km vis-à-vis area of 258,203.68 sq. km in 1951 of SAs become puzzling. Different committees and commissions have been set up to address problems of Adivasis during 1970 and 2004.[15] These committees have dealt with issues which fall broadly into two categories: development and protection. And yet, on both these issues, the outcome for tribal communities has been mixed (MoTA 2014: 26).

This volume at the first level attempts to elaborate the existing differences – paradoxes and puzzles. First, SAs as geographically carved special areas with a purpose of providing protections to the tribal population and ensuring their development, which could be expanded with a Constitution Order by the Prime Minister, but the statutory powers are assigned under the Indian Constitution to the President and the Governor of the respective states. This implies a criss-cross of constitutional authority and political decision-making regarding the functioning of the polity.[16] Second, geographic areas are carved with an aim of improving the life of its residents, and special measures are being taken to ensure the development of STs as a target group. To materialise this aim, separate financial and administrative arrangements are conceived at the time of formation of the SAs; the funds are allocated and the special measures for STs are taken in the form of government schemes and programmes. Despite special funds and special measures, the performance of these schemes and programmes are not carried out from the perspective of governance, especially for SAs; corrective measures are neither planned nor executed specially for SAs. Third, the absence of special financial and administrative arrangement gives a feeling of the continuation of colonial arrangements. No innovative or exclusive government schemes or programmes applicable to SAs are conceived or planned and therefore not executed, as a result SAs are facing *status quo* and regional backwardness continues. Fourth, though 'protection of tribal population' is the aim, it is difficult to spell 'protection' in terms of upholding 'rights' and 'identity' of Adivasis or protection 'against the ills of underdevelopment' or bundle of these concepts. These aspects are articulated by various scholars as Adivasis' underdevelopment, violations of human rights, inadequate funding for STs, etc., but considerable articulations are neither found from the perspective of governance nor the concerns of SAs and regional planning.

This chapter contains two sections – the first section elaborates framework of governance and governmentality, law-making and the rule of law, and the rights of Adivasis in the SAs and describes existing paradoxes and puzzles of SAs in the neoliberal era. The second section presents an overview of how the volume is organised, and it provides details about each chapter and how a chapter is linked and attuned to the overall theme of the volume, focusing on mainly two sub-themes – 'Governmentality: A Neoliberal Perspective on Governance' and 'Politics, Rights and Legalism' in the Scheduled Areas.

Section one

Historically, in the colonial period, the Bengal Regulation XIII, 1833, and Scheduled Districts (Act XIV), 1874, listed the scheduled districts across British India. However, the criterion of geographical backwardness to identify the scheduled tribes (STs) was adopted in the 1901 census. Later on the British government, in due recognition of the freedom-loving spirit of the Adivasis, designated the areas inhabited by the latter as 'excluded areas' or 'partially excluded areas' under the Government of India Act, 1935 (Mazumdar 1937). But what was the nature of these areas before being appropriated by the British? Well, the inconclusive histories of these areas indicate that the Adivasi communities which gave specific features to these areas came to settle in different ways. Neat colonial constructs of 'excluded' and 'partially excluded areas' and special laws applicable to these areas[17] are but an attempt to recognise the distinctness of the inhabitants thereof. While we tend to generally understand these areas and their residents in terms of culture and civilisational aspects, very little has been said about their distinct political structures and arrangements.

Vast literature on Adivasi societies points toward at least three different forms in which the geographical space now known as scheduled areas should be understood in its pre-colonial formation. First, are those areas which were cleared and inhabited by the 'original' settlers.[18] Second category comprises of the areas colonised by the Adivasis by expelling other communities.[19] And the last category is that of the tribal-dominated areas which expanded to acquire the size of kingdoms. This last category is particularly interesting because of its potential to suggest the existence of kingdoms among the Adivasis. However, a close scrutiny by scholars suggests that the nature of Adivasi kingdoms, though similar to that of the ruling castes, were also different in substantial ways. For example, citing the example of Nimar, Shashank Kela (2012: 88) argues that 'incorporation' rather than 'coercion' played a major role in sustaining the tribal kingdoms. Now the question arises: Were these kingdoms inspired by the imitation of Hindu kingdoms? Or, was it entirely based on the local economy and its challenges and opportunities?

Shashank Kela (2012: 91) subscribes to Surajit Sinha's hypothesis on the formation of tribal kingdoms according to which the latter 'emerged either through Rajput conquest, or the crystallisation of ruling elite from within the tribal group.' Nevertheless, Kela (2012: 92) rules out the hypothesis of acculturation forwarded by historians like Kosambi or sociologists like Ghurye. He argues that had acculturation been a dominant issue, few Adivasi societies would have survived into the colonial period given the fact that tribal kingdoms came into vogue during the medieval period. Bhangya Bhukya (2016) who has studied the history of Gonds argues that the assertion of political self-determination and the demand for autonomy in governance by the Gonds even today is guided by the historical notion of their existence as independent kingdoms.

Even in the pre-British era, the SAs were not entirely disconnected with the political systems in the other areas. They existed in loose political linkages with neighbouring kingdoms and enjoyed different degrees of autonomy. British expedition into these areas, however caused severe setback to such political arrangements and led to the creation of hybrid political institutions which, while retaining the label of 'customary,' underwent significant transformation.

In post-independence period, the way the Adivasi population has experienced the state can be summarised into three terms: First, adverse inclusion; second, internal colonialism; and, third, political disenfranchisement. The term *adverse inclusion* is used by scholars to argue that as a result of state-led development projects the Adivasis were separated from their traditional source of livelihood. The illustrious administrator and scholar on Adivasi affairs B.D. Sharma (2010: 19) had identified education and awareness among the Adivasis about the institutions and law of the Indian state as the necessary pre-condition for their integration. However, owing to their poor educational status, they were retained either in blue collar jobs or were rendered jobless. This approach certainly included the Adivasis in the mainstream but in a rather adverse manner. The second phenomenon of *internal colonialism* points toward the spatial aspects of development and underdevelopment. The proponents of this hypothesis apply the lens of dependency theory in examining the inter-regional disparity in development. They argue that the dispossession of the Adivasi-dominated areas was primarily required to develop the urban areas and, hence, the creation of a civil society in urban areas is directly linked with the making of political society in the countryside since almost 85 percent of the Adivasi population still lives in rural areas (MoTA 2014). Studies on regional disparities argue that states such as Jharkhand and Odisha with a dominating Adivasi population have been facing the problem of chronic poverty among Adivasis, with a higher extent of land alienation and indebtedness among them (Guha 2007; Sundar 2016). The third phenomenon of *political disenfranchisement* is typically linked to the post-liberalisation phase of economy. As a result of new economic policy in 1991 and the following development paradigm, the Adivasi population faced evictions from their land at an increased pace and were displaced, dispossessed, alienated from their roots,[20] and reduced to the status of migrants. This converted them into a disenfranchised community who is typified with an aggressive assertion of Adivasi identity.

It is clear that the historical doings have brought two issues to the forefront – carving out geographic area named as 'Scheduled Areas' and tribals as main inhabitants, their culture, traditions, and governance mechanism. With reference to SAs and tribals,development/underdevelopment of the tribals and decision-making over resources, especially natural resources, are key issues. In this discourse, four newer, overarching dimensions have been highlighted – governmentality, rights, legalism, and politics. In such closely inter-connected and overlapping discourses, the present volume attempts to look at the state and the way it deals with the question of underdevelopment of Adivasis, their traditional mechanism of governance, and their decision-making regarding resources, which leads to a critical study of governance, institutions, and laws by locating them in the social milieu within which they work. The aim is to capture the evolving paradigm of governance,[21] which is a means and an end in the discourse of development; institutions reveal the mechanisms and processes undertaken for ensuring development while laws are enacted with the purpose of ensuring development. On the other hand, the chronic problems of the underdevelopment of tribals, who are faring poorly in social sectors like health and education, have captured the attention of scholars and invited them to critically look at laws and institutions and politics that contribute to the present scenario, which are more visible in the post-liberalisation era in India.

Who owns the *temples* of modern India?

The principle of integration was the accepted approach of Indian state towards its Adivasi people which emerged as a compromise between the discourses of 'isolation' and 'assimilation.' In the colonial period the missionaries and the Hindu organisations were both proactive in transforming the Adivasi society with their discreet and micro operations. While the colonial ethnographers recognised the separate religion of the Adivasis as a basis to differentiate them from the others, the Hindu right wing, deriving from Ghurye's description of Adivasis, considered them as 'backward Hindus' ignoring their characteristics like isolation, language, and social structure.[22] Furthermore, the caste system which is so integral to the Hindu religion is believed to be absent among the Adivasis and poses a major challenge to the *Sangh Parivar* attempts to assimilate the Adivasis into the fold of Hinduism. It was in this context that 'integration' was adopted, however without any formal/official recognition (Xaxa 2005: 1366). This approach was entirely in line with India's multi-cultural and plural society and was supposed to accommodate the Adivasi culture and tradition by reconstituting the eclectic nature of the mainstream culture and society. As if against 'assimilation,' which espouses an apparent loss of culture and tradition, the term 'absorption' was used to understand the interaction of Adivasi people with the members of organised religions. This had to be done while ensuring the gradual replacement of Adivasi economy and their incorporation into the material life of the modern state.

The overwhelming thrust of Nehruvian era towards the modernisation of the newly independent state through state-led developmental projects like dams, industries, and mining caused irreparable damage to the Adivasi communities. The temples of modern India had evicted the Adivasis and also their deities/spirits alike to make way for development. While the monumental story of modern Indian state was being written, the story of its dispossessed though archaic and episodic in nature could not be hidden.[23] This is the reason why the discourse of development cannot be discussed without discussing its costs. In context of the Adivasi population, the cost can be seen in terms of their disproportionately high number in cases of 'development-induced-displacement, poor literacy, poverty, and high mortality rate.[24] The High Level Committee (HLC) constituted in 2014 under Virginius Xaxa to study the *socio-economic, education,* and *health* status of the STs disagrees with some of the oft-cited reasons for the abysmal development of the community; first, their social and geographical isolation; second, the poor implementation of programmes; and third, the traditional socio-cultural aspects of Adivasi life (MoTA 2014: 29–30). The committee rather identifies the insensitive bureaucracy, traders, and money lenders as well as the onslaught of private companies as the responsible factors behind underdevelopment of the STs (ibid. 31). These aspects of dispossession can be captured in terms of objective data. Nevertheless, the everyday statecraft also perpetuates marginalisation, which is intangible in nature and requires the socio-anthropological analysis to capture it. This volume aims at capturing governance/institutional mechanism and legal provisions, which has still not been able to deal with the sense of marginalisation and dispossession of the Adivasi community. The volume also discusses the cases of Adivasis' resistance against state usurping their rights over land, forests, customary institutions, and culture on the one hand and why, despite having a separate identity under the Scheduled Areas, this form of marginalisation and manifestations has been observed on the other hand.

In retrospect, one can argue that the modernisation spree should have been preceded by attempts to prepare suitable grounds for a fruitful integration of the Adivasis in the mainstream society rather than projecting a binary of Adivasis' culture (implying backwardness and ancient way of life) versus the modern state's idea of development. Education could have served as the starting point; a domain in which the curriculum development should have been strictly guided by the Adivasi ethos, culture, and traditional governance mechanism that addressed their life problems in holistic manner. The initial facilities to learn in their mother tongue could have prepared a better ground for their integration. All these solutions which present themselves today only exist as a lost opportunity. Furthermore, today the disenfranchisement of the Adivasis has to be understood within the broader discourse of neoliberal development marked with increasing inequality, an unorganised workforce, and the insecurities attuned to the market forces. One can see that laws like Panchayat (Extension to Scheduled Areas) Act, 1996 (PESA), Scheduled Tribes and Other Traditional Forest Dwellers (Recognition of Forest Rights) Act, 2006, which ensure community control over their institutions and resources were also promulgated in the post-liberalisation period. Recently enacted law, Right to Fair Compensation and Transparency in Land Acquisition and Rehabilitation & Resettlement Act, 2013 (RFCT-LARR), as such, needs to elaborate special provisions for the SAs in the broader context of displacement and dispossession of Adivasis. It is within this shift of paradigms and the changing ideologies that we will try to understand the issue of governance of SAs.

Scheduled Areas and governmentality

Consensus exists among scholars regarding the patriarchal approach of the independent Indian state towards the SAs. However, in the post-liberalisation phase governments have apparently shed even this approach and declared explicitly that the objective of governance is to pull out the presumably disturbed SAs out of their pathogenic state owing to the presence of Maoists. In fact, this trend better represents a shift from *statism* to *governmentality*. Talking about this trend, Nikolas Rose (1999: 3) highlights a shift from an alien-centralised authority seeking subordination, or at least obedience, from individuals to an agency which endeavours to shape, guide, and direct the conduct of others. Borrowing from Foucault, Rose (1999) emphasises upon the study of the 'formation and transformation of theories, proposals, strategies and technologies for "the conduct of conduct."' The idea is to understand the programmatic manner in which certain ends are to be achieved by instrumentalising the actions of the individuals in a desired direction. Argued thus, governmentality seems to acknowledge the freedom of the governed (Rose 1999: 4) and helps the state to retain the existing power relations by seeking legitimacy rather than colonising the population. But, as this process requires continued consent of the governed, it is less durable in nature and simultaneously opens a space for critical thought (Rose 1999: 18). Contesting the view that governing is an exercise through which people, their habits, and ultimately their values are transformed according to the dominant ethos, Rose (1999: 32) argues that

> Governable spaces are not fabricated counter to experience; they make new kinds of experience possible, produce new modes of perception, invest percepts with affects, with dangers and opportunities, with saliences and attractions . . . they are modalities in which a real and material governable world is composed, terraformed and populated.

While Rose's views on governmentality extracts the possibility of spaces of negotiation for the governed, one cannot oversee the fact that the prospect of this opportunity is defined according to the context. In his compelling analysis of capitalism in post-colonial India, Kalyan Sanyal (2007) identifies a major shift in the discourse of development which took place in the 1970s. He argues that, following the address of the World Bank President Robert McNamara in 1973, developing countries world over shifted the target of governance from pursuing economic growth to addressing poverty. This approach looks upon the problem of poverty as an ailment which is in need of the suitable administering of medicines as a panacea. In this framework the state comes to *work upon* the population rather than *working for* the citizens. Thus, the neoliberal state has changed governance into *governmentality* wherein the target population is subjected to techno-managerial interventions for addressing the problem of poverty. Borrowing from Michel Foucault's notion, Kalyan Sanyal (2007: 171) argues that, in the West,

> Governmentality refers to the management of the social body in terms of interventions on the part of the state aimed at promoting the welfare of society. The purpose of these interventions is to activate and arouse the subjects, rather than constrict and repress them.

There is a certain power dynamics operating in this model as sovereignty gets replaced with governmentality. Subject for the sovereign is the citizen whereas for governmentality the social space comprises of population with peculiar variables like birth and death rates, life expectancy, etc. Sanyal agrees with Foucault that in such a state power is no more located in sovereignty which is internal in nature, but it is rather generated in the decentralised form through the use of administration to perform the instrumental role of social welfare. However, Sanyal criticises Foucault for failing to relate governmentality to the 'question of the reproduction of capital's conditions of existence' (Sanyal 2007: 173). Here the state seems to be more occupied with the task of creating legitimacy for the market in the eyes of the governed by directly targeting those who are 'outside of capitalism'[25] through its welfare programmes. Sanyal further argues that at the core of this poverty-oriented approach are the two issues of 'entitlement' and 'capability' identified by Amartya Sen. This helps us to understand the relation between capital and development which exists in their mutuality as well as contradiction (Sanyal 2007: 175). Poverty does not exist anymore on a politically contestable terrain as governmentality will level the accusation that growth has failed to eradicate poverty without holding the former responsible for the latter. In exploring the issues of governance in SAs, this theoretical framework is applied throughout the volume.

The technical approach of governance has also failed to recognise the normative views that the Adivasi community holds regarding their land, forest, and water. Since the Forest Conservation Act of 1980, stringent measures were established to control and discourage the Adivasis from extracting resources even for household uses. It was under the National Forest Policy, 1988, that the state acknowledged the symbiotic relationship between the Adivasi people and forest for the first time. Joint Forest Management started as a programme with the dual target of increasing forest cover through community participation and address issues of poverty in these areas. Further rights over forest resources were recognised through Scheduled Tribes and Other Traditional Forest Dwellers (Recognition of Forest Rights) Act, 2006 (FRA), which is encapsulated in the language of entitlement. Thomas Sikor and Johannes Stahl (2011: 2) argue that rights-based agenda in forestry is marked by three features: First, redistribution based upon entrenched historical inequalities; second, more grassroots movements than trans-national movements recognising forest people's identities, vision, and experiences; and third, people's individual as well as collective rights. In locating the yet another narrative of equity, participation, and recognition, William Sunderlin (2011: 23–24) argues that the shift from the comprehensive government control of forests to greater access and ownership by forest people has taken place due to the failure of state forest management decentralisation, resource management devolution, democratisation, and international solidarity campaigns. While these arguments borrow too heavily from the vibrant discourse of civil society action, a critical approach requires building upon the grassroot experiences of communities in dealing with MFPs and Non-Timber forest products under the changed circumstances. The evidence brought forward by Siddharth Sareen in this volume points toward a rather perplexed situation on forest governance and community rights which fits into the approach discussed in the preceding paragraph.

Regarding land one can see that in the SAs land was operated under the principle of collective command and individual use (CCIU). This mode of land governance was never recognised by the state. In fact, the large-sized multi-purpose societies (LAMPS) which was established to cater to all the credit needs of the Adivasi people could not succeed because it was based upon recognition of individual ownership of land. As money lending is identified as one of the major reasons behind the alienation of Adivasi land in SAs, we can notice a vivid disconnect between government policy and the objectives it is supposed to achieve. With the promulgation of Right to Fair Compensation and Transparency in Land Acquisition, Rehabilitation and Resettlement Act, 2013 which has replaced the Land Acquisition Act, 1894, the vocabulary of rights is being used. However, even this new law fails to recognise the community ownership model, and the discourse of land acquisition is marred with multiple protests by the Adivasis. Most of the resistance against land acquisition is articulated in the name of Adivasi culture and world view. The amorphous nature of Adivasi identity has served its purpose to galvanise and unite the community on several occasions with positive results. However, there have been cases where the resistance movements have failed to achieve their desired objectives. This failure is contingent upon several issues and need to be understood as a part of Adivasi politics today.

Scheduled Areas, rights, legalism, and politics

The discourse of governance as 'a field of strategies' (Samaddar and Sen 2012) – a two-way or multiple axis process – and the concept of the 'rights of tribals' occupy centrestage while studying SAs. The concept of 'rights' include the vision and aspirations of Adivasis, claims and entitlements, access, availability, and control and management of resources. One of the main aims of this volume is to study how Adivasis both deal with the dynamics of power, and assert and/or establish culture-based identity (and in turn the traditional mechanism of governance, even when subjugated to the modern rule of law for ensuring their right to development – which includes participation and decision-making, avenues, scope, and abilities – in the specially carved geographic areas/SAs). Is this or could this process and strategy differ from non-SAs? The volume attempts to explore and understand governance as a dynamic process between those who rule and those who react to rule of law or process of governance. For understanding the strategies of Adivasis, the volume explores whether Adivasis accept the rationale of modern rule of law or the traditional way of governance – process, mechanism and operations; whether they modify the rationale of modern institutions including law and polity; or whether they question and resist the rationale of existing governance process; or whether they are able to create and establish a parallel process and structure of mechanism.

In order to understand strategies, it is important to understand various rights that have been evolved and articulated in the last two to three decades; such as the rights over natural resources – like forest, water, and land; the economic and material rights, especially in the context of land acquisition, land alienation, and dispossession; the ability to exercise political rights in terms of state's accountability and transparency and avenues created for participation at various levels of governance; cultural rights, identity questions, and their linkages with the process of development; and jurisprudence of rights (i.e., how the judiciary has interpreted existing laws – Forest Rights Act and PESA – in relation to the importance of Gram Sabha and the cultural practices of Adivasis). This leads to further study into the agency that establishes rights – the judiciary, the administrative structure, local governance mechanism, traditional governance mechanism or parallel-created mechanism such as left wing extremism (LWE). Are there different shades of 'rights?' In other words, does the judicial interpretation based on cultural rights vary from the statist perspective of governance or the LWE versus statist perspective of administration?

If one has to conceptualise the nature of SAs, then how does one do that? Should one consider them exclusively as Excluded or Partially Excluded Areas? Or shall they be recognized as dynamic spaces witnessing the socio-cultural as well as the political transformation of its inhabitants? Nandini Sundar (2016: 21–23) has cited several works to state that the SAs were rather dynamic spaces which got transformed due to their interaction with 'regional economies and polities . . . on adverse basis.' Scheduled Areas are not simply the habitat of Adivasi people. Apart from the Adivasis, it also constitutes people which can be broadly put into two categories; first, the people who have stayed with the Adivasis for a relatively longer time and were functionally linked with them. This largely comprises of the service providing 'lower' caste groups who enjoyed a symbiotic relationship with the original inhabitants. The second group of people was 'outsiders' who entered the Adivasi areas initially as traders and after independence mostly as the new workforce required to work in the industrial and other ventures. This group also comprises of the administrative and landlord class which had emerged during the colonial times. In Jharkhand, the colloquial terms used to imply these two groups of people are *sadan*[26] and *diku*,[27] respectively. Over a period of time some of these people have come to own land and act as a major factor in determining the scenario of land acquisition. Apart from this, Nandini Sundar (2016: 7) points towards the problem of 'descheduling.' She argues that the scheduling of areas with the purpose of directed welfare expenditure is not as contested as the scheduling of communities. However, in the absence of absolute moratorium on the flow of non-tribals in the SAs will ostensibly lead to, and has indeed led to, demands for descheduling of areas (ibid.). This will possibly enable the non-tribals to grab tribal land and dereserve the ST constituencies. Attempts are made by urban governing bodies to notify new areas under municipal administration to deschedule them through backdoor policies. Similar attempts in Chaibasa where several villages were brought under municipal authority were protested by the people successfully. Moreover, studies have already found that out of the total 229 administrative units in SAs, 95 also include urban areas. Thus, PESA does not apply to almost 41 percent of the administrative units under SAs (Wahi and Bhatia 2018: 24).

In addition to this demographic profile of SAs, it is important to capture the issues of class and identity to gain a more nuanced understanding of politics. For example, there has been a rise of Adivasi elite and middle class who can be either a product of their political integration through the reservation of seats in legislature and/or state's affirmative policies. These new classes among the Adivasi population play a very confusing role in terms of understanding Adivasi politics.[28] While a good number of them have been found to be associating themselves with the votaries of neoliberal growth model many of them also play a crucial role in organising resistance against the resource grab. Identity formation is a crucial process in the articulation of resistance, and scholars have argued that in post-independence India initially the construction of Adivasi identity was a 'process from without' and only with the advent of modern education and the threats posed to the Adivasi *way of life* has made it a 'process from within' (Xaxa 2005: 1363). However, the idea that the politics organised around identity is spearheaded by a middle class because of modern education seems to be little problematic. Does this mean that the Adivasis are striving to ensure their cultural autonomy by adopting modern education as a tool? Isn't it paradoxical to think that 'modernity,' which has the visible tendency to usurp and subsume local customs and culture, can also serve as a tool to redeem the latter? In the past whenever Adivasi identity emerged as a galvanising tool against their exploiters, a crucial role was performed by charismatic leaders without any formal education. However, there are also cases where the identity construction took place by leaders like Birsa Munda who were aware of modern education and also received it partially.

It is worth mentioning that Adivasi identity also comprises of heterogeneous constructs which are more localised and particularly articulated around the basic units of ethnicity like *language and culture*. For example, the Hos, Santhals, Oraons, Mundas, Gonds and so on are different Adivasi groups with different ethnicities. However, the commonality among them can be drawn more on the grounds of the particular nature of religion (mostly naturalism), the sharing of tradition and practices, and also their geographical locations. Another aspect of forming a shared identity to create a discourse of shared interest as well as common enemy works through the creation of *others*. This *other* not only differs in the culture and outlook but holds a material view of the world which does not fits into the Adivasi world view. A significant contestation around the resources has also acquired a violent dimension in the form of left wing extremism regarded by the state as the 'greatest internal threat' to India.

The march of capitalism in India also seems to have created a situation where the STs and their habitations are seldom viewed outside some discomforting narratives. Coincidentally, areas of Maoist domination are contiguous with the huge presence of Adivasi population primarily living in the SAs. A highly prejudiced general perception prevails among the people about the SAs wherein the latter is regarded as consisting of nation's wealth in the form of minerals upon which the Maoists have laid claim through the active support of the Adivasis. Protests to safeguard their traditional source of livelihood are regarded in common parlance as anti-developmental. In a nutshell, some sense of despise and concern exist among the mainstream people who confess to the need of an *area combing* method in order to drag the Adivasis out of their backwardness and poverty. Nevertheless, the post-independence Indian government also realised several virtues of these 'backward' areas and their inhabitants. As a result of this realisation, a certain degree of autonomy was conferred on them to preserve their political institutions only to be followed by their 'development through integration'[29] (Wahi and Bhatia 2018: 17). The 'broken promises' have caused retaliation from the Adivasi community who try to reclaim their constitutional rights through popular movements.

Organisation of the volume

After presenting an overview on the SAs and how the process of untangling governance, law, and politics takes place, this section describes each chapter briefly and its linkages with the overall theme of the volume. The chapters are organised around mainly two themes – (1) governmentality and process of governance; and (2) sources and agencies that shape rights of Adivasis (i.e., law, judicial interpretations, articulation of resource rights by the state and Adivasis, resistance, participation, and the creation of parallel mechanism of governance). There are five chapters in the first sub-section on governmentality and four papers in the second sub-section on rights, legalism, and politics. The chapters of the first sub-section on governmentality cover topics on local governance/Panchayati Raj, financial governance, economic development, and instrumentality of governance for environment conservation in Schedule VI areas. The second sub-section on 'rights, legalism, and politics in the scheduled areas' cover four chapters, each one articulating a different right, and different dimensions of right, such as agency, process of right's articulation, exercising and expansion by Adivasis, and resistance by Adivasis.

The first chapter of the first sub-section, 'Manki-Munda system of West Singhbhum: historical overview of village governance and development' by Asoka Kumar Sen seeks to historically study the ideologies behind the formation and function of the indigenous Manki-Munda system in Kolhan region of the erstwhile Singhbhum district. During pre-colonial times, the institution developed as an autonomous system of social governance to bond the Ho community[30] and promote their welfare. This was co-opted by the British as a lower unit of Raj bureaucracy and invested with new rights and jurisdictions. The ideology at work was to consolidate colonial rule by creating the façade of ruling through the tribal social agencies. As elsewhere in India, the British rulers were inspired by the 'civilising mission' that inaugurated a paternalistic regime in which the traditional Manki-Munda system functioned as a political tool to promote the aforementioned purposes. After Indian independence, the system encountered the challenge of an alternative form of village governance known as Panchayati Raj that systematically displaced it from the helm. Divided in three broad sections, the first section traces the genesis and development of the indigenous institution and its function as an agency of development and change; the second critically examines the process of the incorporation of the institution as a political tool to consolidate British colonialism and promote change and development; and the last postscripts the experiments that state and Union governments have made since independence in mainstreamising and democratising the mechanism of rural governance and the final form that it took.

The second chapter, 'Issues of financial governance of Scheduled Areas' by the author duo Varsha Bhagat-Ganguly and Bhanu Shree Jain, explores and analyses various sources of fund allocation and utilisation for the welfare of the Scheduled Tribes from the perspective of governance. The main thrust of the chapter is the 'governmentality perspective' which includes how financial decisions, planning, and implementation address underdevelopment of tribals in SAs (i.e., whether there is consultative approach while aforesaid situations take place). While analysing the same, the author duo came across a web of issues which are financial and other than financial. The other than financial covers issues that are of a socio-economic and political nature. The problematic financial issues include a reduction in fund allocation, fund diversion, non-utilisation, and a lack of accountability of the government in the financial governance. Divided in three sections, the first section describes various sources of fund allocation, the following section undertakes an analysis of the fund flow of two components – (1) Tribal Sub-Plan and (2) a scheme, Vanbandhu Kalyan Yojana. Based on the study of these two components, the chapter tries to identify the linkages and problems in fund allocation in order to understand governmentality. The third section presents four puzzles to characterise governmentality (i.e., by describing the differentiation between the 'administration of funds' and 'governance as a tool for development' and whether this differentiation in financial governance approach facilitates movement and ensuring tribals' development in SAs). It also talks about upholding a bottom-up and participatory approach to governance, which has the potential for area-specific planning/regional development such as SAs and focusing on target group like STs; thus the government would be able make a shift from community-centric development to region-centric development.

The third chapter, 'Role of tribal autonomous council in economic development in the Sixth Scheduled Areas' by Sumarbin Umdor, focuses on the low financial autonomy of TAC by analysing the different sources of revenues of the councils. The chapter further shows the low contribution of own revenue and the financial dependence of the councils on the state governments. The third issue is explored by highlighting the lack of actions taken by the councils to protect the economic interest of the tribals through the enactment of appropriate legislations and their implementation over the years.

In continuation, the fourth chapter of the volume, 'Instrumentalities of governance in a multi-ethnic nation-state: Sixth Scheduled Area governance' by author duo Chandra Bhushan Kumar and Sonali Ghosh, studies the Bodoland Territorial Areas District (BTAD) of Assam as a case in order to understand and articulate the journey and relevance of the instrumentality of governance in the Sixth Scheduled Area. As the governance as an instrument is expected to entwine the 'community' and the 'public,' the authors bring these together for the larger common good on common ground as well as a mechanism for conflict resolution, especially in case of natural resources (such as forests and wildlife) within the statutory limits set in the nation-state. The paper situates a case study of Manas World Heritage Site, perceived as a successful model of governance in a scheme of a large project of nation-state. The chapter begins with tracing the historical journey that captures the aspirations of the Bodo community in the state of Assam and how congenially they responded to the site. The chapter describes the relationship of the Bodo community with the state and whether the community found the manoeuvring space in the present institutional architecture or the relationship with the state remained tenuous. The chapter looks at evolving nature and shape of the process of governance in the participation of the Bodos to conserve the site and draws upon learning related to the process of participation, the mechanism of conflict resolutions in a contested terrain (with special reference to natural resource ownership and management), and the complexities of governance in the state of Assam based on study of the BTAD Bodoland Territorial Council.

The following chapter, 'Mahua for Jharkhand's Ho? An accountability analysis of minor forest product governance,' is written by author duo Siddharth Sareen and Emma Jane Lord. The chapter shows how governance varies across resources in India's Scheduled Areas by studying the governance of minor forest products, which has been relatively neglected. The chapter elaborates a triple conjuncture of recognition: resources defined as MFPs, communities defined as Scheduled Tribes, and land territorialised through recognition as SAs and on occasion also as forest. Access to MFPs in SAs is governed by hybrid formal and customary laws. In practice, it is also determined by numerous trans-legal factors such as financial capital, social networks, epistemic politics, hierarchies based on intersectionality, and the very materiality of a specific resource. The chapter adopts an accountability analysis approach and contextualises minor forest product governance within the larger regional political economy by taking up the case of mahua (*Madhucaindica*) flowers, or *matkam*, in a Fifth Scheduled Area of Jharkhand where Ho communities reside. It analyses the local *matkam* value chain prior to use as distilled liquor and introduce two large external interventions that loom on the horizon vis-à-vis compensatory forestry and carbon forestry. A thorough understanding of accountability relations and the practices of legitimation that perform them problematises the implications of these interventions, which have the potential to reconfigure existing benefit allocations. Tracking relations of accountability within this dynamic, multi-scalar and multi-sited resource access assemblage throws the allocation of benefits extracted from *matkam* into relief and brings to light an accountability crisis in resource governance.

The chapter 'Politics of dispossession: land, law, and protest in Jharkhand' by Sujit Kumar is the second in Part II. This chapter emphasises that the land acquisition, particularly in the Scheduled Areas, has to be viewed in context of the specific laws apart from the umbrella legislation dictating the terms of acquisition. It studies how protective legislations like the Chotanagpur Tenancy Act, 1908, and the Santhal Parganas Tenancy Act, 1949, which are operational in Jharkhand, have framed the community perception towards land acquisition; and how this perception evokes responses ranging from 'jury politics' to protest movements. This chapter thus attempts to capture the politics revolving around the legality of land acquisition by analysing cases of land acquisition for Sponge Iron Projects (SIPs) in West Singhbhum of Jharkhand based upon empirical evidence from three SIPs. It builds upon the argument that the companies follow certain strategies to circumvent legality while the people subscribe to historical imagining of laws in organising protest movements. There exists a convoluted legal discourse inconsistent with people's aspirations and the space for legal ambiguities sometimes compromises the legitimacy of people's movements. A plausible solution to deal with these ambiguities is to embark upon people's rights in defining a set of laws ensuring their consensual participation in development and governance by strengthening the already existing laws like PESA and FRA.

The eighth chapter of the volume is 'Historical wrongs and forest rights: nascent jurisprudence on FRA and participatory evidence making' by Shomona Khanna. Forest law in India has undergone a paradigm shift since the colonial times to the more recent FRA. This statute is a trendsetter in participatory governance, turning the tables on entrenched mechanisms on administration of forest resources, which have been a gated resource since colonial times. From the centrality of state ownership of forest resources, the legal regime has evolved to recognise peoples' rights upon them. Even more significantly, the law dismantles established mechanisms for the determination of the nature and extent of such rights, and replaces them with a counter cultural mechanism where the village Gram Sabha is at the centre of the decision-making mechanism. Through the juxtaposition of two judgments of the Indian Supreme Court separated by almost three decades, namely the *Banwasi Seva Ashram* case from Uttar Pradesh (1986) and the *Niyamgiri* case from Odisha (2013), the chapter delves into the paradigm shift brought by the Forest Rights Act not only in the substantive content of forest rights, but also the procedural requirements of establishing such rights. The chapter, in particular, examines closely the nature of evidence and evidentiary rules which the Forest Rights Act seeks to rely upon, and the complex tensions which have come into play in the operation of such evidentiary rules in a system of forest administration which continues to be based on colonial legal architectures, and the compounding of such complexity by the digital revolution.

The ninth chapter 'Left wing extremism: Re-examining challenges for development and governance in the Scheduled Areas' is by Richard Hemraj Toppo. The Naxalite Movement(s) in India, broadly referred to as left wing extremism (LWE) in the official parlance, have had pre-occupied the domain of developmental-governance discourse in the Adivasi population in the Eastern and Central parts of the country. The principal state agency tasked with internal security, the Ministry of Home Affairs, has squarely put the blame on Naxalites for any underdevelopment and lack of governance in these regions. On the other hand, several scholars have questioned such discursive constructs, that of a terror-wielding Naxalite and a victimised-impoverished Adivasi, which would pave the way for 'counter' insurgency operations in the region. These scholars, instead, blame the state functioning and functionaries to have caused profound grievances amongst the Adivasis, from which Naxalite is only a manifestation. This chapter goes beyond these projected oppositional entities to explore the fluidity between the Adivasis, Naxalites, and the state, and how these fluid interactions have shaped the processes of development and governance in the Scheduled Areas of Eastern and Central India. It raises important questions on the traditional understanding of development and governance as state's monopolistic project, and rather argues for conceptualising them as a complex set of doings between different actors. The chapter draws inputs from fieldwork in Jharkhand, and the secondary sources are used either to substantiate or explore new insights.

The last chapter of the volume titled '*Pathalgadi* movement and conflicting ideologies of tribal village governance' by Anjana Singh talks about a form and cause of resistance by Adivasis to the existing system of governance in the SA of Jharkhand State. By studying the '*Pathalgadi*' (erection of stone slabs) movement, evolved as a popular form of Adivasi protest, the chapter shows different the aspirations and responses of Adivasis to the ground reality (i.e., in those villages where Adivasi's have lost hope of development). It captures the recent form of assertion by Adivasis for traditional rights of Adivasi villages as 'Gram Ganarajyas' (village republics) and how it has taken sharp political overtones in last year. While discussing the modern model of governance for augmentation of industrial growth by the government, the chapter depicts how the present model of governance gives undue advantage to the capitalists and the powerful and, in the given situations, how the marginalised communities resort to derive strength from laws – both traditional and modern. By adopting an empirical approach to understand the conflict of ideologies and evolving system of tribal village administration after enactment of PESA, 1996, the chapter seeks to unfold the nature and spectrum of the conflict, the causes of discontent against the present system of governance, the polarisation of the state and people, and the recent modality of tribal protest drawing legitimacy from an official act, yet using it as a tool against the state itself.

The diversity of issues pertaining to the development of SAs and STs, models of governance, and forms of governmentality revealed different types of rights of Adivasis articulated by different agencies from both the SAs – Fifth and Sixth – and how Adivasis as inhabitants of SAs have responded to the existing models of governance, laws, and politics that have addressed the existing paradoxes and puzzles of India's SAs. The key areas of governance in SAs are addressed and problematised (e.g., land question, left wing extremism, and identity-based movements to assert political autonomy, customary institutions, and minor forest produce [MFPs]). Through a variety of strategies/governance models, linking SAs and STs, the volume attempts to bring familiarity to little-known SAs of India, which is a pioneering contribution in the existing literature on India's Scheduled Areas. The case study approach in a given geographic area (SA) has a limitation (i.e., most of the study of cases are pertaining to the Jharkhand State) which happens to be a dynamic representative of SAs with the scope for keeping the analysis of governance area centric rather than falling in line with the conventional community or ST/Adivasi[31] centric analysis. Moving from a tribe-centric approach to a region-centric/SA-centric approach is a formative and trend setting approach in this context; Jharkhand presents for a dynamic investigation into issues of governance in SAs and the combination of SAs and STs.

Notes

1 Adivasi literally means original settlers/inhabitants.
2 While the term 'indigenous' implying 'original settlers' is more suitable to be used in context of North and South America and Australia, in South Asia it acquires a controversial dimension based upon the theory of Aryan invasion. Nevertheless, many Adivasi communities use the political construct of 'Adivasi' (original settlers/inhabitants) for self-reference although this term is not recognised by the Government of India (MoTA 2014: 25). Officially these tribes are known as 'Scheduled Tribes' and usually mentioned as 'tribals.'
3 Odisha, Madhya Pradesh, Chhattisgarh, Jharkhand, Maharashtra, Gujarat, Rajasthan, Andhra Pradesh and West Bengal. About 12 percent inhabit the North-eastern region, about five percent in the Southern region and about three percent in the Northern States (MoTA 2014).
4 All parts of Meghalaya State and parts of the states of Assam, Tripura, and Mizoram. Originally, the Sixth Schedule areas were created in 1952; they were reorganised in 1971, i.e. Mizoram and Meghalaya were carved out of the composite Assam. These areas have been given special provisions under Part XXI of the Constitution. The extension of such provisions to newer areas has been the result of political mobilisation and social movements (MoTA 2014: 25).
5 As per Article 244(2) and 275(1) of Indian Constitution. Article 244(2) mandates formation of District Council for each autonomous district, not more than 30. Four out of 30 members could be nominated by the Governor and the rest could be elected.
6 As per paragraph 6(1) of the Fifth Schedule [Article 244(1)] to the Constitution of India, the expression 'Scheduled Areas' means 'such areas as the President may by order declare to be Scheduled Areas.' In accordance with the provisions of paragraph 6(2) of the Fifth Schedule to the Constitution, the President may at any time by order increase the area of any Scheduled Area in a state after consultation with the Governor of that state; rescind, in relation to any State or States, any order or orders made under this paragraph; and in consultation with the Governor of the State concerned, make fresh orders redefining the areas which are to be Scheduled Areas (https://tribal.nic.in/writereaddata/News/2018042503 23288187946PressReleaseScheduledAreas.pdf accessed on 1 May 2018).
7 The executive power of the Union under Para 3 of the Schedule V extends to give directions to the State as to the administration of the SAs.
8 Available at https://tribal.nic.in/writereaddata/News/201804250323288187946 PressReleaseScheduledAreas.pdfaccessed on 1 May 2018.
9 Assam and Tripura are tribal minority States as an exception with 12.45 percent and 31.76 percent ST population respectively to the total population according to the 2011 Census.
10 The Lokur committee constituted in 1965 looked at the matter of scheduling the groups as Scheduled Tribes and the criteria used by it are accepted even today. The committee accepted five criteria: (i) primitive traits, (ii) distinct culture, (iii) geographical isolation, (iv) shyness of contact with the community at large, and (v) backwardness.
11 The word 'tribals' is used referring to ST and 'Adivasi.'

12 Jaipal Singh, Shibban Lal Saksena, Brajeshwar Prasad, and K M Munshi
13 Advisory Committee on Fundamental Rights and Minorities,
14 For details see *The Framing of India's Constitution: Select Documents, Vol. III (pp. 681–779), Vol. IV (376–391)*
15 Bhuria Committee (1991) and the Bhuria Commission (2002–2004) – Bhuria Committee recommendations paved the way for the enactment of the PESA Act, 1996, while the Bhuria Commission focused on a wide range of issues from the Fifth Schedule to tribal land and forests, health and education, the working of Panchayats, and the status of tribal women. The most recent committees have been the Bandopadhyay Committee, which looked at development and governance in Left-Wing Extremist areas, and the Mungekar Committee, which examined issues of administration and governance (MoTA 2014: 26). The High Level Committee was organised by the Prime Minister's Office in 2014 on researching the socio-economic, health, and educational status of tribal communities of India, and was led by Dr Virginius Xaxa.
16 For instance, the Regional Councils, for an autonomous region, and District Councils, within the Autonomous Districts, have the powers to assess and collect revenue, levy taxes on lands and buildings in accordance with the principles of the state of which such councils and districts are a part. But the federal and state governments retain powers to acquire land in exercise of the power of eminent domain. In addition, they have the powers to grant licenses for prospecting for mining in the Autonomous Regions and Districts, except that the state has to share royalties with the District Councils as agreed upon by the state governments. Like in the Fifth Schedule Areas, the President may by notification apply or restrict the application of central acts, and the Governor may do so with respect to state Acts in the autonomous districts or regions of any of these states (Wahi and Bhatia 2018: 17).
17 The British colonial state attempted to classify tribal communities through customs, dialects, traits (listing of criminal tribes), backwardness, and need for tribal 'rights and privileges' to be conferred at the will by the British state (Wahi and Bhatia 2018: 13).
18 The Mundari-Khuntkatti villages in Jharkhand are the ones originally established by the Adivasis by clearing the forest areas. In post-independence India, these villages are accorded special status with due recognition to the rights of its inhabitants (Sen 2012).
19 Historians like Asoka Kumar Sen (2012) and Sanjukta Dasgupta (2011) have argued that the Ho Adivasis in Kolhan region of Jharkhand migrated to these areas and colonised it by removing the earlier settlers like *Saraks* and *Bhuiyans*.
20 The indigenous/tribal peoples who constituted 8 percent of the total population of India at 1991census make up 55 percent of the total displaced persons due to development projects up to1990. According to the MoTA, nearly 85 lakh tribals were displaced until 1990 on account of mega developmental projects like dams, mining, industries, and conservation of forests etc. (http://socialissuesindia.wordpress.com accessed on 18 April 2018).
21 Samaddar and Sen (2012: 1) refer to governance as a process of production of subjects and governance as a field of strategies in the context of participatory democracy. As a field of strategies, they have tried to indicate how strategic imperatives of rule (such as law-making, constitutionalism, producing the combined discourse of the rule of law and rights, promise-making in politics and other forms of legitimacy exercise, developmentalism as a strategy of governance, governance as a means of ensuring security, etc.) take their shape. By a 'process of production of subjects' they want to say that governance is not a one-sided affair starting and ending with those who rule and govern us, producing fiats,

decrees, and diktats, but a productive process – one that produces the subjects of governance who then react to the process and make the field of governance a contentious one. As this volume focuses on SAs, specially carved areas, the application of these terms is different from the context of participatory governance. Some of the components such as 'imperatives of rule' and 'contentious processes' are applied in the context of politics, rights, legalism, and governmentality.

22 Virginius Xaxa (2005: 1363) argues that religion and caste became the accepted units of sociological analysis because of their ability to transcend region and language barriers. It is because of this that even the colonial administrators and anthropologists first accepted animistic religion as the criteria to differentiate between the caste and Adivasi people. Features like primitive conditions of living, geographical isolation, etc. were added as a corollary to the primary postulate of religion.

23 Michel Foucault (1969: 7–13) argues that the hegemonic form of history writing considers the selected historical monuments to construct an overwhelming document in which the episodic contents have been deliberately silenced. However, history writing as an archaeological exercise has tried to uncover these hidden layers and resort to writing a 'series of series' even at the risk of being accused by the writers of monumental history as having subscribed to unaccepted tools of methodology.

24 Scholars like Walter Fernandes (2004: 1192) put the final figure of project-affected people till 2000 at around 50 million out of which almost 70 percent are the STs. In comparison to the national average of almost 74 percent the literacy of ST is around 59 percent as per the 2011 census. In 2004–2005, as against 37 percent of the average population, 60 percent of the STs were below the poverty line and the infant mortality was as high as 62 per 1,000 live births (MoTA 2014: 26).

25 This, according to Kalyan Sanyal (2007), comprises of those people who are not accommodated within the capitalist structures of growth.

26 The term *sadan* is used to refer to the people who have been living by the side of the Adivasis for a relatively longer period and were primarily allowed to settle in Adivasi areas due to functional utility of these occupational groups.

27 *Diku* is a derogatory term used by the Adivasis to refer to those outsiders who migrated into the Adivasi areas with the clear purpose of exploiting them. This group is generally comprised of landlords and money lenders. The term has broadened to include even industrialists and others who invest in Adivasi areas in mining and other projects.

28 For an intricate analysis of Adivasi politics in Jharkhand, please see Sujit Kumar (2018) Adivasis and the State politics in Jharkhand. *Studies in Indian Politics*, 6(1): 103–116.

29 Namita Wahi and Ankit Bhatia (2018) argue that the Faizpur resolution of All India Congress Committee adopted the 'development through integration' approach for the tribal population which continued even after independence. This approach was to adopt the affirmative policies of reserving seats in legislative bodies, jobs, and education. However, identity intertwined with geography serves the purpose of retaining autonomy.

30 One of the four major Adivasi communities of present-day Jharkhand.

31 Nandini Sundar, Ramchandra Guha, and other scholars' writings focus on STs and issues of LWE, underdevelopment, violation of their rights, identity question, and so on. Their analyses are community/tribe focused, not on the SAs as a region. The existing writings refer to central India, Madhya Pradesh, Chhattisgarh, and rarely on Andhra Pradesh and to some extent Maharashtra states, which are part of SAs.

References

Bhukhya, B. 2016. *The Roots of the Periphery: A History of the Gonds of Deccan India*. Oxford: Oxford University Press.

DasGupta, S. 2011. *Adivasis and the Raj: Socio-Economic Transition of the Hos, 1820–1932*. Hyderabad: Orient Blackswan.

Fernandes, W. 2004. 'Rehabilitation Policy for the Displaced.' *Economic and Political Weekly*, 39(12): 1191–1193.

Foucault, M. 1969. *Archaeology of Knowledge*. London: Routledge.

Government of India. 1961. *Report of the Scheduled Areas and Scheduled Tribes Commission*. Available at https://books.google.co.in/books?id=GVXRAAAAMAAJ&printsec=frontcover&source=gbs_ge_summary_r&cad=0#v=onepage&q&f=false

Guha, R. 2007. 'Adivasi, Naxalites and Indian Democracy.' *Economic and Political Weekly*, 42(32): 4107–4113.

Hindustan Times. 2018. 'Centre Approves Scheduled Areas Extension in Rajasthan.' 25 April 2018. Available at www.hindustantimes.com/24aipur/centre-approves-scheduled-areas-extension-in-rajasthan/story-pX3DghggI2NQHe36zlFL9O.html (accessed on 1 May 2018).

Kela, S. 2012. *A Rogue and Peasant Slave: Adivasi Resistance, 1800–2000*. New Delhi: Navayana.

Kumar, S. 2018. 'Adivasis and the State Politics in Jharkhand.' *Studies in Indian Politics*, 6(1): 103–116.

Majumdar, D.N. 1937. *A Tribe in Transition: A Study in Culture Pattern*. Calcutta: Longman, Greens & Co. Ltd.

Ministry of Tribal Affairs (MoTA). 2014. *High Level Committee on Socio-Economic, Health and Educational Status of Tribal Communities in India*. Government of India.

PTI. 2018. *Union Cabinet Approves Extension of Scheduled Areas in Rajasthan; Over 45 lakh Tribals Stand to Benefit in State* (26 April 2018). Available at: www.firstpost.com/india/union-cabinet-approves-extension-of-scheduled-areas-in-rajasthan-over-45-lakh-tribals-stand-to-benefit-in-state-4446199.html (accessed on 2 May 2018).

Rose, N. 1999. *Powers of Freedom: Reframing Political Thought*. Cambridge: Cambridge University Press.

Samaddar R. and Sen, S.K. 2012. *New Subjects and New Governance in India*. India: Routledge.

Sanyal, K. 2007. *Rethinking Capitalist Development: Primitive Accumulation, Governmentality and Post-Colonial Capitalism*. New Delhi: Routledge.

Sen, A.K. 2012. *From Village Elder to British Judge: Custom, Customary Law and Tribal Society*. New Delhi: Orient Blackswan.

Sharma, B.D. 2010. *Unbroken History of Broken Promises: Indian State and the Tribal People*. New Delhi: Sahyog Pustak Kuteer.

Sikor, T. and Johannes, S. 2011. 'Introduction: The Rights-Based Agenda in International Forestry.' In T. Sikor and J. Stahl (Eds.), *Forests and People: Property, Governance and Human Rights* (pp. 1–13). London: Routledge.

Sundar, N. 2016. 'Introduction: Of the Scheduled Tribes, States and Sociology.' In N. Sundar (Ed.), *The Scheduled Tribes and Their India: Politics, Identities, Policies and Work* (pp. 1–45). New Delhi: Oxford University Press.

Sunderlin, W. 2011. The Global Forest Tenure Transition: Background, Substance, and Prospects. In T. Sikor and J. Stahl (Eds.), *Forests and People: Property, Governance and Human Rights* (pp. 14–30). London: Routledge.

Wahi, N. and Bhatia, A. 2018. 'The Legal Regime and Political Economy of Land Rights of Scheduled Tribes in the Scheduled Areas of India.' *Research Report. CPR Land Rights Initiative*. New Delhi: Centre for Policy Research.

Xaxa, V. 2005. 'Politics of Language, Religion and Identity: Tribes in India.' *Economic and Political Weekly*, 40(13): 1363–1370.

Part I

Governmentality

A neoliberal perspective on governance

2 Manki-Munda system of West Singhbhum

Historical overview of village governance and development

Asoka Kumar Sen

Introduction

During 1947–2010, Bihar (Jharkhand since 2000) state and Union governments made attempts to lay the basis of a uniform democratic system of village governance known as the Panchayati Raj system. This stoked a debate in the public domain between pan-Indianism, represented by the Panchayati Raj, and regionalism by the indigenous Manki-Munda system. The new experiment with village governance was conducted steadily through the Bihar Panchayat Raj Act, 1947 (Bihar Act 7 of 1948), article 243 B of the Constitution Act 1992 (73rd Amendment, Part IX) laying down three-tier Panchayat (village, intermediate, and district levels), the Panchayats (Extension to the Scheduled Areas) Act by the Indian Parliament in 1996,[1] the Jharkhand Panchayati Raj Act (JPRA) in 2001 (amended in 2003),[2] the Jharkhand Panchayati Raj (Amendment) Ordinance of 2010, and the Jharkhand Raj Panchayat (Amendment) Act, 2010 (Bill No 93-F of 2010). While recognising the specificity of tribal customs and institutions, these measures sought to introduce a uniform and elected system of village self-rule. However, the concept of Panchayati Raj remained contentious, stirring up social protests in Bihar and Jharkhand. The issues were whether it was proper to retain a hereditary mode of governance in a democratic polity, and whether the Manki-Munda system should continue to function in the Kolhan region of erstwhile Singhbhum, when the Panchayati Raj system governed other parts of the country. The Adivasi community in Jharkhand contended that the indigenous system was a symbol of their collective identity, an institution most capable of governing their lives and resources. Spanning between the pre-colonial period down to the lived present, this chapter seeks to explore what the traditional system was, what was the ideology behind it, and how this system was invented during colonial rule. Divided in three broad sections, the first deals with its pre-colonial form and content, second, studies its hybridisation during British rule, and it is followed in the last section by its systematic replacement by the Panchayat Raj.

The Manki-Munda system during the pre-colonial period

The Adivasi communities in Jharkhand had developed Manki-Munda and *parha-parganait* systems long before the advent of the British in their territories. These governed their villages (*hatus*) and the supra village formation known as pir-parha-pargana. The origin of the institution was coeval with the adoption of a settled village life. In the case of the Hos of Kolhan, this had occurred when the breakaway Munda groups migrated to Singhbhum from Chotanagpur plateau since the 10th century AD. Since the 18th century AD, they raised their permanent villages in the southern parts of Singhbhum, better known as Kolhan. In the history of Adivasi political expansion across Jharkhand, the issue of leadership was differentially crucial. Among the Mundas, we find Risa Munda as their legendary culture hero, who with 21,000 followers set up the cradle of the Munda community in Murima village and his adherents Koromba and Sutia, respectively, in Koromba and Sutiambe villages (Hallett 1917: 22). But the story is different in the case of the Hos. The Ho history of colonisation relates the story of village-specific founders, and not that of a generic culture hero as the maker of a unified cradle. The origin of the position of village head is closely related to this history of Ho political expansion. This determined the nature of the post and the ideology governing it.

Village governance and Munda-in-Panchayat

Adivasi communities attributed different names to their village head: Munda by the Munda and Ho; Manjhi by the Santal and Mahato by the Oraon. The significance of this office lay in performing a crucial role in the steady graduation of the community from itinerancy to settled village life. This shaped their understanding of what should be the basic character of this post: Whether this should be communitarian rather than authoritarian, and what role the Munda should play in shaping the entire course of village making. Making a village had different stages: First, the selection of the village site in the forests of Singhbhum by the village founder, called *Ham* in Ho; second, the demarcation of the village boundary and performance of the ceremonial prayer to propitiate the *bonga*, supposedly governing the space; third, the building of the huts of the early man and his associates; fourth, the invitation to others; and last, the allocation of village spaces among later comers for building their huts and preparing lands for cultivation. In setting the norms of settled rural life and cultivation, the leadership of the village founder was crucial.

For performing the historic role of village making, the original founder or the early man became the head or Munda of the village (Roy 1970: 63–64; Bodding 1994: 101). Since he offered prayer to the spirit of the space, he acted as the village priest, called *Deuri* (Ho), *Pahan* (Munda, Oraon), and *Naeke* (Santal) (Roy 1970: 63–64; Roy 1984: 28).[3] Conjunction of the mundane and sacerdotal duties to the same person[4] implied that originally the duty of the Munda was to ensure the material and moral well-being of the village and its inhabitants. However, the offices of the Munda and Deuri were bifurcated later, causing the disjunction of the profane and religious roles of the village head.

The next important function of the early man was to set the demographic pattern of the village. He invited members of his family and killi (i.e., *haga*, also members of those killis, called *bala*). However, peopling the village was a gradual process that continued under the later Mundas also. This way the ethnic character of the villages took shape, converting the villages of Kolhan into multi-killi formations from their original uni-killi character. Demographic profiling took final shape when the Mundas of this region allowed functional castes to settle in conducting village socio-economy. This consummated the making of the village community. Negotiating homogeneous relations among villagers for the maintenance of peace and harmony within his area was the prime duty of the village head.

Distribution of village lands was his third important function. This privilege accrued to him by virtue of Adivasi traditional norm, which accorded ownership of a village to the founder and his family/killi. Initial land distribution among the founder, his family, and associates, generally his agnates, was made at the behest and supervision of the founder. Allocation of village lands among later comers (killis and communities) was often done by the subsequent Mundas. At this stage, the village ceased on all practical purposes to belong solely to the founding killi, giving birth to the concept of village land/resources belonging to the village community, as headed by the Munda.

The post of the Munda was hereditary; it descended on the male line and remained confined to the founding family/killi, unless the family became heirless. In the absence of a son, it passed to the nearest male kin of the same family. There was no custom of enacting the practice of social consensus among the Hos as we find among the Santals. Among the latter, the ritual of renewal of social selection of the village head was annually enacted when the Manjhi had to surrender the post and get himself socially selected again. But the tradition of social support was implicit among the Hos also. This can be derived from the fact that the person on whom the post devolved had to be physically and mentally fit to serve the office to the satisfaction of the village community.

The Munda did not govern the village by virtue of his wealth and power. His landed property, though often greater than others, was in no case considerably disproportionate to those owned by the latter, nor had he the power to acquire extra wealth by appropriating revenue like a *zamindar*. He did not head or own an armed force to enforce his command and authority like a feudal lord. He was the social leader for whom villagers felt attachment, rather than fear.[5] The basis of village governance was therefore communitarian rather than authoritarian. As representing the social will of the village community, the Munda functioned more as 'first among the equals,' than as their overlord. In governing the village, he was assisted by the village Panchayat comprised of village elders and respectable members of the same village.

We do not have any oral or literate evidence of the jurisdiction and precise functioning of Munda-in-Panchayat before the advent of British rule. But on the basis of sparse colonial ethnography and colonial-day mechanism of village governance, we can form an approximate idea of the system during this period. This body had two major functions: Resolution of disputes for the maintenance of peace and harmony in the village and governance of village common property. Disputes at family and intra-killi levels were solved internally by the head of the family and elders of the killi comprising killi Panchayat. Disputes of general nature occurring among killis and communities, as also those which could not be resolved at the familial and killi levels, came up before the village Panchayat, headed by the Munda. These were generally land- and marriage-related issues, as also crimes like murder and theft committed within the village (Majumdar 1937: 60–65; Roy 1984: 28.).[6] This social tribunal was held at a central place in the village like the *manjhi than* among the Santal or the *akhara* (i.e., village meeting place) and dancing ground as in Chotanagpur plateau (Man 1983: 88; O'Malley 1999: 111; Roy 1935: 242). The issues were raised, discussed in the presence of the villagers, arbitrated openly, and a consensual rather than adversarial judgment was finally delivered. The sole purpose was the maintenance of village peace and harmony (Sen 2012: 54–55). It does not appear that there was a supra-village body for appeal among the Hos like the *Council of Five Manjhis* under the *parganait* found among the Santals (O'Malley 1999: 112; Archer 1984: 15–24).

The second duty of the village council was to govern the common property of the village. This comprised the village forest, uplands, and natural water resources like the spring and river, besides tanks left behind by the pre-Ho settlers of Kolhan like the Saraks (a community of lay Jains) and Bhuiyans. Customarily, the concept of commonness originated because the ethnic communities in general believed that being *Singbonga*'s free gift to them, these natural resources were common properties to be enjoyed by villagers alike. A significant fact was that this notion of commonness that was customarily defined and asserted in respect of the over-ground natural resources only, and not over underground resources like minerals (Sen 2017: 41–46). Significantly therefore, the spelling of the items of village property, as done either by the PESA Act and subsequent Ordinances, elaborated later, was an extension of the ambience of village property itself. We cannot however deny that both the Union and Jharkhand Governments were responding to the claim of rights over natural resources, including mines and minerals, asserted by the Adivasi intelligentsia in the state during post-independence decades (Sen 2018: Chap X).

This question may be begged: Did the indigenous mode of governance promote village development the way the term is meant today? Presumably, the administrators of the village did not make any conscious or noteworthy effort to either conduct or guide the course of village development through building of roads, weekly markets, tanks for irrigation, health facilities, educational institution etc. We cannot however deny that material and moral changes were in motion. Villagers participated in the intra- and inter-village barter economy for which forest pathways had developed. Villages adjacent to non-Adivasi villages showed remarkable agricultural growth, a fact lauded in early colonial ethnography.[7] The social institution of *Gitiora* had developed to educate village youth about the traditional social norms. This way, 'traditions and customs,' which the PESA Act sought to safeguard, had instilled a sense of distinct Ho 'cultural identity' and ethnicity.[8] However, the most remarkable and conscious attempt initiated by the Mundas was to invite functional castes and allot lands to settle in their villages. Caste groups paved the way for the advent of modern technology that fulfilled the need of iron implements, clay utensils, cloth, and wooden furniture which promoted the growth of agro-rural life among the Hos.

Governance of pir and the office of the Manki

The higher unit of village governance was pir, parha, or pargana (Roy 1970: 238–248),[9] comprising a varying number of villages. The head of a pir was called the Manki. We cannot definitively say how and when the institutions of pir and Manki originated. One view, as adduced from the Munda[10] history, informs us that parha and Manki organically developed out of an indigenous matrix. The parha was originally 'a wider brotherhood,' rather a socio-political body of 'allied and associated villages,' formed to 'afford greater protection to the communities against the aggression of other village units that surrounded them' (Roy 1970: 235–236; Hallett 1917: 23). 'Munda of the parent village, or the strongest and most influential of the headmen' was generally selected as the Manki. Oraon parha system also had the similar origin. But among them the head of parha was called the Raja (ibid.: 23–24). But colonial ethnography on the Ho offers another explanation. The local chiefs of Porahat, Mayurbhanj, Seraikela, and Kharsawan created the institutions of pir and Manki and imposed them on the autonomous villages to establish feudal control over the Hos. They were assigned the duties of the collection of land revenue and maintenance of law and order within their territories (Tuckey 1920: para 32). Village revenue was collected by the Munda, which was remitted to the chief's treasury through the Manki. We do not have any idea whether Manki and pir had any judicial function as we found among the Munda, Oraon, and Santal. Among the latter, the pir council functioned either as a primary or appellate court (Hallett 1917: 66–68).

However, the political control of the local chiefs over the Hos gradually dwindled since AD 1620. This seemed to have sapped the feudal hierarchisation of village administration and the practice of imposing the control of the Manki and pir over the Mundas and villages. Consequently, the villages regained their earlier autonomy, and the primacy of the Munda and

Panchayat was restored. But the Manki and pir were not completely obliterated. This can be substantiated by the fact that after the Ho territory was conquered by the British, the new administrative unit named Kolhan Government Estate (KGE), formed by them in 1837, comprised 622 villages under 26 pirs.

After the formation of Jharkhand, Adivasi intelligentsia appropriated this historical institution to articulate their protest against the Panchayati Raj System. K.C. Hembrom, the leader of the *Kolhan Raksha Dal*, who considered the Manki-Munda System as an essentially Adivasi institution, gave the call *Ho Dostur abua* (Welcome to Ho system) and *Diku Dostur Kabua* (Down with the Diku system).[11] They underlined that their system of village governance was characterised by the ideologies of social selection, people's direct participation, and consensual functioning; it was conducted by the Munda and Panchayat, comprising *Moy Ho* (i.e., five members). This was therefore antithetical and superior to the party-centric Panchayati Raj formed through secret ballot and arbitrarily run by the *mukhiya* and *sarpanch*.[12] Interestingly, this self-narrative suffered from an identification problem. They were confused whether to locate their identity in a pre-colonial original institution or the hybridised institution during the colonial period. Confusion was created mainly because of fragmentary knowledge about the pre-colonial past, as compared to the colonial. Consequently, they often identified their mechanism of village administration as filtered by the British to be their original system. This will be elaborated in the next section.

British rule and the changing system of village governance

Instead of implementing the system as it existed, the British restructured it to suit their ideology of governance. Bentinck-day[13] ideology was to give due recognition to indigenous mode of village administration. As the existing rural governance represented to the British 'a tribal and communal system of self-government of a purely natural growth,'[14] they incorporated it into British bureaucracy. Through this co-option, British rulers wanted to impress the Hos that they would continue to be governed by their social leaders. This was obviously a ploy to stave off the fear of tribal unrest. Second, colonial rulers avowed that this system was intended to save them from the non-Adivasis by fencing them off from the mainstream. To quote: 'In the Kolhan we are dealing with a protected race. The Hos have been protected against contact with the outer world by the complete recognition of their communal system of government.'[15] Furthermore, the British wanted to politico-economically integrate Kolhan within the Raj framework. The village and pir were therefore brought under the progressive control and superintendence of the district, divisional, provincial, and central administration. In this administrative hierarchy, the lowest official was the Munda; Manki was his superior; and the deputy commissioner was the head of the district administration. This structure functioned under the superintendence and control of the commissioner and the provincial and central administration. It was natural therefore that the Manki-Munda system lost its pre-colonial autonomy and the social functionaries were converted into government officials.

Bureaucratisation of social functionaries was done by bringing them under clearly defined powers and jurisdictions. First, specific rules of their appointment, service, and dismissal were framed. The British more or less legitimised the traditional familial, hereditary, and male-centric norms of appointment to these posts.[16] They legalised seniority and adulthood criteria in the appointment to these offices. Digressing from Ho tradition, British administration made the literacy criterion obligatory so that village officials could effectively serve the administrative machinery run by written laws and procedures.[17] More notable was however the invention of the customary norm of social approval. Knowledge of this is relevant particularly because of contemporary claim, as related earlier, that the Manki-Munda system was a socially selected and consensually functioning customary institution. It seems that during the pre-British period incumbency of the familially chosen candidate, not suffering from infirmity, inefficiency, or misconduct, received tacit social approval, though formal enactment of the annual social approval like the Santals was not in practice among the Hos. In normal cases, the British allowed the aforementioned practice to continue. But while appointing a Munda from outside the original family, due either to the extinction of the direct line or family taint owing to the past record of dismissal, it became imperative to elicit the opinions of the Manki and villagers. Similarly, support of villagers of the pir was made necessary for appointing a Manki.[18] Besides the framing of appointment rules, the British introduced the punitive measure of dismissal and the imposition of a fine on village officials for disobedience and misconduct. When a village official was dismissed, the said family was debarred from succession to the post. During British rule, due to recurring cases of misconduct, appointment outside the derelict family became the rule.[19]

Under colonial rule, village officials were assigned the power to collect revenue, maintain the law and order, deliver justice, and promote development within their territory. The rights and duties were elaborated in the *pattas* issued to a Manki and Munda during the land revenue settlements of 1838, 1867, 1895, and 1914. The British officials believed that this 'system of village polity is clearly one which should be carefully fostered and the introduction of any law which would tend to weaken or break it up is to be deprecated.'[20]

It was made incumbent on the Manki to oversee and ensure the due and timely collection of land rents of villagers and their remittance at the district treasury by the Mundas. The duty of the Munda was to collect rent from villagers in two unequal installments. The default in payment was a penal offence for which he could be subjected to forfeiture of commission, fine, attachment and sale of property, and finally dismissal.[21] On being sanctioned by the Deputy Commissioner, the Munda could appoint a *Tahsildar* whose duty was to maintain accounts and grant receipts for rents to payers. The village head was required to ensure that that the Tahsildar followed the rules strictly.[22] For the performance of their duties, the Manki and Munda were entitled respectively to 10 and 16% commission of the total amount collected by them.[23] These measures made fundamental changes in the process of resource mobilisation within a village. First, the right of the village community to mop up a resource was withdrawn; instead of indefinite and irregular payment of subscription, fixed and timely payment of rent was introduced and default in payment was made a punitive offence for the villagers and collectors.

The village and pir heads were the primary agencies for the maintenance of law and order within their areas.[24] The police had no jurisdiction in Kolhan.[25] As a local police functionary, the duty of the Manki and Munda was to see that peace and order were not disturbed in the village and pir. Furthermore, they had to apprehend criminals and deliver them to the nearest *thana*.[26] The village and pir *Dakua* or *Chaukidar* helped them in apprehending the offenders and carried the report to the thana. Interestingly, while the post of pir dakua was officially recognised, that of the village was not (Sahu 1985: 134). A significant fact was that during the early decades, an elaborate mechanism of maintenance of law and order had not developed and thanas and police personnel were very few in number. So the district administration heavily depended on village officials for keeping Kolhan free from any disturbances and crime.

As enunciated through Wilkinson's[27] civil and criminal rules and his letter written to his assistant Lt. S.R. Tickell,[28] Manki, Munda, and village Panchayat were accorded specific judicial powers. Wilkinson instructed Tickell to make 'as much use as possible of Panchayats taking care to select the most respected and intelligent amongst the Coles to compose the Panch.'[29] This body was to comprise 'three or five persons to be selected by the agents or assistants from amongst the persons most conversant with the matter at issue' (Sen 1999: 88). This imprecision in the composition rebuts the contemporary claim that the village Panchayat comprised Moy Ho (Five Hos). Furthermore, it was also not imperative to keep the selection among the Hos only. Wilkinson's rules stipulated that in inter-village disputes, Panchayat was to be 'selected from amongst the head, most influential, and respectable men of the adjacent villages' (ibid.: 89). However, confining the selection from among village and pir heads as well as substantial *raiyats* became the normal practice.[30] The Manki-Munda-Panchayat came to be invested with primary and original jurisdictions in the Kolhan court system. It was their duty to make local enquiries, adduce and interpret customs, give their award in a properly constituted Panchayat. On this basis, the final judgment was awarded by the district administration (Sen 2012: Chap IV). Wilkinson's civil rules (ibid.: 68) and section 76 of Chotanagpur Tenancy Act (CNT Act) of 1908 (Datta 1928: 185) made 'common law' and tribal customs the basis of delivering justice. In normal practice, village officials appropriated customs from village elders and interpreted them before the local courts. But during British rule, the judges reinterpreted the customs as per the British ideology of equity, uniformity, and justice (Sen 2012: 81–137). Local administration claimed that in this Kolhan system 'the Hos have nothing to do with the numerous petty officials of the Khas Mohal, Tahsildars, Excise Officers, etc.'[31] In fact, the village court system was kept under the revenue officers like Settlement Officer and Assistant Settlement Officer with the Deputy Commissioner as the final authority (Sen 2012: 73–80).

The British deployed village and pir heads as agencies for promoting the development of the area. Since rich forest and mineral resources of Kolhan provided the essential raw material for material growth, the primary concern of the local administrators was to assert state control over these resources. But the local administration had two immediate problems to resolve. First, they found that delinquency of tribals extended beyond their militant uprisings, as they indulged in the rampant destruction of natural resources, particularly the forests. Therefore, the fear was rife that 'If left to their own devices the aboriginals will clear everything in less than one generation.'[32] Protection and judicious management of state resources became understandably the prime purpose of governmentality. Second, while implementing state ownership of land, water and forest, they had to resolve the disjuncture from the Adivasi notion of village community as the ultimate owner and manager of these resources. Colonial rulers were careful not to trigger tribal protest by ignoring Ho customary forest and land rights.

Drawing on the pre-colonial tradition, the local administration therefore created a shared realm of the management of village natural resources to elicit local support. The records of rights entrusted the Munda and Manki to 'protect' and 'look after' the trees of the protected forest and village or his circle; to protect the forest from fire, damages, and encroachments by villagers; and to report the same to the Deputy Commissioner. They were required to repair and protect *bandh* or tank, irrigation works, boundary pillars, and village roads with the help of 'his raiyats.'[33] Instead of assigning local development projects to private contractors, the normal practice was to advance money to the Mundas and Mankis to get these done at the local level 'at half the rate'.[34] Similarly, to regulate the management of village land, the Munda was required to prevent any transfer or alienation of land and 'to inform the Deputy Commissioner of the transfer of land by gift, sale, mortgage or when land passes into the hands of another by partition or of settlement of waste or relinquished land.' Besides these, the village and pir heads were required 'to encourage all works of improvement and measures calculated to add to the prosperity of the people' Significantly, as regards the moral growth of people, the Manki was enjoined to 'promote education among the people and to have his own heirs educated.'[35] Furthermore, the Mankis and Mundas had to supervise and execute officially commissioned projects for developing the system of transport and irrigation. Understandably, for the allotment of funds and the preparation of the schemes, they had to rely on the district administration. Money was generally allotted from the Kolhan Improvement Fund.[36]

During the entire span of British rule, village officials generally collaborated with local administration. They regularly collected and deposited land revenue in the district treasury as evident from high percentage of revenue collection.[37] They managed their police duties to the best of their capability. The efficacy of the system during early part of British rule earned official recognition. The Superintendent of Police, Singhbhum, admitted: 'The Manki and Munda system I believe worked well in former years when the Kols were the principal inhabitants of the Kolhan and when they acknowledged and respected the authority of their headmen.'[38] These officials could resolve 'all the minor disputes among the villagers,'[39] which ably fulfilled the colonial policy of expeditious justice and distancing Adivasis from British courts and lawyers. Protection of natural resources from the destruction of villagers and rapacity and infringement of outsiders was the other job more or less done well.

The Mankis and Mundas could build a bridge between the villagers and the government. They could act 'as a political intermediary between Government and the raiyats. . . . All Government orders and intentions are communicated to the people through them and through them the latter lay their grievances to the Government authorities in charge of the Kolhan.'[40] This became amply clear when the government proposed the periodic enhancement of land revenue during Hayes (1867) and Craven land revenue settlement (1895–1898) by convening the meetings of the Mankis, Mundas, and villagers of Kolhan (Dalton 1973: 184).[41] Similarly, village and pir heads worked in tandem with the local administration in trying to lower the rate of *gonong* (ibid.: 192), curbing the growing incidence of illicit social relations and fixing a uniform date for the *Maghe parab*.[42]

Conjunction and collaboration made however one aspect of this relationship. We have instances when the Manki-Mundas were at variance with the local administrators. During Craven land revenue settlement, when the Deputy Commissioner proposed that all *gora* lands be taxed, 44 Mankis and 85 Mundas initially raised their objections. The village heads permitted dikus to settle and own lands in tribal villages in contravention of the provisions of Wilkinson's civil rules (1837) and Thomson's rules[43] (1900). Presumably, this was their ploy to assert their pre-colonial customary right of the ownership of villages. Furthermore, despite official instructions, the Mundas refrained from reporting all cases of land transfer through gift, sale and mortgage, inheritance, and partition to the district administration (Sen 2011: 213). In a memorial presented to the Lieutenant-Governor of Bihar and Orissa, the Mankis, Mundas, and the *raiyats* of Kolhan asserted: 'That formerly the Mankis and the Mundas as well as their tenants had absolute right in the forest produce, to clear the forest land for extension of cultivation . . . and to graze their cattle there.'[44]

These reasons tended to create doubt in the efficiency and sincerity of the Mankis and Mundas. Due to the supposed reason of lack of education, officials believed that the Manki and Mundas were unable to report all cases of transfers, partitions, and settlements of lands in their villages. So the Commissioner of Chotanagpur suggested that a special establishment consisting of a sub-deputy collector, a clerk, and 11 amins be appointed.[45] To keep vigil over the diku settlement, the post of Kolhan Inspector was created. In one of his reports, the official observed: 'From my long experience of the Manki and Mundas I regret to report in general of the untruthfulness in bringing light the sale and mortgage cases.'[46] Similarly, the efficacy of the existing village level police system under the headmen was doubted by the district police head. He maintained: 'it is found necessary to depute an officer for making an enquiry . . . of late years they have become more litigious and resort more to the law courts and there has been a great influx of foreigners into the Kolhan.'[47]

Last, the district administration held that the Manki-Munda system was incapable of efficiently promoting the policy of development. The paradox was that, though the development projects could not as a matter of policy be assigned to diku contractors, in the eyes of the district administration the role of local agency was 'unsatisfactory'. A common complaint was that the Mankis and Mundas were 'dilatory in carrying out their work'; the quality of work done through their agency was bad.[48] Local administration therefore subjected the entire system to the control and supervision of Kolhan deputy collector, Kolhan Inspector, Kolhan Overseer, and sometimes the district *Kanungo*.[49]

Postscript

During the post-independence decades, the powers and jurisdictions of the Manki-Munda system shrunk further. Under Bihar and Jharkhand governments, the village and pir heads were allowed to function, at least on paper, as revenue, judicial, and police agencies. But they were actually to share their domain with the Circle Officer and *karmacharis*, the regular police department and the district administration (Sundar 2009: 194–199). Perhaps the worst phase began when they had to encounter the challenge from the alternative system of rural self-government known as Panchayati Raj. The questions were raised whether it was proper to retain a hereditary mode of governance in a democratic polity and whether a regional system should continue to function when the Panchayati Raj system governed other parts of the country. This presaged the progressive introduction of the new system, as narrated earlier, culminating in the passage of the PESA and subsequent Acts. The Panchayati Raj system has transformed the system of rural governance further, though the modified system of village governance is to a great extent an amalgam of the traditional and modern.

It will be interesting to know how this mechanism has been structured, and to what extent it is an interface of the traditional and modern. First, the introduction of adult franchise has put an end to the hereditary nature of the traditional system. Second, strict and definite procedure for the composition of the Panchayat is clearly innovative. Accordingly, the Panchayat has been brought under the constitutional provision of the reservation of posts in proportion to the population of the concerned communities. It is stipulated that the Scheduled Tribe (ST) membership can in no case be one-half of the total; the posts of Chairpersons of Panchayats at all levels are to be reserved for the STs. These changes tend to strengthen the indigenous character of village governance which more or less characterised Ho-dominated villages. But we notice a clear digression from the tradition in the provision of Jharkhand Raj Panchayat (Amendment) Act, 2010, of reserving at least 50 percent seats for the Scheduled Castes, Other Backward Castes (OBC), and women. Reservation of seats for women marks a movement from the patriarchal tradition of the Manki-Munda system. De-recognition of the supra-village pir/parha formation registers yet another shift from the tradition (Sundar 2005: 4432).

We cannot however deny that Panchayati Raj system has considerably strengthened the rural governance mechanism. The elected body of Gram Sabha (GS) has been vested with wider and more powers than the colonial-day Manki-Munda system. This has been empowered to 'safeguard and preserve the traditions and customs of the people, their cultural identity, community resources and the customary mode of dispute resolution.' We can read this as a recognition of Ho tradition and cultural identity. The next registers a clear-cut policy of co-opting the GS as a developing agency. This marks an extension of the colonial-day role of the traditional system. Accordingly, the Panchayat in conjunction with GS has been empowered to implement plans, programmes, and projects for social and economic development and acquire land for development purposes; GS is entrusted with the planning and management of water bodies; the recommendation of GS is made mandatory for the grant of prospecting license or mining lease or for the exploitation of minor minerals. Furthermore, the pre-colonial day practice of a village community headed by the Munda as the owner and Governor of village resources is re-invented in the next provision of the Panchayat system. This legitimises the village Panchayat as the owner of minor forest produce; it is empowered to prevent the alienation of tribal land and effect its restoration if done in an unlawful manner, to manage village markets, to exercise control over institutions and functionaries in the social sectors and to control over local plans and resources for such plans including tribal sub-plans.[50] But at the same time, under the new system the right of ownership of minor forest produce and the right to recommend licenses/leases of minor minerals and regulate liquor sales have been withdrawn (Sundar 2005: 4433). Another area of change-in-continuity is the re-invention of the office of the Munda. Though, the Munda is virtually denied any role, the Jharkhand Panchayat Raj Act (JPRA) in 2001 (amended in 2003) has empowered a traditional village head to preside over the GS and has extended a wide range of powers to administer the affairs of the village and regulate its welfare in the light of the PESA

Act.[51] But the right extended to the state government to deny or modify the existing powers of GS considerably dilutes the extended autonomy to the village bodies (Sundar 2005: 4433).

The entire period of the introduction of Panchayati Raj during 1947–2010 charged the public domain unprecedentedly. It will be topical therefore to have a look at the political scenario, particularly the debates around the Panchayati Raj system and responses of the Adivasi communities to diverse changes.[52] This inaugurated a new brand of politics that involved Adivasi communities of Bihar-Jharkhand, the non-tribal elements known as *Sadans-Mulbasis* who had been living here for centuries and the state and Union governments, who debated over such issues as Adivasi identity, the status of the Sadans-Mulbasis, and the efficacy of pursuing the policy of centralisation or giving recognition to the traditional mode of governance. This chapter would however seek to concentrate on the responses of the Adivasi communities to the diverse modifications of the system during the period under review.

On the whole, the attitude of the Adivasi communities in Jharkhand to the changes in their traditional system was ambivalent. First, there was a regional polarisation of Kolhan-Porahat, where the Manki-Munda system had survived and the rest of tribal region in Jharkhand where it had progressively been side-lined.[53] Demographical polarisation was also visible at two levels. While attitude of Ho and other Adivasi communities varied, even the Ho society stood divided between votaries and detractors of the Manki-Munda system and Panchayati Raj.

Furthermore, even advocates of the Manki-Munda system were divided into radical and moderate factions. The former were vocal against any kind of dilution in the traditional mode of governance. After the first Panchayat elections in 1978, K.C. Hembrom, the head of the *Kolhan Raksha Dal* and A.K. Sawaiyan, a local lawyer, argued that as the institution of Manki-Munda was an inviolable system of tribal governance, Panchayati Raj could not be enforced here.[54] During the movement for the creation of a separate state which sharpened after 1947, Adivasi political groups of Jharkhand region like *Jharkhand Pradesh Parha Raja*, *Majhi Parganait Manki Munda*, *Doklo Sohor Mana Samiti*, Manki-Munda Sangh, Kolhan Raksha Sangh, and the National Indigenous Party (NIP) reiterated that their system of social governance through the Manki-Munda was basic to their identity. They were united in opposition against the holding of Panchayat election when the state government planned to hold it in 2005 (Sen 2018: 130).[55] When the state government announced the dates of election in 2005, some of these bodies formed a common forum called the *Kolhan-Porahat Panchayat Birodhi* and *Sanjukt Sangharsh Samiti* to resist election at all costs.[56]

However, the moderate group took a middle position between the traditional and exotic systems. They mainly veered around the PESA Act. Johar, a Kolhan-based NGO, set up over 800 Gram Sabhas between 1996 and 2001.[57] *Adivasi Mahasabha* and the *Adivasi Adhikar Morcha* strongly advocated for Panchayat elections.[58] At the meeting of *Jharkhand Buddhijivi Manch* held at Ranchi Central Library, R.D. Munda affirmed that as the PESA Act reflected the essence of Jharkhand movement, its implementation would strengthen democracy at the grassroots, which represented the true identity of an Adivasi.[59]

It becomes clear therefore that over centuries as the system of village governance was reinvented, the attachment of Adivasi communities to their traditional institution waned considerably. The primary reason for this was its progressive marginalisation under feudal and colonial rules when alternate form of authority wielded by the feudal and colonial states displaced society as the fountain of authority. The emergence of this alternate source of authority as the Governor of the tribal landscape eroded the loyalty of the people in general and respectable and educated villagers in particular to the traditional system. What was somewhat latent and subterranean during the colonial period became more manifest and sharp during post-independence period. This inflated the ranks of the votaries of Panchayati Raj. We can imagine that these elements raised demands that factored the pro-Adivasi modification of the Panchayati Raj mechanism itself. We cannot ignore another heterogeneous trend and this was the emergence of gender aspiration whom the colonial state had empowered through legitimisation of their right to property (Sen 2012: 98–121). Their stand received decisive support when the *Bharatiya Janata Party*, *Jharkhand Mukti Morcha*, *Jharkhand Vikash Morcha*, *All-India Jharkhand Students Union*, and local leaders of the Congress Party openly supported the Panchayat election.[60] During the Panchayat elections held in 2010, it was not unnatural that 70 percent polling was registered with pronounced gender support.[61] The fact however cannot be denied that despite dissipation, votaries of the Manki-Munda system, which include the ranks of the Manki-Mundas as also a section of the Ho Adivasis, continue to articulate their support to this institution as a marker of their collective selfhood.

Notes

1 The Provisions of the Panchayats (Extension of the Scheduled Areas) Act, 1996, No. 40 of 1996, The Gazette of India, Extraordinary, Part II – Section I, Ministry of Law and Justice (Legislative Department), New Delhi, 24 December 1996, The Controller of Publications, Delhi, 1996.
2 Jharkhand Panchayat Raj Act, 2001 (Jharkhand Act-6 of 2001)
3 TSKP, Sini, 3, VN 16.
4 Ibid., Gundijowa, 3–9, VN 71.
5 E. Roughsedge to Mr Secretary Metcalfe, 9 May 1820, para 19, No. 38, Extract Bengal Political Consultations, 3 June 1820.
6 Captain T. Wilkinson to Lt. Tickell, 13 May 1837, paras. 13, 17–21, Governor General's Agent, SWFPDR, 13 May to 1 December 1840, vol. 231.
7 Roughsedge to Metcalfe, 9 May 1820, paras 16–18.
8 S.R. Tickell, the first Assistant Political Agent of Kolhan Government Estate wrote: 'They [Hos] have separated themselves entirely from the race from which they sprang viz. the Mondas of Eastern Chootia Nagpoor. . . . When the separation

took place, it is impossible to say but it has become marked not only in manners, dialect and dress, but in appearance' (Tickell 1840: 803).

9 Wilkinson to Tickell, 13 May 1837, para 4.

10 The ethnic group from which the Hos originated.

11 Prabhat Khabar, 24 January, 23 September, 7/23 October, 2010; 14 January, 14 April, 4 May, 19/23 September; 7/22 October, 2010; Ranchi Express, 14 January 2010; Dainik Jagaran, 23 January, 1/25 October 2010.

12 Hindusthan, 4 May 2010.

13 Lord William Cavendish-Bentinck, the Governor General of India, 1828–35.

14 Note on the Kolhan resettlement recorded by Mr J.D. Sifton, ICS, Settlement Officer of Chota Nagpur on the 30th May 1914, Appendix A [Enclosure (3) to Progs. No. 6], para II, vide Resettlement of the Kolhan Government estate in the district of Singhbhum. Government of Bihar and Orissa, Revenue Department, FN S/6 of 1915, Nos 1–12.

15 ibid.

16 CSVN, FL, Mis Case No 235 of 1907–8, Goi Munda of Argundi tendered resignation of his Mundaship and prays that it should be accepted, Argundi, 2–8, FS 9, VN 758.

17 CSVEP, FL, Mis. Case No 162 of 1908–9, Petition of Manki Ho, Ghuntia,1–3, FS 4, VN79;CS,Village Note, FL, Mis. Case No 661 of 1910–11, Kolhan Inspector's report on succession of UchbaManki'silaka, Dhobadhobin, 2–3, FS 5, VN 494.

18 CSVEP, FL, Case No 124 of 1900, Pasubera, 1–2, VN 128; Mis. Case No 226 of 1911, Man Singh Ho's Application for Mankiship, Binj, 1–7; Mis. Case No 484 of 1910–11, Kolhan Deputy Collector of Singhbhum's report about the case arising out of Criminal case No 344 of 1910, Barbil, 2–9, FS 25.

19 CSVEP, FL, Mis Case No 241 of 1905–6, BandhuManki vs Chamru, Pradhan, Sangi &Toklo Munda, Pandrasali, 1–19, FS3, VN 68.

20 Note on the Kolhan resettlement recorded by Mr J.D. Sifton, para II

21 Wilkinson to Tickell, 13 May 1837, paras. 8, 18–21, 30–33; 'Translation of a Sunnud given by Captain Tickell to Raoria, Mankee of Kowsillapossi in Bur Peer, dated 10thDecemeber 1838' (Aitchison 1930: 361–2).

22 *Hakuknama* (Record of Rights), Kolhan Government Estate, District Singhbhum, Settlement1897, 12.

23 'Translation of a Pottah given by Captain Tickell to Raoria, Mankee of Kowsillapossi in Bur Peer, dated 19th March 1838'(Aitchison 1930: 363).

24 *Hakuknama* (Record of Rights), Kolhan Government Estate, District Singhbhum, Settlement1897, 12, 17.

25 Note on the Kolhan resettlement recorded by Mr J.D. Sifton, para II (iii-iv).

26 Rules for the administration of Criminal Justice in the Colhan of Singhbhoom and Bamanghatty under the Political Agent of the South Western Frontier, 6 June 1837, No.615, SWFPDR, Vol. 231, paras.4–7.

27 Thomas Wilkinson was the Political Agent to the Governor General of the South Western Frontier Agency.

28 Wilkinson to Tickell, 13 May, 1837

29 ibid., paras. 18–21

30 CSVEP, Form of Order Sheet, Land Dispute Suit no 86 of 1895–96 between Sridhar Kol & others of Rajabasa vrs CharaKol of Goontia, Gara Rajabasa, 38–42, VN74.

31 Note on the Kolhan resettlement recorded by Mr J.D.Sifton, para II (iii–iiv)

32 Report of L.B. Burrows, para 6, Appendix to DC, Singhbhum's letter to the Commissioner, No.181R of 15 May, 1912, vide Constitution of the Kolhan Reserved Forest Division.

33 *Hakuknama* (Record of Rights), Kolhan Government Estate, District Singhbhum, Settlement1897, 12–7.

34 LRAR 1907–8, DCOS, RB, CN XI Returns, FN 16, para 21

35 '*Hakuknama* (Record of Rights), Kolhan Government Estate, District Singhbhum, Settlement 1897, 12–7.
36 LRAR 1907–8, DCOS, RB, CN XI Returns, FN 16, para 21.
37 ibid.
38 From A.S. Judge, District Superintendent of Police, Singhbum to the Deputy Commissioner of Singhbhum, No 610 of 24 June 1890, para 2, vide Gleanings of Thanna Jurisdiction, FL, DCOS, Judicial Department, CN 1 Criminal, FS 2, FN 40 of 1890
39 Note on the Kolhan resettlement recorded by Mr J.D. Sifton, para II, (iii-iiv).
40 Note, dated the 11th September 1914, on the Kolhan resettlement recorded by Babu DahnMassi Panna, Sub-Deputy Collector and Assistant Settlement Officer of Chota Nagpur, Appendix K. [Enclosure (13) to Progs. No. 6], para 2, vide Resettlement of the Kolhan Government estate in the district of Singhbhum. Government of Bihar and Orissa, Revenue Department, FN S/6 of 1915, Nos 1–12.
41 R.H. Renny, Dy. Commissioner Singhbhum to the Commissioner of Chotanagpur Division, Chaibasa, 29July/ 3August 1893. No 307R. Fly Leaf 1892–3, 1893–4 DCOS, RB, CN III Settlement, FN1893–4, Kolhan Settlement in Singhbhum, paras 9–17.
42 CS, FL, Mis. Case No. 1021 of 1909–10, Kolhan Dy. Collector's report about celebrating Mage Parab before proper date, FS 11, Dumria, 1–2, VN 514.
43 Rules issued by W. B. Thomson, the Deputy Commissioner of Singhbhum, prohibiting the transfer of arable land to a *Diku* and ordering their exclusion.
44 Copy of memorial presented by the Hos at Chaibasa, para 7.
45 E. G. Collin, Officiating Secretary to the Board of Revenue, Lower Provinces, to the Secretary to the Government of Bengal, No 593A, 20 June 1898, Civil Suit Rules, FL,DCOS, RB, CN I GR, FN 57 of 1903–4, FS 17, para 2.
46 Note of BagunJarika, Kolhan Inspector of 24 August 1903, para 1, enclosure to the letter of Deputy Commissioner of Singhbhum to the Commissioner of Chotanagpur, FS 9, Civil Suit Rules.
47 From A.S. Judge, District Superintendent of Police Singhbhum to the Deputy Commissioner of Singhbhum, para 2.
48 LRAR 1907–8, DCOS, RD, CN XI Returns, FN 16, para 21.
49 LRAR 1910–11, Appended to LRAR 1911–12, DCOS, GD, RB, CN XI, FN 1 of 1911–12, para 21.
50 The Provisions of the Panchayats (Extension of the Scheduled Areas) Act, 1996, No.40 of 1996
51 Jharkhand Panchayat Raj Act, 2001, (Jharkhand Act-6 of 2001)
52 For more detailed information see (Sen 2018: 125–132).
53 Oraon *parha panchayat* ceased to function by the second half of the last century, and, among the Mundas, this institution was operative in a few blocks only. Nandini Sundar (2009) 'Framing the Political Imagination: Custom, Democracy, and Citizenship'. In Nandini Sundar (ed.), *Legal Grounds: Natural Resources, Identity, and the Law in Jharkhand*. New Delhi: Oxford University Press, p. 197.
54 Nandini Sundar, 'Custom' and 'Democracy' in Jharkhand', p. 4433.
55 Prabhat Khabar, 1/2/5 September 2005; Ranchi Express, 5 September 2005; Dainik Jagaran, 10 September 2005.
56 Prabhat Khabar, 24 January, 23 September, 7/23 October, 2010; 14 January, 14 April, 4 May, 19/23 September; 7/22 October, 2010; Ranchi Express, 14 January 2010; Dainik Jagaran, 23 January,1/25 October 2010.
57 Through election a committee was formed which elected its head who was generally the Munda. Nandini Sundar, 'Custom' and 'Democracy' in Jharkhand', p. 4433.
58 Ranchi Express, 9 September 2005. Dainik Jagaran, 10 September 2005.
59 Dainik Jagaran, 7 February 2010. D.S. Bhuria declared at Ranchi that Pesa Act represented the fundamental right of Adivasis. Ranchi Express, 17 March 2010.

60 Ranchi Express, 23 January 2010; Hindusthan, 8 October 2010; Prabhat Khabar, 8 October 2005, 6/10 October 2010; Dainik Jagaran, 9 October 2005.
61 Hindusthan, 8 October, 14 December 2010; Prabhat Khabar, 12 October, 8 December 2010; Ranchi Express, 9 December 2010.

Archival sources

District record room, Chaibasa

Manuscripts

Craven Settlement Village Papers.
Forest Department Papers.
From A.S. Judge, District Superintendent of Police, Singhbhum to the Deputy Commissioner of Singhbhum, No 610 of 24 June 1890, para 2, vide Gleanings of Thanna Jurisdiction, FL, DCOS, Judicial Department, CN 1 Criminal, FS 2, FN 40 of 1890.
Hakuknama (Record of Rights), Kolhan Government Estate, District Singhbhum, Settlement1897.
Khuntkatti Papers.
Land Revenue Administration Report.
R.H. Renny, Dy. Commissioner Singhbhum to the Commissioner of Chotanagpur Division, Chaibasa, 29 July/3 August 1893. No 307R. Fly Leaf 1892–3, 1893–4 DCOS, RB, CN III Settlement, FN1893–4, Kolhan Settlement in Singhbhum.
Tuckey Settlement Khuntkatti Papers.

Bihar state archives, Patna

Manuscripts

South West Frontier Political Dispatch Register.

- Vol. 26 from 6 October 1819 to 10 November 1820.
- Vol. 231 from 13 May 1837 to 1 December 1840.

Printed

Resettlement of the Kolhan Government Estate in the District of Singhbhum. Government of Bihar and Orissa, Revenue Department, FN S/6 of 1915, Nos 1–12.

Reports/Gazetteers/Acts

Craven, J.A. 1898. *Final Report on the Settlement of the Kolhan Government Estate 1897*. Calcutta: Superintendent Government Printing Bihar and Orissa.
Hallett, M.G. 1917. *Bihar and Orissa District Gazetteers: Ranchi*. Patna: Superintendent, Government Printing Bihar and Orissa.
Jharkhand Panchayat Raj Act, 2001 (Jharkhand Act-6 of 2001).
O'Malley, L.S.S. 1999. *Bengal District Gazetteers: Santal Parganas*. New Delhi: Logos Press.

The Provisions of the Panchayats (Extension of the Scheduled Areas) Act, 1996, No. 40 of 1996, The Gazette of India, Extraordinary, Part II – Section I, Ministry of Law and Justice (Legislative Department), New Delhi, 24 December 1996, The Controller of Publications, Delhi, 1996.

Tuckey, A.D. 1920. *Final Report on the Resettlement of the Kolhan Government Estate in the District of Singhbhum 1913–1918*. Patna: Superintendent Government Printing Bihar and Orissa.

Books/Journals

Aitchison, C.U. (Complier). 1930. *A Collection of Treaties, Engagements and Sanads: Relations to India and Neighbouring Countries*, Vol. II. Calcutta: Government of India Central Publication Branch, No. XIX.

Archer, W.G. 1984. *Tribal Law and Justice: A Report on the Santal*. New Delhi: Concept Publishing Company.

Bodding, P.O. (Translator). 1994. *Traditions and Institutions of the Santals: Horkoren Mare HapramkoReak Katha*. New Delhi: Bahumukhi Prakashan.

Dalton, E.T. 1973. *Tribal History of Eastern India (Original Title Descriptive Ethnology of Bengal)*. New Delhi: Cosmo Publication.

Datta, S.N. 1928. *The Chotanagpur Tenancy Act (Bengal Act VI of 1908) With Notes, Judicial Rulings, Rules, Notifications*. Patna: The Students Emporium.

Majumdar, D.N. 1937. *A Tribe in Transition: Study in Cultural Pattern*. Calcutta: Longmans Green & Co., Ltd.

Man, E.G. 1983. *Sonthalia and the Santhals*. New Delhi: Mittal Publications.

Roy, S.C. 1935. 'Ethnographical Investigation in Official Records.' *Journal of the Bihar and Orissa Research Society*, XXI, part IV, 231–250.

Roy, S.C. 1970. *The Mundas and Their Country*. Calcutta: Asia Publishing House.

Roy, S.C. 1984. *Oraons of Chotanagpur*. Ranchi: Man in India Office.

Sahu, M. 1985. *Kolhan Under the British Rule*. Calcutta: No Publisher.

Sen, A.K. (Ed.). 1999. *Wilkinson's Rules: Context, Content and Ramifications*. Chaibasa: Tata College.

Sen, A.K. 2011. 'Collaboration and Conflict: Environmental Legacies of the Ho of Kolhan (1700–1918).' In D. Kumar, V. Damodaran and R. D' Souza (Eds.), *The British Empire and the Natural World: Environmental Encounters in South Asia* (pp. 202–227). New Delhi: Oxford University Press.

Sen, A.K. 2012. *From Village Elder to British Judge: Custom, Customary Law and Tribal Society*. Hyderabad: Orient Blackswan.

Sen, A.K. 2017. 'Claiming Mining Rights: A Rare Instance of Adivasi Assertion Over Underground Resource.' *Journal of Adivasi and Indigenous Studies*, VI(I), February, 41–46.

Sen, A.K. 2018. *Indigeneity, Landscape and History: Adivasi Self-fashioning in India*. London and New York: Routledge.

Sundar, N. 2005. '"Custom" and "Democracy" in Jharkhand.' *Economic and Political Weekly*, 40(41), October 8–14: 4430–4434.

Sundar, N. 2009. 'Framing the Political Imagination: Custom, Democracy, and Citizenship.' In N. Sundar (Ed.), *Legal Grounds: Natural Resources, Identity, and the Law in Jharkhand* (pp. 189–215). New Delhi: Oxford University Press.

Tickell, Lt. S.R. 1840. 'Memoir on the Ho desum (Improperly Called Kolehan).' *Journal of Asiatic Society of Bengal*, XI, part II: 694–709, 783–808.

Newspapers

Dainik Jagaran.
Hindustan.
Prabhat Khabar.
Ranchi Express.

3 Issues of financial governance in Scheduled Areas

Varsha Bhagat-Ganguly and Bhanu Shree Jain

Web of funds scenario: patterns and problems

The Government of India has largely adopted a community-centric approach for development activities, many of which are backed by regulatory provisions. In this approach, governance – including adequate financial planning, allocation and utilisation, and the performance of mechanisms – takes place to achieve desired results and the development of the target group are stressed upon. Both Scheduled Areas (SAs) and Scheduled Tribes (STs) are well defined in the Indian Constitution[1] and they are inter-linked, which aims at protecting the tribal population and ensuring their development. If the fund scenario – allocation, utilisation, and lapses – are examined from the perspective of governance, then how financial decisions, planning, and implementation address underdevelopment of tribals in SAs is the central enquiry of this chapter from the perspective of 'governmentality.' It is the state that plans, allocates, and utilises the funds; however, are the processes involved inclusive of the beneficiaries or does the state shows face value of the beneficiaries and decide on their behalf? While undertaking the said investigation, what emerges is a web of issues – financial as well as 'other than financial' (i.e., of the socio-economic and political nature and their complex linkages). The web of financial issues includes multiple sources, varied institutional channels for routing and disbursement of funds, and sectoral priorities: What happens when the funds are not utilised? The sectoral priorities in form of schemes/programmes need to address the following concerns – (1) which sector and why that sector (e.g., infrastructure and non-infrastructure [social sector] or development based projects); and (2) their channels for receiving funds (i.e., a nodal agency run by the government or public-private partnership which contributes to fund generation and utilisation). Pre-budget allocation consists of budget approval and the budget utilisation processes, which require other financial processes including proactive planning, consultative process with the beneficiaries and, in this case, the receiving agency's administrative structure and multiple levels of routing of funds and implementation (i.e., district, taluk/block/tehsil, and village). Further, with reference to the Scheduled Areas, it is important to clarify that they are not homogenous. Therefore, there is added difficulty of homogeneity in fund allocation for these areas. The Fifth Schedule Areas are struggling for effective implementation of PESA (Panchayati Raj Extension to Scheduled Areas Act), 1996, and for administrative and financial autonomy while the Sixth Scheduled Areas have administrative autonomy but are struggling for financial autonomy. Thus, at every level, many issues are inter-twined, entangled, and move parallel to each other. Reduction in fund allocation for welfare and development of STs[2] has been one of the most important concerns for those championing the cause of STs, including political leaders, community leaders, civil society organisations/actors, and academia. Along with reduction in fund allocation, fund diversion, non-utilisation, and lack of accountability of the government in the financial governance are three other problems which are of importance. The reduction is result of unutilised funds which shows lack of financial planning as there is still huge gap in the human development indicators in case of Scheduled Tribes.[3] Dungdung (2015: 1–2) has raised questions against the top-down approach of financial governance, especially related to the tribal sub plan (TSP), and he extended his concern in replacing TSP with TSDP (Tribal Sustainable Development Plan) in order to drastically reduce influence of the Naxals. Furthermore, the Ministry of Tribal Affairs states that the 'availability of funds is not the real constraint in achieving the intended targets. Instead, effective monitoring, accountability and management thereof appear to the issues of concern' [emphasis removed]. This means that there is major lacuna in the strategies for addressing development challenges. If governance is a tool to achieve desired development, then it is important to flag the issues of financial governance from the perspective of governmentality.

This chapter explores and studies governmentality in regard to a gamut of financial and 'other than financial' related processes and mechanism in the SAs and see whether these are inter-linked and coordinated to their principal beneficiaries (i.e., STs). The governmentality framework focuses on whether the fund allocation is reduced and if so whether it has been done through mode of participatory processes such as the consultation, transparency, and accountability in decision-making; the functional autonomy for implementing decisions; and the role of culture and traditional mechanisms for governance in the given financial governance. It is equally important to study the financial processes in the context of the reduction in fund allocation, because these processes contribute to ensure the ST's development and welfare through adequate funding. This includes whether the allocation of funds is proportionate to the ST population; whether the disbursement of funds are timely and adequate; and whether the smooth fund flow – from central government to state government and to the local governance –is ensured. This also includes a matching up of requirements with grants and earmarked funds and their utilisation, etc. The real goal is for autonomy – financial as well as administrative. Who is empowered with statutory powers for carrying out development activities: The state, the people's representative, or their institutions (Panchayati Raj for local governance)?

The chapter is presented in three sections: first section describes various sources of fund allocation, the following section undertakes analysis of fund flow of two components – (1) the Tribal Sub-Plan and (2) the Vanbandhu Kalyan Yojana scheme. Based on a study of these two components, the chapter tries to identify the linkages and problems in fund allocation in order to understand governmentality in the second section. The third section presents three puzzles to characterise governmentality (i.e., by describing the differentiation between the 'administration of funds' and 'governance as a tool for development') and whether this differentiation in the financial governance approach facilitates tribal development in SAs. The first puzzle is related to the lack of differentiation in budget heads and the overcharging of the total amount for development activity. The second puzzle is related to a category of non-transferable and non-lapsable funds. The third puzzle is related to disproportionate funds.

Multiple sources of fund allocation for Scheduled Areas and Scheduled Tribes

Since the first five-year plan, funds were allocated for the tribal development. However, for the initial two five-year plans, funds were released by the central government only under Article 245 (1) of the Constitution of India (Planning Commission 2011). No other specific schemes were formulated at that time. The government later on realised that there was a need for collaboration between the Union and states in regard to the development of tribes, and funding for such development must flow from both the central government and state government (ibid.). Thus, with the passage of time, various sources of funds were developed. Currently, the funding for tribal development can be divided under five main heads: (1) Article 275(1) of the Constitution of India, (2) Centrally Sponsored Scheme (CSS), (3) Tribal Sub Plan (TSP), (4) Special Central Assistance (SCA), and (5) Multiple Project Funding.

Article 275(1) of the Constitution of India, the provision for grants from Union to certain states, mentions the following:

> Such sums as Parliament may by law provide shall be charged on the consolidated Fund of India in each year as grants-in-aid of the revenues of such States as Parliament may determine to be in need of assistance, and different sums may be fixed for different States: Provided that there shall be paid out of the Consolidated Fund of India as grants-in aid of the revenues of a State such capital and recurring sums as may be necessary to enable that State to meet the costs of such schemes of development as may be undertaken by the State with the approval of the Government of India for the purpose of promoting the welfare of Scheduled Tribes in that State or raising the level of administration of the Scheduled Areas therein to that of the administration of the rest of the areas of that State.

As per the proviso to the Article, it is permissible for the Union to give grants-in-aid from the Consolidated Fund of India to meet the cost of schemes of development undertaken by the state with the approval of the Government of India (Union Government) when such schemes are intended to promote the welfare of the Scheduled Tribes in the state or are for raising the level of administration of Scheduled Areas to that of the administration of the rest of the Areas of the state.[4]

Further, under Article 275(2), the President may by order exercise powers conferred upon the Parliament under clause (1), subject to any provision that is made by the Parliament.[5] This is a Central Sector Scheme and 100 percent of the grants are provided to the states by the centre. Funds are charged from consolidated fund of India and the state government has to take the approval of central government for schemes under this Article.[6] The grants are provided in proportion to the ST population of the state to the total tribal population of India. The said funds are released by the state government against the specific projects for the welfare of the ST population and to strengthen the administration of tribal areas.

The states can also take up activities for strengthening the infrastructure in the sectors which are critical to the enhancement of human development indices such as education, income generation, health irrigation, roads, bridges, forests, forests villages, electrification, communication, rural marketing, agriculture, animal husbandry, food processing, processing of minor forest produce (MFPs), human resource development in technical and vocational spheres, water harvesting, resettlement of displaced persons, tribal land management, and sports promotion. Also included is the generation of community welfare assets like residential schools; maintenance of schools; providing skilled teaching in tribal language; nutritional support to needy: Children, mothers, and elderly people; community grain storage; and assured drinking water. In a report prepared by Joint Committee of Ministry of Tribal Affairs (2010), it clarifies that other activities meant for the welfare of tribal population different from conventional development can also be taken up. Funds under this Article are also utilised to establish an Eklavya Model Residential School which provides quality education to ST students from classes VI to XII. The Ministry of Tribal Affairs released revised guidelines for the utilisation of the grant on July 2, 2002, to extend the financial assistance to forest villages, model schools, expansion and integration schemes, etc.[7]

Centrally Sponsored Schemes (CSS): complicating factor for SAs

These schemes are sponsored by the central government. Thus, apart from funds that are released via Article 245(1) of Constitution of India, the central government also releases funds to the state governments in schemes which are centrally sponsored (Planning Commission 2011). The funding proportion varies, that is, it can go from 100 percent centrally sponsored to a 50/50 split by the central government and state government. However, there is a lot of overlapping between the funds released under Article 275, and under these schemes. Further, many times it has become a problem to identify what is the source of funding (i.e., whether it is disbursed under Article 275 or CSS with State Government's due share). A reference in this regard can be made to the third instalment released by the Central Government under Article 275(1) of the Indian Constitution to the State of Andhra Pradesh[8] and Order No. DDCP/404 of 2018 dated 27 August 2018 relating to release of funds under Art. 275(1) of the Indian Constitution[9] wherein the funds released under Art. 275(1) are charged against the TSP and CSS, respectively. In the context of SAs, it is very difficult to know whether the tribals benefited belong to SAs or not.

In this regard, National Democratic Council[10] (NDC) on several occasions has emphasised on the need to reduce the central government's contribution to both these schemes and also a number of CSS. It is also been advised that the flexibility and autonomy must be given to the state government in deployment of funds under these schemes[11] (Kapur and Srinivas 2016). This shows that, pre-2014, the Planning Commission and Finance Commission, the administrative and finance agencies, were planning and allocating a proportion of funds while NDC, comprised of elected representatives, played a role in deciding the proportion of funds between the Union and State government for various development activities. There is very little scope for SAs to be in focus, as the approach to planning is community based.

Tribal Sub Plan (TSP): plan and performance

Among other sources, TSP is one of the most known and popular source of fund flow among the STs and those working for tribal development. TSP was started in 1974. TSP as a strategy is meant to ensure that outlays and benefits from the general sectors of the Plan flow to STs at least in proportion to their shares in the total population, both in physical and financial terms. These allocations are meant for umbrella programmes under which various schemes implemented by the government need to be dovetailed for addressing the different needs of STs. The Planning Commission has issued several government orders and guidelines to the central government ministries and state governments with regards to the implementation of these strategies of TSP. The guidelines also insist on designing relevant programmes/schemes for STs that directly affect ST families and on designing special mechanisms and making the special agency responsible and accountable for the formulation and implementation of TSP; this ensures both a timely release of funds and that the TSP funds should be non-divertible and non-lapsable.

The funds for TSP are sourced through the following instrumentalities: (1) State plans; (2) funds under TSP components of CSS, which are administered by Central Ministries/Departments; (3) SCA to TSP; (4) Grant-in-aid under Article 275(1) of the Constitution of India and other schemes implemented by Ministry of Tribal Affairs; and (5) the Institutional Finance including Corporate Social Responsibilities (CSR) of Corporate Entities (Joint Committee of Ministry of Environment and Ministry of Tribal Affairs 2010). Thus, there is multiple overlapping in the funding. As the broad objectives of TSP[12] are closely related – (1) reduce poverty and unemployment by the creation of productive resources/assets for STs, (2) develop human resources in STs by providing them with education and health services, (3) safeguard the STs physically and financially from all types of exploitation and oppression – it is a mechanism through which it is able to source funds from different agencies (Dungdung 2015).

The *revised guidelines for implementation of TSP by the States/UTs (Union Territories), 2013*,[13] mention a need for TSP's formulation at the district level; a need for preparing a realistic budget matching sectoral priorities and in consultation with other departments; a need for the service delivery to be standardised; and a need for the synchronisation of the gap filling role of SCA to TSP to be facilitated. There is a specific guideline regarding SAs: In the states having Scheduled Areas, the Gram Sabhas should undertake an exercise to identify the areas needing priority attention in villages (No.M-11012/03/2013-SJ&SW, Planning Commission, SJ&E Division: 16). However, the MoTA report mentions that, since 1976, there have been efforts to ensure that the Scheduled Areas coincide with the Tribal Sub-Plan areas through several orders, although this task is still not complete (MoTA 2014a: 65).

The fund allocation details of TSP are available based on ST population, not on SAs. The analysis of the Union budget by the Centre for Budget and Governance Accountability (CBGA) presents information on budgetary outlays.[14] Total allocation to TSP was 256,020 million in 2016–2017, which was increased to 319,200 million rupees in 2017–2018; of this 48,270 million in 2016–2017 and 53,290 million in 2017–2018 were allocated to MoTA. Under SCA, 12,000 million rupees in 2016–2017 and 13,500 million rupees in 2017–2018 were allocated to TSP (CBGA 2017a: 55–56). Schemes under proviso to article 275(1) of the Constitution, 12,600 million rupees in 2016–2017 and 1,500 million rupees in 2017–2018 were allocated (CBGA website)[15].

The allocations made under the Tribal Sub Plan for a period of five years (from 2012–2013 to 2016–2017)[16] reveals three trends: (1) TSP allocations have consistently increased;[17] (2) tribal development is increasingly dependent on state funds as opposed to central funds;[18] and (3) the allocations made under the TSP fall far short of the recommended allocations under the central and state TSP as per the Planning Commission's revised Guidelines of 2014.[19] Both the central and state governments failed to comply with the Planning Commission's Guidelines in discharging their responsibility for tribal welfare (CBGA 2017b: 22).

Some state governments have suggested changes in TSP for SAs. The fund allocation details of TSP are available based on ST population, not on

SAs. The state government of Chhattisgarh noted that while it has about 81,669 sq. km as Scheduled Areas, there are 88,000 sq. km in the state under the Tribal Sub-Plan (TSP), thus creating a disparity which must be addressed by making Scheduled Areas coterminous with TSP areas (MoTA 2014: 65). Thus, at a deliberation and discussion level, SAs do emerge as a point of consideration, but not much is observed at the implementation level. The Article 275 recognises only states with substantial a tribal population to be eligible for special grants. So can these funds be extended to cover only SAs or to all the states that have tribal populations? When such a shift in decision-making happens, the government would be able to make a shift from either a community-development approach or territory-centric approach to an area to analysing issues of financial allocation.

Special Central Assistance (SCA): specific role for tribal development

This Programme was started in 1974–1975. The Ministry of Tribal affairs has provided an additive to State TSP in the form of a 100 percent grant to fill the critical gaps especially in family-based income activities for the tribals living Below the Poverty Line (BPL) (Joint Committee of Ministry of Tribal Affairs 2010). The ultimate objective of extending SCA to TSP is to boost the demand-based income-generation programmes in tribal areas and thus raise the economic and social status of Tribals. Not more than 30 percent of the fund can be used for infrastructure development which is incidental to income generating schemes. The scope of SCA is expanded to cover the employment-cum-income generation activities and the infrastructure incidental thereto is not only family based, but also community based through a cluster approach (ibid.). It is meant for income-generation schemes which are family oriented in indigenous sectors like agriculture, horticulture, sericulture, and animal husbandry.[20]

Multiple project funding

The prime objective of these schemes is to enhance the reach of welfare schemes of the government and fill the gaps in service-deficient tribal areas, in the sectors such as education, health, drinking water, agro-horticultural productivity, social security etc. through the efforts of voluntary organisations, and to provide an environment for the socio-economic upliftment and overall development of the STs. This funding is for different development projects for the welfare of the tribal population and for the development of Scheduled Areas. Any other innovative activity having direct impact on the socio-economic development or livelihood generation of STs may also be considered through voluntary efforts (MoTA website).[21]

The Constitution envisages a centralised framework for the administration of tribal areas under the aegis of the President and the Governors of all the states, the responsibility of financing the costs of progressive changes for the tribals increasingly vests with the state governments. The fragmented nature of the constitutional protections for the STs are also replicated in the administrative and financial apparatuses designed to effectuate these protections, thereby reducing the efficacy of provisions designed to safeguard the rights of the tribal peoples (Wahi and Bhatia 2018: 22).

Studying Vanbandhu Kalyan Yojana

The scheme Vanbandhu Kalyan Yojana (VKY) is a centrally sponsored scheme; the Ministry of Tribal Affairs is the implementation agency. This scheme is for the welfare of the friends of forest and has been included as a Central Sector Scheme in the Annual Plan of Ministry of Tribal Affairs. The mission of the scheme is to enhance the socio-economic status of the Scheduled Tribes population of the country, preserving their dignity and culture, so as to work towards removal of gaps in the Human Development Indices (HDIs) of tribals vis-à-vis other social groups through an outcome-based approach, particularly focusing on quality education, health, livelihood, infrastructure development by way of an appropriate convergence of available resources and the re-engineering of processes in the Fifth Schedule Areas.[22]

This scheme has witnessed ups and downs in fund allocation. An initial fund allocation of rupees 112,000 million was made which was reduced to rupees 10,000 million for the year 2014–2015 (CBGA website).[23] The fund was six times more in the consecutive year (i.e., 62,900 million rupees in 2015–2016). The following three years witnessed a reduction in the fund allocation under this scheme. The said fund is allocated to various departments so as to achieve the objects of the VKY scheme. Furthermore, a lot of funds are released by the state government for the implementation of the scheme.

The total expenditure by the central government shows that the actual expenditure on VKY for the year 2015–2016 was rupees 628,890 million. However, the budget estimate was only for rupees 504,780 million, which was revised to rupees 472,400 million. Thus, there is gap in the actual estimates and the financial estimates done by the central government. The said gap is on account of the fact that the financial estimates of the government lack proper supervision and control and planning. Further, it also showcases that the central government might have released more funds than estimated in the said scheme. There is no mechanism to check as to where the said extra funds might have been used. Thus, there is lack of inter-linkages in the estimated funds and the actual released funds and where the actual released funds are used. Contrary to this statistics, Ministry of Tribal Affairs reported that only 12.5 percent of the funds (rupees 249.3 million) were utilised by the states in 2015–2016. The Rs. 200 crore [rupees 2,000 million] that were earmarked for 20 blocks in BJP rules states – Gujarat, Madhya Pradesh,

Chhattisgarh, and Maharashtra – remained unspent under the VKY scheme (Sharma 2017).

The fund is allocated on the basis of the CAG (comptroller and auditor general) report by the finance commission. MoTA and ITDA (Integrated Tribal Development Agency) are created as nodal agencies for looking into the implementation of funds. Since the flow of funds is complex, it also leads to a problem in analysing how the funds are spent, which further leads to the problem in setting accountability on various departments. As there is vagueness in the law, there also remains vagueness in expenditure. Thus, the whole fund allocation machinery is full of problems as there are no inter-linkages; also there is not a direct release of funds to the affected persons.

As there is a lack of appropriate machinery to check the fund flow; at times, more fund is released than the required. The same is in the case of VKY, wherein excess funds were released in the financial year 2015–2016. However, since the said funds are used by various departments to achieve the object of the VKY scheme, there is no effective mechanism through which the beneficiary of the said scheme can be identified. This situation leads to a huge gap between the expenditure and the actual beneficiaries, which becomes a handicap due to which success of this scheme cannot be ascertained at the ground level. Further, the fund which is not utilised gets diverted to the other plans; it is likely that the excess funds of the VKY are diverted to the other schemes of the government. Whether the diverted funds are allocated to SAs or not is a matter of investigation.

Flow of funds: allocation machinery and accountability

There are various sources from which funds are released for the development of tribals. If the fund is flowing from the Central Government under Article 275(1) or CSS or part of SCA or TSP then the same is allocated by the central government to the respective state governments. Thereafter, the state government releases the funds to the specific/concerned department[24] which looks after Tribal Area development. This specific department in turn releases the funds to the concerned district-level agency which in turn releases the funds to the Taluk/block and village Panchayats under PESA/ADC, which ultimately utilises the funds according to the plans given to them by the state government, which were approved by the central government. A similar mechanism is also followed by the funds released by the state government; however, there is no specific budget head for SAs.

In absence of specific machinery for a specific scheme or programme, the routing of funds is not standardised. In this situation, three possibilities could be thought of: First, the direct release to the concerned department/agency; second, a mix-up [i.e., two departments (PWD and Irrigation departments)] in the case of dams and canal development or PWD and water and Sanitation Department in the case of school infrastructure development; and third, for specific activity for tribal development activities, and the funds are released to the specified department. In the second possibility, it is difficult to derive the ratio in which fund has been utilised for the development of the tribal activities as the fund may be utilised for other activities by the specified department. This point is directly linked to the accountability for funds – utilisation of funds, number of beneficiaries of the scheme – by the concerned department(s). There also remains a possibility of diversion of funds within a department or two departments for other developmental activity. No elected representative of local governance has any say or no avenue for vigilance in this way of fund flow. This is one of the indicators of 'governmentality' – the administration of funds without participation or consultation of the beneficiary target group or elected representatives who are accountable for development of tribals residing in the SAs.

Flagging some puzzling questions regarding financial governance

The welfare and development of tribes is one of the main motives for which the funds are released. The same can be taken care of by proper fund channelisation wherein there is inclusive participation of the beneficiaries (i.e., planning based on consultation with the beneficiaries) or participative and decentralised decision-making regarding funds, realistic allocation, fund routing through a specified agency/department, analysis of fund utilisation linked to benefits of development, etc. Without undertaking the said exercise, many a time the fund allocation remains merely a financial exercise where the beneficiaries are targets/subjects and the number game continues without the beneficiaries getting any benefit of the allocated funds. The central questions of the governmentality perspective are these: Is there a possibility or an avenue for bringing corrections in the financial process with the help of people's participation? Is there a way to make the 'administrative' process a process of 'governance' wherein citizens' participation, contribution in decision-making, and/or accountability to citizens could be ensured? Four problems (three financial and one other) are shared here in order to discuss governance in the SAs, especially for tribals.

The first puzzle is related to the lack of differentiation in budget heads and overcharging the total amount for development activity. For tribal development, the funds released under Article 275(1) of the Constitution of India are utilised in the TSP, CSS, SCA, as well as in multiple project funding. If rupees 100 are released as grants-in-aid under Article 245(1) as the first budget head, then out of rupees 100, rupees 20 are allocated to TSP, and rupees 10 to multiple project funding. In this case, essentially rupees 100 are being spent, but since it is shown under different heads of TSP and multiple project funding, the total funding of rupees 130 could be shown because tracing back to different budget heads are difficult. This creates a false, misleading picture in relation to the funds that are released for the development of the tribal population. The financial process is so insulated that the governance process (citizen centric and participative) does not provide scope for either altering the existing process or allowing other than financial process to be effective.

The second puzzle is related to a category of non-transferable and non-lapsable funds (i.e., funds will not be diverted to other schemes and it will not lapse). In this case, the fund allocated has to be 100 percent utilised during the specified period of time for tribal development. However, in practice, it has been a trend that such funds get diverted, either by the state government or by the central. The same is evident from the reported utilisation of funds (CBGA 2011; Dungdung 2015). In this puzzle, is there any possibility for accountability of the government official towards tribals? PESA (Panchayati Raj Extension to Scheduled Areas Act), 1996, is one of the legal instruments which provides the right to the elected representatives of the local governance to participate in the decision-making related to resource utilisation. Dungdung (2015: 5) observes lacuna in this possibility as well. For instance, the Jharkhand Panchayat Raj Act of 2001 denies the Gram Sabha's rights on the management of community resources, whereas 'section 4(d) of the PESA Act 1996, provides that 'every Gram Sabha shall be competent to safeguard and preserve the traditions, customs of the people, their cultural identity, community resources and community mode of dispute resolution.'[25] The PESA Act and Rules enacted by the state governments are not in favour of the Scheduled Tribes.

The non-utilisation and diversion of funds is in clear breach of government guidelines by the implementing agency/the government itself. Moreover, whenever situations arise where the fund or additional funds are required, for example, a higher number of children going to schools, this fund is reportedly 'non-transferable' and therefore does not get diverted for development cause. An implication of this situation is that beneficiaries of the scheme have to wait for the next cycle of budgetary provisions. Conversely, in a situation where large-scale seasonal migration takes place from specific areas, even though budgetary allocation has taken place, the government would face a problem of under-utilisation. Further, in the case of a natural calamity or man-made disaster, utilisation of this fund remains a puzzling question. Financial autonomy of ADC needs to be examined in such situations. Currently, no financial autonomy is given to ADCs/Panchayats regarding the utilisation of funds; also, ADCs are not allowed to use the revenue which they have generated from their place of residence/Sixth SA. Since statutory powers are not assigned to the people's forum, the citizens remain outside the financially related decision-making processes.

Third puzzle is related to disproportionate funds. As per Constitutional mandate, funds have to be released in proportion to the tribal population (i.e., tribal population of the state to total tribal population of India). Thus, if a state has a low tribal population then less funds are released to that state than the state which has a greater tribal population. However, it is constantly seen that the same is not done. The funds are not in proportion to the tribal population and are always less (ibid.). An implication of this situation is that an inequality among the tribal population inhabiting in SAs is created; some of them have been developed by the funds and some have not received the fruits of the development due to the lack of funds. In Meghalaya (Sixth Schedule Area), the residents are claiming to allocate funds based on backwardness rather than the proportion to the population, because it has a small proportion of tribal population (ActionAid 2016). In such a circumstance, how do we ensure development of the region?

These three puzzles raise issues of financial governance from the perspective of governmentality (i.e., the need for planning, accountability, transparency, a bottom-up approach) and the need for consultative and decentralised processes in the financial zone. It is also pertinent to discuss the issue of corruption which has been faced by the Dima Hasao region of Assam wherein there is rampant financial corruption. Absence of a committee for the purpose of monitoring and evaluating the transfer of funds and the no accountability in the functioning of the council are considered to be the key reasons for rampant corruption. In 2011, Dima Hasao Autonomous District Council was allegedly involved in the misappropriation of funds worth rupees 10,000 million, reported by the National Investigation and the Central Bureau of Investigation (ActionAid 2016: 21).

A problem pertaining to governance is related to the conception of a scheme/programme and fund allocation combined with socio-economic dynamics at the implementation level, which has implications on tribal development. Under SCA, a programme is launched for the enhancement of livelihood by providing 'microcredit' and starting a new economic micro-enterprise. In this conception, microcredit is a necessary component, but it is not the only condition for a sufficient micro-enterprise promotion. For any micro-enterprise, other than inputs/components, other factors also require evaluation, such as the identification of livelihood opportunities, the selection and motivation of the micro-entrepreneurs, some business and technical training, the establishment of market linkages for inputs and outputs, the common infrastructure, and the sometimes regulatory approvals. In the absence of these, microcredit by itself works only for a limited but familiar set of activities like small farming, livestock rearing, and petty trading, and even those where market linkages are in place. This means that any micro-enterprise is simply not a matter of economics; it has to be holistic, including legal, technical skill, technological understanding, etc. If TSP is looked upon as a plan which is holistic in nature, this programme under SCA needs to be combined with TSP as well. Collaboration with the private sector in imparting skill training could be a useful approach. For instance, some of the ITIs in forested districts can be handed over to industrial houses for better enhancement (GoI 2010). Two implications of this situation could be thought of: first, micro-enterprise is an economic venture, yet it requires a variety of materialistic inputs (technology, technical and infrastructure related) and, therefore, it needs to be combined with a holistic plan like TSP. Second, linkages of funding with non-materialistic inputs such as cultural and political aspirations – for any economic venture – need moral and community support, in such cases political support could be of added value. Could financial governance be holistic in this manner, specifically for tribals residing in SAs?

Moving towards financial governance as a tool for development

Getting consistent data related to funds planned and allocated for SAs – from every source, its channel for disbursement to utilisation, and what happens to unutilised funds – is the most difficult task. Even by joining dots (i.e., by connecting all the sources of finance) one would not be able to create a clear picture, mainly because fund utilisation is the lack of inter-linkages between various plans and the under-utilisation of the allocated funds of plans; this problem is closely linked to planned allocation of the funds and approaches thereto (Dungdung 2015). There is vagueness in respect to the flow of funds, or one can say that multiple levels of operations by one department of a state government brings vagueness. While looking at utilisation, all the funds are combinedly shown (i.e., there is no special fund for SA) it is allocated and utilised under the Tribal Sub Plan (TSP) for tribals in the given state, which makes it difficult to differentiate the schemes and beneficiaries against the different sources of funds (SEEDS 2007: 211). In the given situation, this chapter flags three puzzles in order to articulate governmentality. There are two ways in which governance as a tool supported with proper, effective fund arrangement could be thought of. First, some rule-based structural changes are presented, such as that funds must be non-lapsable and non-transferrable and thus the problem of diversion will be tackled. The other is a suggestion regarding the differentiation of the 'administration of funds' and 'governance as a tool for development' and the shift towards this goal that needs to be made. For example, in order to deal with a problem of backward areas and backwardness in terms of a lack of basic amenities, such rule-based financial decision-making may help and bring success. While upholding a bottom-up and participatory approach to governance, the financial rules need flexibility and accountability components. If any ADC or village Panchayat presents a proposal for development, it could be addressed with a holistic approach that TSP provides on paper. This approach has potential for area specific planning/regional development such as SAs and focusing on target group like STs. A timely disbursement of funds by one department to one district-based and lower level agency (i.e., under one budgetary head) which may augment the process for sectoral development in the SAs. Along with a financial audit, social audit, and accountability audit on a regular basis, this may be a step towards the formation of people-centric governance in the SAs. The accountability audit may be carried out in the form of a public hearing at a cluster of villages.[26] Having suggested a combination of financial and otherwise processes, changes in the conception of a development program and associated structural changes in the framework of SA governance is necessary (i.e., timely disbursal of funds under one budget head) released by one department and executed by one agency at the village to district level; thus reducing overlapping roles and the pressure of coordinating the funds and development activities in a given region. This may bring execution on par with rule-bound, legal compliance. The Jharkhand PESA example is alarming and enunciates a need for tribal-empowering laws. The proper combination of rights and legalism may also make finance governance more people-centric.

Notes

1 Article 366 (25) of the Constitution of India refers to Scheduled Tribes as those communities, who are scheduled in accordance with Article 342 of the Constitution (MoTA 2016: 29). The Fifth Schedule under Article 244(1) of Constitution defines 'Scheduled Areas' as such areas as the President may by order declare to be Scheduled Areas after consultation with the Governor of that State. The Sixth Schedule under Article 244 (2) of the Constitution relates to those areas in the States of Assam, Meghalaya, Tripura and Mizoram which are declared as 'tribal areas' and provides for District or Regional Autonomous Councils for such areas. These councils have wide-ranging legislative, judicial and executive powers (ibid.: 33).

2 In the budget of 2015, no new programme for tribal welfare or development was announced. The budgetary allocation showed reduction – from Rs. 26,715 crore [267.15 million rupees] during 2014–2015 down to Rs.19,980 crore [199.8 million rupees] (Dungdung 2015: 1).

3 A report of the Ministry of Tribal Affairs and United Nations Development Programme on the Brainstorming Consultation on Convergence of Resources for Tribal Development, 13 December 2014 reported that 'As far as the Scheduled Tribes are concerned, there is still a huge gap in human development indicators, since 47.4 percent of the tribal population in rural areas, and 30.4 percent in urban areas, are below the poverty line. Households covered by a health scheme are merely 2.6 percent, 68.5 percent of tribal women are anaemic, the population with drinking water facility readily available is just 19.7 percent, literacy rate is 58.9 percent, and the child mortality rate remains at 35.8 percent' (quoted in Dunddung 2015: 2). The reduction in fund allocation is interpreted as government's lack of sensitivity towards underprivileged and disadvantaged, also as lack of priority for tribals which is a constitutional mandate (CBGA 2011; Dungdung 2015).

4 Pulusam Krishna Murthy vs. T. Sujan Kumar and Ors. [2002 (2) ALT 77].

5 *Samasta Gujarat Rajya Mochi Samaj vs. Union of India (UOI) thro' Secretary* [2004 GLH (2) 67].

6 For more details on grants under Article 275(1) of the Constitution of India, Ministry of Tribal Affairs, Government of India, visit the following link:http://tribal.nic.in/Content/Grants%20under%20Article%20275%20of%20the%20Constitution%20of%20India.aspx (Last visited on February 21, 2017).

7 Article 275(2) (I), *Guidelines No. 14011/9/2001-SG&C* dated 02/07/2002, GOVERNMENT OF INDIA, Ministry of Tribal Affairs.

8 Available at: https://tribal.nic.in/writereaddata/sentionOrder/201801151113212915656AndhraCap3rd1.pdf (Last visited May 21, 2018).

9 Available at: http://poonch.gov.in/NoticeBoard/ReleaseFundsArticle275i.pdf (Last visited 21 May 2018)

10 This is an apex body for deliberations and decision-making on development issues. It comprises of the Prime Minister, the Chief Minister of all states or their substitutes, representatives of Union Territories, and members of Planning Commission (of NITI Ayog after year 2014).
11 Read more at: Unshackling the states from central schemes; available at: www.livemint.com/Opinion/mJerCMbfcXOpCaXOA8ikfM/Unshackling-the-states-from-central-schemes.html Accessed on 21 May 2018).
12 As per the guidelines of the Planning Commission (Govt. of India), issued on 31 October 2005.
13 No.M-11012/03/2013-SJ&SW Planning Commission (SJ & E Division)
14 For more details visit http://unionbudget2017.cbgaindia.org/scheduled_tribes/highlights.html (accessed on April 20, 2018).
15 see CBGA website http://unionbudget2017.cbgaindia.org/scheduled_tribes/scheme_under_proviso_to_article_of_the_constitution.html (accessed on 10 June 2019).
16 The data on these allocations was collected from the Annual Reports of the Ministry of Tribal Affairs for the years 2015–2016 and 2016–2017 (Wahi and Bhatia 2018: 21).
17 From INR 76,875 crore [768,750 million] in 2012–13 to INR 129,005 crore [1,290,050 million] in 2016–2017 with a Cumulative Average Growth Rate (CAGR) of 13.8% (Wahi and Bhatia, 2018: 21).
18 Relative proportion of Central TSP has come down from 26.3 percent to 14.9 percent during 2012–2013 and 2016–2017, compared to the state TSP, which has gone up from 71.6 percent to 81.4 percent (Wahi and Bhatia, 2018: 22).
19 The total shortfall in the state TSP allocations made to 23 states as compared to the recommended allocations under the Planning Commission's Guidelines over a five-year period (from 2011–2012 to 2015–2016) was INR 52,216 crore. Of this amount, approximately 87% of the shortfall amounting to INR 45,180 crore [451,800 million] was contributed by the Fifth Schedule Area states and the states of Assam and Tripura. The total shortfall for the central TSP for the four-year period from 2013–2014 to 2016–2017 was INR 16,593 crore [165,930 million] (Wahi and Bhatia, 2018: 22).
20 Special Central Assistance to Tribal Sub Plan, Ministry of Tribal Affairs, Government of India, *available at*: www.tribal.nic.in/Content/SpecialCentralAssistancetoTribalSubPlan.aspx (accessed on 21 February 2017).
21 SCHEME OF GRANT-IN-AID TO VOLUNTARY ORGANISATIONS WORKING FOR THE WELFARE OF SCHEDULED TRIBES, F.No.22040/31/2007-NGO (with effect from 1st April 2008), Government of India, Ministry of Tribal Affairs.
22 Convergence Model, Ministry of Tribal Affairs, Government of India (Last visited to http://vky.tribal.nic.in/ circular/BackgroundNoteonconvergence.pdf accessed on 1 March 2018).
23 During the year 2014–2015, it was proposed to implement a pilot project in one block each in the ten states having Fifth Schedule Areas. These ten blocks have been selected primarily base on low literacy criteria. The scheme is to be implemented through state governments and it has been decided to release Rs. 10 Crore [10 trillion] to each of the selected states as a gap-filling measure (MoTA 2018).
24 For example, if the fund is for infrastructure development, Public Works Department (PWD) is usually a channel for fund flow.
25 WRIT PETITION (CIVIL) NO. 180 OF 2011 Orissa Mining Corporation Ltd versus Ministry of Environment & Forest & Others.
26 General public hearings organised by Majdoor Kisan Shakti Sangathan in village of Bhim in Rajasthan State starting from year 2002 till date could be considered an example in this respect.

References

ActionAid India. 2016. *Functioning of Autonomous Councils in Sixth Schedule Areas of North Eastern States*. New Delhi: Natural Resource Hub and Democratisation Hub, ActionAid India.

Centre for Budget and Governance Accountability (CBGA). 2011. *Implementation of Scheduled Castes Sub Plan & Tribal Sub Plan in the Union and State Budgets of India: A Study Report*. Available at: http://www.cbgaindia.org/wp-content/uploads/2016/05/Study-Report-SCP-and-TSP-04.01.12.pdf (accessed on 10 June 2019).

Centre for Budget and Governance Accountability (CBGA). 2017a. *Union Budget Analysis Tools 2017–18*. Available at: http://unionbudget2017.cbgaindia.org/scheduled_tribes/index.html (accessed on 20 April 2018).

Centre for Budget and Governance Accountability (CBGA). 2017b. *What do the numbers tell?: An analysis of Union budget 2017–18*. Available at http://www.cbgaindia.org/wp-content/uploads/2017/02/Analysis-of-Union-Budget-2017-18-4.pdf (accessed on 10 June 2019).

Dungdung, G. 2015. 'The Need for a New Approach to Adivasi Development.' *Countercurrents.org*. Available at: www.countercurrents.org/dungdung230315.pdf (accessed on 30 March 2018).

Government of India (GoI). 2010. *Report of National Committee of Forest Rights Act: Joint Committee of Ministry of Environment and Ministry of Tribal Affairs*. New Delhi: Government of India.

Joint Committee of Ministry of Environment and Ministry of Tribal Affairs. 2010. *Report of National Committee of Forest Rights Act*. New Delhi: Government of India (December).

Kapur, A. and Srinivas, V. 2016. *Why the Centre Needs to Give States More Control Over Schemes It Co-Finances* (29 March 2016). Available at: https://scroll.in/article/805191/why-the-centre-needs-to-give-states-more-control-over-schemes-it-co-finances (accessed on 21 May 2018).

Ministry of Tribal Affairs (MoTA). 2002. *Article 275(2) (I), Guidelines No. 14011/9/2001-SG&C dated 02/07/2002*. New Delhi: Government of India, Ministry of Tribal Affairs, ANNUAL REPORT 2015–16. Available at: http://tribal.nic.in/WriteReadData/CMS/Documents/201606060452201526687EnglishAR.pdf (accessed on 29 March 2018).

Ministry of Tribal Affairs (MoTA). 2008. 'Scheme of Grant-In-Aid to Voluntary Organisations Working for the Welfare of Scheduled Tribes.' *F.No.22040/31/2007-NGO* (with effect from 1st April 2008). New Delhi: Government of India.

Ministry of Tribal Affairs (MoTA). 2014a. *Report of The High Level Committee on Socio-economic, Health and Educational Status of Tribal Communities of India*. Available at: www.kractivist.org/wp-content/uploads/2014/12/Tribal-Committee-Report-May-June-2014.pdf (accessed on March 29, 2018).

Ministry of Tribal Affairs (MoTA). 2014b. *VANBANDHU KALYAN YOJANA*. New Delhi: Press Information Bureau, Government of India. Available at: http://pib.nic.in/newsite/PrintRelease.aspx?relid=112081 (accessed on 28 February 2018).

Ministry of Tribal Affairs (MoTA). 2016. *Annual Report 2015–16*. Available at https://tribal.nic.in/writereaddata/AnnualReport/AnnualReport2015-16.pdf (accessed on 10 June 2019).

Ministry of Tribal Affairs (MoTA). 2017. *Special Central Assistance to Tribal Sub Plan*. New Delhi: Government of India. Available at: www.tribal.nic.in/Content/SpecialCentralAssistancetoTribalSubPlan.aspx (accessed on 21 February 2017).

Ministry of Tribal Affairs. na. *Convergence Model*. New Delhi: Government of India. Available at: http://vky.tribal.nic.in/ circular/BackgroundNoteonconvergence.pdf (accessed on 1 March 2018).

Ministry of Tribal Affairs. *Annual Report 2017–18*. Available at https://tribal.nic.in/writereaddata/AnnualReport/AR2017-18.pdf (accessed on 10 June 2019).

Planning Commission. 2011. *Report of the Committee on Restructuring of Centrally Sponsored Schemes (CSS)*. New Delhi: Government of India.

Planning Commission. 2013. *Revised Guidelines for Implementation of Tribal Sub-Plan (TSP) by the States/UTs*. Available at: planningcommission.gov.in/sectors/guide_state1208.pdf (accessed on 19 May 2018).

Pulusam Krishna Murthy vs. T. Sujan Kumar and Ors. [2002 (2) ALT 77].

Samasta Gujarat Rajya Mochi Samaj vs. Union of India (UOI) thro' Secretary [2004 GLH (2) 67].

Sharma, N. 2017. 'Centre to Rethink Replication of Gujarat Model of Tribal Welfare Across the Country.' *Economic Times*, June 16. Available at https://economictimes.indiatimes.com/news/politics-and-nation/centre-to-rethink-replication-of-gujarat-model-of-tribal-welfare-across-the-country/articleshow/56577486.cms?utm_source=contentofinterest&utm_medium=text&utm_campaign=cppst (accessed on 19 May 2018).

Socio Economic and Educational Development Society (SEEDS). 2007. *Research Study on Livelihood Options Assets Creation Out of Special Component Plan (SCP) & Tribal Sub Plan (TSP) Schemes and Its Impact Among SCs and STs in India*. New Delhi: Planning Commission, Government of India, p. 211. Available at: http://planningcommission.nic.in/reports/sereport/ser/stdy_scp.pdf (accessed on 29 March 2018)

Wahi, N. and Bhatia, A. 2018. *The legal regime and political economy of land rights of Scheduled Tribes in the Schedules Areas of India*. New Delhi: Centre for Policy Research

4 Role of tribal autonomous councils in economic development in the Sixth Scheduled Areas

Sumarbin Umdor

Introduction

The Autonomous Distirct Councils (ADCs) occupy a unique position in the constitutional arrangement for local governments in India. The decentralisation of power to sub-state governments was introduced in the country through the 73rd and 74th constitutional amendment acts (CAAs) creating a *third tier of governance* through the constitution of Panchayati Raj institutions (PRIs) in rural areas and municipalities in urban areas from 1992 onwards. However, much before the aforementioned two CAAs, the Constitution of India as adopted in 1951 included special provisions that allows some measure of autonomy and self-governance to tribal areas in the northeast region of India through the institution of autonomous district councils. The application of the 73rd and 74th CAAs are therefore are not applicable to the areas under the jurisdiction of autonomous district councils as they operate under a set of provisions contained in the Sixth Schedule of the Indian Constitution.

These tribal autonomous councils constituted under the Sixth Schedule are local self-government institutions mandated to protect and promote tribal interest and the preservation of their culture and custom including administration of traditional tribal institutions (Karlsson 2005). The councils were envisaged to provide some measure of self-government to the different tribes in the region that would enable them to preserve and continue with their distinct culture and traditional grassroot institutions, and as succinctly argued by a member in the constitutional assembly debate 'to rule themselves according to their culture and genius' (Lok Sabha Constitutional Assembly Debates 1949).

The autonomous councils have been entrusted with legislative, executive, judicial, as well as fiscal powers in subjects laid down in 21 articles of the Constitution referred to as paragraphs [Articles 244(2) and 275(1)]. However, the functioning of these councils has been marred by the limited role that they play in promoting development in areas under their jurisdiction. This chapter examines the three issues argued as being responsible for the subdued development role of the councils which include a limited development mandate, a low level of financial autonomy, and the failure of the councils to formulate legislations to protect economic interest of the tribals.

For examining the first issue, we compare the allocation and devolution of development functions to the councils which show that apart from the three councils in Assam, the Sixth Schedule has not envisaged a substantial development role for the councils in the other states as reflected in the allocation of development functions to them. Further, even in states like Mizoram and Tripura where we find that the state governments have devolved some additional functions to the councils, the transfer of activities is limited to the implementation of specific programmes with very little control vested with the councils in terms of funds and functionaries.

Low financial autonomy of the councils is examined by analysing the different sources of revenues of the councils which show low contribution of own revenue and the financial dependence of the councils on the state governments. The third issue is explored by highlighting the lack of actions taken by the councils to protect the economic interest of the tribals through enactment of appropriate legislations and their implementation over the years.

Background

The origin of the Sixth Schedule of the Constitution can be traced to the Cabinet Mission sent to India by the then British Prime Minister Attlee in 1946 to discuss and finalise plans for the transfer of power to Indian leadership and to prepare a post-British governing institution, which had raised the issue of a separate arrangement for the administration of tribal and excluded areas and its inclusion in the Constitution. This led to the formation of the sub-committee – The North-East Frontier (Assam) Tribal and Excluded Areas – on 27 February 1947, under the Chairmanship of the then Premier of Assam, Gopinath Bardoloi. The sub-committee was constituted by the Advisory Committee on the Fundamental Rights, Minorities, and Tribal and Excluded Areas under the Chairmanship of Vallabhbhai Patel.

The committee brought to fore the existence of traditional village councils in tribal areas, which are participatory and democratic in their functioning, while in the same vein it also mentioned the absence of any statutory local self-governing bodies in these areas and therefore implicitly alluded to the danger of replacing the tribal village councils with modern self-governing councils. The committee also argued for an administrative arrangement that would protect the distinct social customs of the tribes and their religious belief and also safeguard and promote the rights and interests of the tribals who formed a minority in the then composite province of Assam (Hansari 2010).

These recommendations of the Bardoloi Committee were incorporated in the Sixth Schedule of the Indian Constitution. At the time when the Constitution was adopted the Sixth Schedule was to be applied to the tribal areas of Assam contained in table appended to Paragraph 20 of the Sixth Schedule containing in two parts – Part A with the following areas (1) The

United Khasi and Jaintis Hills District, (2) The Garo Hills District, (3) The Lushai (later substituted by the word Mizo) Hills District, (4)The Naga Hills District, (5) The North Cachar Hills District, (6) The Mikir Hills District (later changed to the Karbi Anglong District); and Part B with (1) Northeast Frontier Tract and (2) The Naga Tribal Area.

The provisions of the Sixth Schedule were never extended to areas in Part B which now forms part of the states of Arunachal Pradesh and Nagaland. Further, since the adoption of the Constitution there have been many changes to the areas listed in Part A of paragraph 20 of the Schedule that were necessitated by the reorganisation of tribal areas in Assam and the creation of new states. Today there are ten such autonomous councils: three each in Assam,[1] Meghalaya,[2] and Mizoram[3] and one in Tripura.[4] While some of the councils such as the BTC have been newly created in 2004 and TTAADC (Tripura Tribal Area Autonomous District Council) was included under the Schedule in 1985, ADCs in Meghalaya have been in existence since the 1950s.

In terms of coverage of population, we find that in Assam about 44 percent of the population falls under the jurisdiction of the three tribal autonomous councils while in Meghalaya, except for the population in Shillong municipality area, in the whole state, as much as 88 percent of the population falls under the coverage of the three councils. In Mizoram, the three ADCs extend their coverage over two districts covering 16 percent of the state's population, while the TTAADC in Tripura is spread over all four districts and covers about 80 percent of the state's population.

Limited development mandate of ADCs

The developmental role envisaged for PRIs and municipalities are diametrically opposite to ADCs. For instance, the 73rd CAA has clearly enunciated the role of the PRIs in facilitating a bottom-up approach in preparing and implementation plans for achieving economic development and social justice originating from the primary unit of governance at the village level (the Gram Sabha); this is achieved through the delegation of specific functions, funds, and functionaries to the local bodies so that they can be an effective unit of self-government. To this end, 29 and 18 different subjects encompassing every facet of human development have been assigned to PRIs and municipalities, respectively.

In the case of ADCs, not much emphasis has been entrusted to the councils as can be seen for the limited subject assigned to them when compared to the PRIs and municipalities. Rather, the rationale for their constitution as originally envisaged has more to do with providing an institutional mechanism to protect the socio-cultural and economic interests of the minority tribal population in the then composite state of Assam. Corollary to this, under paragraph 3 of the Sixth Schedule, which applied to ADCs in

Meghalaya, Mizoram, and Tripura, the legislative powers of the councils is confined to ten subjects related to the administration of land and forest management, the administration of villages and towns, the administration of the institution of chieftains and social customs, all of which are governed by traditional socio-cultural norms and practices. These law-making powers assigned to the councils on the use of land and forest resources and the administration of tribal socio-cultural institutions are bounded and limited by age-old practices and traditions followed by the tribals, which are distinct to each community. For example, in Meghalaya, land and forest are owned by clan and community and the role of the councils is the administration of resources and institution as per traditional norms and practices followed by the community.

The provisions under paragraph 3 of the Sixth Schedule were subsequently amended in 1995 and 2003, which delegated additional legislative powers on 15 subjects to Karbi Anglong Autonomous Council (KAAC) and Dima Hasao Autonomous Council (DHAC) (paragraph 3A) and on 40 subjects to Bodoland Territorial Council (BTC) (paragraph 3B). However, the extensive legislative powers provided to the three councils in Assam are an outcome of the protracted and violent demand for separate statehood for these tribal regions of Assam, and the enhanced autonomy and legislative powers to these councils are measures used by the Union government to placate the various groups agitating for statehood. For the seven other tribal councils under the Sixth Schedule, the legislative powers are confined to subjects listed in paragraph 3 as described in preceding paragraph.

Paragraph 6 of the Sixth Schedule has devolved only a limited number of socio-economic activities to the ADCs comprising of establishment and management of primary schools, dispensaries, markets, cattle pounds, ferries, fisheries, roads, roads transport, and waterways. However, there is an enabling clause under sub-paragraph 1 of the paragraph 6 that provides for the transfer of additional functions relating to agriculture, animal husbandry, community projects, co-operative societies, social welfare, village planning, or any other functions from the state government to the ADCs, which has been used by the state government of Mizoram and Tripura to devolve additional functions to the tribal councils in their respective states.

In Mizoram, the state government in 1986 has handed over the executive functions of certain activities of some departments to the three ADCs operating in the state. These relate to agriculture, animal husbandry, community projects, social welfare, industries, forest and soil conservation. In 1993, the state government issued another notification entrusting the executive functions of 20 departments to the three councils in the area within their jurisdiction. From our scrutiny of annual plan schemes of the three ADCs in Mizoram, we have identified the following socio-economic activities devolved to the three councils in Mizoram.

However, due to the limited funds available with the councils, the actual expenditure in the above activities is very meagre amount. For instance, the

Table 4.1 Activities and functions managed/performed by the three ADCs in Mizoram

Sl. no.	*Activities*	*Nature of involvement*
1	Primary schools	Establishment, management, and control
2	Markets	Management and control
3	Roads (village roads and footpath)	Construction and maintenance
4	Roads Transport	Maintenance of vehicles and construction of garage
5	Waterways	Management of boats
6	Fisheries	Procurement of fish seeds for free distribution to reliable fish farmers, development of identified fishery ponds Supply of fish breeding and feeding materials.
7	Agriculture and horticulture	Agriculture demonstrator farm Construction of agriculture link road, land development, extension service, procurement of seedlings Maintenance of agriculture orchards, construction of minor irrigation (Kutcha), development of horticulture garden
8	Animal husbandry	Purchase of fodder Construction and maintenance of veterinary farm
9	Community projects	Clearance and maintenance of inter Village path Construction of seasonal wooden bridges at IVP roads Distribution of GCI Sheets to needy families
10	Co-operative society	Assistance to co-operative society training and seminar
11	Social welfare	Assistance to orphans, physically challenged persons, poor patients old-aged, NGOs Awareness campaign on drug abuse elimination

Source: Annual Plan of ADCs in Mizoram (various issues)

total outlay of Lai Autonomous District Council (LADC) in Mizoram under the 11th Five Year Plan for 18 departments is only Rs. 53 crore. Moreover, more than 50 percent of the development expenditure of the councils goes towards salary and other components of revenue expenditure, which results in very limited impact and recognition of the council role in developmental activities in areas under their jurisdiction. Further, even though some activities of departments have been officially entrusted to the ADCs, many of the departments and their staff continue to be under the direct control and administration of the state government, with some department such as that of Agriculture and Sericulture functioning as a dual department of the state government and the councils.

In LADC, it is reported that in primary school education over which the Council has full administrative control, the teaching staff of the state government whose services have been transferred to the council are treated as on deputation on foreign service. Further, the necessary funding for departments/activities devolved to the council has not been transferred, as a result, the Council is not in a position to exercise complete control over these departments/activities (Thomas 2008).

The primary developmental activity of TTAADC is centred on the management of primary schools which have been fully transferred to the ADCs along with staffs and funding since 1985. In 2014 there were about 1,475 primary schools, 228 Senior Basic Schools, and 1 higher Secondary School with 88,137 enrolled under the management of TTAADC. In 1986, the state government also transferred the management of all social education centres and adult literacy centres to the council. Other developmental functions of the council are the construction and maintenance of roads, bridges, and culverts; managing of vocational training centres and a hospital; rehabilitating shifting cultivators; providing veterinary and fisheries services; and implementing promotional schemes for farmers. However, except for primary education, the council intervention in other development activities is limited in scope and funding.

As far as the ADCs in Meghalaya are concerned, there are hardly any development activities where the involvement of the three councils is having any significant impact on the community. The councils are involved in minor community projects such as the construction and maintenance of footpaths, sanitation facilities, approach roads, bridges, drinking wells, community hall, check dams, and fishery units. Even in the case of primary education which is one of the main activities of ADCs in the other three states, the government of Meghalaya has all but taken over this activity from the three councils since the mid-1980s due to their inability to manage the administration and finances of the primary schools.

Low financial autonomy

The Sixth Schedule empowers ADCs to collect taxes for generation of its own revenue. Under paragraph 8 of the Sixth Schedule, the councils can levy and collect taxes on the following: (1) Taxes on lands and buildings; (2) taxes on professional trades, callings, and employments; (3) taxes on entry of goods into markets for sale therein, and tolls on passengers and goods carried and ferries; (4) taxes on animals, vehicles, and boats; and (5) taxes for the maintenance of school, dispensaries, and roads. Paragraph 9 of the Schedule also gives the tribal councils the right to receive a share of the royalties accrued each year from licenses or leases for the purpose of prospecting for or the extraction of minerals granted by the state government with respect to any area within the jurisdiction of councils. The share of royalties on minerals (major and minor minerals) and also from motor vehicle tax, both of which are collected by the state government, constitute the shared revenue of the councils.

Studies carried out on the finances of the ADCs have shown that the functioning of the councils has been marred by many problems, one of which is the lack of financial resources and their total dependence on the transfer of funds from higher governments (Rao and Brunner 2010; Stuligross 1999). According to the Expert Committee on Planning for Sixth Schedule (GoI 2006), the lack of financial resources have denied these institutions the flexibility required to emerge as a vibrant institution for promoting local development in the region.

The sources of the revenue of ADCs can be divided into three categories: (1) Tax and non-tax revenues which are collected and appropriated by the councils, (2) shared revenue which are levied and collected by the state government and a percentage and the proceed shared with the councils, and (3) grants from Union and the state government. The source revenue includes professional taxes, proceeds from the sale of timbers, the royalty on forest products, market receipts in the form of rent from stalls and entry tax on goods, trading licence fees and fines collected from non-tribal traders, the receipts from toll gates, land revenue, stamps, and registration fees and other minor receipts. Shared Revenue is comprised of mainly motor vehicle tax and royalty on minerals. However, in case of TTAADC, many of the taxes assigned to the council is collected by the state government, which it then shares with the Council in the following proportion: (1) Forest revenue – 75 percent; (2) agriculture income tax – 50 percent; (3) land revenue – 40 percent; (4) professional tax – 25 percent; (5) motor vehicle tax – 25 percent; and (6) royalty from natural gas – 30 percent.

Grants from Union and the state governments constitute the third component of revenue receipts of ADCs. Grants from the Union government consist of assistance from the Tribal Affairs Ministry, the Government of India under Article 275(1) of the Constitution, the Union Finance Commission, and, under the Non-Lapsable Central Pool of Resources under the Ministry of Development of North Eastern Region, the Government of India as assistance for development projects of the councils. The state government also provides funds to the autonomous councils mainly towards supporting expenditure under non-plan schemes particularly the salaries and pension's components of the council expenditure. The state government also provides assistance to the councils towards financing of minor projects of the councils.

Compared to PRIs, the Constitution has assigned limited powers to ADCs to levy and collect tax and non-tax revenues. While PRI has as many as 32 taxes and fees assigned to it as own revenue, there are only 20 different sources of own revenue available to councils in Meghalaya. Even with these assigned revenue sources, the lack of economic development in the tribal areas severely limits the councils' ability to impose taxes and generate funds. Further, many of the councils are also reluctant to impose taxes like the house and property tax on its tribal population, thus affecting its

Table 4.2 Revenue sources of ADCs

Sources	*Meghalaya*	*Mizoram*	*Assam*	*Tripura*
A. Own revenues	1 Taxes on profession, trade, calling, and employment 2 Land revenue – ordinary land revenue, mortgage and survey fees, land valuation charges 3 Stamps and registration fees 4 Forest – sale of timbers, weight bridges, royalty on forest products, etc. 5 Administration of justice – Court fee, application and certifying fees 6 Trades – trading license fees and fines 7 Markets – collection from councils markets and other markets 8 Stationery and printing – sale of forms, tender fees, etc. 9 Toll gates – collection from toll gates 10 Water works – water supply charges. 11 Income from fisheries. 12 Miscellaneous receipts	1 Taxes on profession, trade calling and employment 2 Land Revenue – ordinary land revenue, miscellaneous receipts 3 Stamps and registration 4 Vehicle tax – tax on vehicles entering council area 5 Public works – rent on council's buildings 6 Administrative services – certifying and application fees 7 Education fees – tuition fee, examination Fee, other fees 8 Rent from council markets, other receipts 9 Forest – royalty and sale of timber and forest products 10 Road and transport Services	1 Taxes on property and capital transaction 2 Interest receipts, dividends, and profits 3 Public works, miscellaneous 4 Education, sports, arts, and culture 5 Crop husbandry, fisheries, 6 Other rural development programmes 7 Minor irrigation 8 Village and small scale industries 9 Roads and bridges 10 Tourism 11 Other general economic services	1 Trade license 2 Rent or sale of sale stalls 3 Auction of village markets 4 Sale proceed of fishery farms 5 Sale proceeds of piggery farm
B. Shared revenue	1 Motor vehicle tax. 2 Royalty on minerals.	–	–	1 Forest Revenue 2 Agriculture income tax 3 Land revenue tax 4 Professional tax 5 Motor vehicle tax 6 Royalty from natural gas
C. Grants and transfer-red funds	1 State government grants 2 Central government grants	1 Non Plan grants – general secretariat and education 2 Plan grants – minor work	1 Non-plan grants 2 Plan grants – central plan schemes, centrally sponsored schemes 3 Special plan grants	1 Plan grants 2 Transferred funds

Source: Annual Budget of respective ADCs

ability to generate sufficient resources for undertaking development work (Umdor and Syiem 2014). The weak financial position of the councils is further compounded by the financial irregularities and lack of financial transparency and accountability on the part of the councils (Goswami 1996; Syiem 2007).

Among all the ADCs, the reliance of ADCs in Mizoram on transfers from higher governments is as high as 98 percent of total revenue receipts of the councils. Similarly, other councils are also highly dependent on funds from the state and Union government, which mainly go towards meeting salary, pension and other revenue expenditure of the councils. Therefore, the inability to generate sufficient own resources coupled with high revenue expenditure have severely constrained the development initiative and activities of the councils (Umdor 2014).

Another problem plaguing the functioning of the ADCs is the high proportion of revenue expenditure of the councils, which severely curtails their ability to plan and implement appropriate community development projects for the benefit of people under their jurisdiction. To explain this issue, we take a look at the expenditure of Khasi Hills Autonomous District Council (KHADC), which has been disaggregated into revenue and capital expenditure. Revenue expenditure includes all that spending which is recurring in nature and is incurred during the normal running of the departments and the maintenance of services of the council and which does not lead to the creation of assets. Examples of revenue expenditure are the salaries of government employees, repairs, travelling, entertainment, etc. Capital expenditure, on the other hand, is that expenditure which leads to creation of concrete assets such as expenditure on purchase of land, buildings, machinery, vehicles, renovation of buildings, community projects, etc.

Expenditure of KHADC has also been classified into development and non-development categories as per function or service under each expenditure major heads. Development expenditure has been broadly defined to include all direct and indirect expenditure under economic and social services, including those secretariat expenses under these two expenses that are intended to promote economic development and social welfare. Expenditure appearing under general services, which include major heads such as the organs of the state and fiscal services, has been included under non-development expenditure.

The annual expenditure of the KHADC for the period 1994–1995 to 2013–2014 in real terms has been obtained by deflating nominal expenditure by GDP deflator. Further, a three-year moving average of expenditure has also been computed to smooth out the year-to-year fluctuations of expenditure and show the trends more clearly. Table 4.3 shows the expenditure of KHADC in terms of nominal and real values both as actual and also as a three-year moving average.

In 1995–1996, the nominal expenditure was rupees 49.5 million, which rose to rupees 372.3 million in 2012–2013. In terms of real expenditure,

Table 4.3 Trends in the expenditure of KHADC, 1994–1995 to 2013–2014

Period	*Nominal expenditure (Rupees in million)*	*Real expenditure (Rupees in million)*
	Three-year moving average	*Three-year moving average*
1995–1996	49.5	100.6
1996–1997	51.6	96.9
1997–1998	56.2	97.4
1998–1999	59.3	92.2
1999–2000	67.4	95.5
2000–2001	73.5	95.3
2001–2002	84.1	104.5
2002–2003	95.4	114.1
2003–2004	122.9	135.3
2004–2005	143.3	147.8
2005–2006	152.0	145.4
2006–2007	147.2	131.6
2007–2008	160.9	131.8
2008–2009	194.2	151.1
2009–2010	235.7	175.5
2010–2011	287.7	204.7
2011–2012	326.7	220.7
2012–2013	372.3	238.8
AAGR	12.9*(31.5)	5.5*(10.5)

* Growth rates have been estimated by fitting a log linear trend equation of the form Ln(y)=a+bx. The t ratios of growth coefficients are given in brackets with the level of statistical significance (one tailed t-test) denoted as: *= 1 percent level)

Source: Author's computation from budget documents of ADCs (various years)

the corresponding increase was from rupees 100.6 million in 1995–1996 to rupees 238.8 million in 2012–2013. AAGR (average annual growth rate), using the three-year moving average of nominal expenditure, is 12.9 percent, while the AAGR for real expenditure is 5.5 percent, both the growth rates being significant at 1 percent (Table 4.3).

During the period of study, we see a major proportion of expenditure of KHADC going towards meeting revenue expenditure with spending in real terms increasing from rupees 70.8 million in 1995–1996 to rupees 167.5 million in 2012–2013. The corresponding increase in capital expenditure in real terms is from rupees 29.8 million in 1995–1996 to rupees 71.3 million in 2012–2013. As percentage of total expenditure, the share of revenue expenditure ranged from 63 percent (2004–2005) to 86 percent (1998–1999). Within revenue expenditure, the bulk of the expenditure went to salaries and pensions, varying from 78 percent (1998–1999) to 89 percent (2011–2012) of total revenue expenditure (Table 4.4). Another important component of revenue expenditure is travelling allowances (TA) and POL (petroleum, oil, and lubricants), which are grouped under 'TA & POL,' on which expenditure is ranged from 5 percent to 9 percent of revenue expenditure of the Council.

Table 4.4 Growth and composition of expenditure of KHADC, 1995–1996 to 2012–2013, three-year moving average

Period	*Revenue expenditure (Rupees in million)*		*Capital expenditure (Rupees in Million)*	
	Amount	*Percent*	*Amount*	*Percent*
1995–1996	70.8	70	29.8	30
1996–1997	75.2	78	21.7	22
1997–1998	80.3	82	17.1	18
1998–1999	78.9	86	13.2	14
1999–2000	79.6	83	15.9	17
2000–2001	78.8	83	16.5	17
2001–2002	86.0	82	18.5	18
2002–2003	90.7	79	23.4	21
2003–2004	91.7	68	43.6	32
2004–2005	93.3	63	54.5	37
2005–2006	93.2	64	52.2	36
2006–2007	95.5	73	36.1	27
2007–2008	96.6	73	35.1	27
2008–2009	103.0	68	48.0	32
2009–2010	118.8	68	56.8	32
2010–2011	141.3	69	63.4	31
2011–2012	161.2	73	59.5	27
2012–2013	167.5	70	71.3	30
AAGR	**4.5*(9.3)**		**9.1*(6.0)**	

* Growth rates have been estimated by fitting a log linear trend equation of the form Ln(y) = a + bx. The t ratios of growth coefficients are given in parentheses with the level of statistical significance (one tailed t-test) denoted as: *= 1 percent level)

Source: same as in table 4.3

The major components of capital expenditure for KHADC are the construction of buildings, markets, and minor projects (which include construction of approach roads, bridges, drinking wells, community hall, etc) represented as 'Buildings, markets and minor projects.' the bulk of capital expenditure is under this head ranging from 82 percent (1995–1996) to 95 percent (2004–2005 and 2005–2006) of capital expenditure. Other two components of capital expenditure with substantial outlays are the purchase of furniture, tools, and vehicles under 'Furniture, tool, and vehicles' and on plantation projects of the Council under 'Plantation Scheme.' Other minor capital expenditure items are in the form of repairs/maintenance of quarters of patrolling squads, fishery ponds, purchase of uniforms, and badges of staff, which are included under 'Miscellaneous' capital expenditure.

Lack of legislative action to protect the economic interest of tribals

Under the Sixth Schedule of the Constitution, ADCs are mandated to legislate and enact laws with respect to land, forest, water resources, the establishment of village or town committees or councils and their powers, village or town police, public health and sanitation, the appointment or succession of Chiefs or Headmen, the inheritance of property, marriage and divorce, and social customs. Land and forest are important resources for the tribals as for many of them are directly dependent on these two resources for their livelihood. In recent years, we find that in many of the tribal areas the community ownership of land is gradually being replaced by private ownership.

In Meghalaya, it is found that the privatisation of community/clan land has taken place at a rapid rate through the creation of legal property rights on land that was previously regarded as a common property, which is taken place due to usurping of community land by the tribal elites and also land acquisition by the state and central government for developmental projects (Nongkynrih 2008; Kumar 2008). In many of these cases, transfers of land to non-tribal entities takes place due to the absence of appropriate laws to regulate the process of securing prior informed consent of the community for transfers of land out outside entities. Staying with the example from Meghalaya, we find that among the rural households it is very common for people to possess a customary landownership certificate issued by traditional institutions which are not accepted by the banks for used as collateral for obtaining loans. As local government, ADCs are in a position to provide legal sanction to the customary landownership certificate which would enable households to use them for borrowing from formal lending institutions. However, in both these cases the ADCs in the state have failed to intervene by way of enactment of appropriate legislation to protect and facilitate the economic interest of the tribal population.

In Tripura, the immigration of non-tribals to the state from neighbouring country and states have led to the large-scale alienation of tribal land, which has affected the tribal population's access to land and forest resources. Under the present arrangement, the regulation of land holdings and reforms is government by the Tripura Land Revenue and Land Reforms Act of 1960 enacted by the state government with no role of the TTAADC in regulating land related issues even in tribal areas of the state (ActionAid India 2016). This relegation of the council's role in this area has aggravated the loss of tribal land and feeling of alienation by the tribals of the state. The above two examples highlight the lack of proactive action by the ADCs in exercising their legislative and executive powers to protect vital economic resources of the tribals.

Indicator of subdued development role of the councils

The extent of involvement of ADCs in the development programmes of the state is measured in terms of the extent of fiscal decentralisation – the devolution of taxing and spending powers enjoyed by the ADCs measured in terms of revenue and expenditure decentralisation ratios. The two ratios

Table 4.5 Fiscal decentralisation statistics of Meghalaya, 2001–2002 to 2011–2012

	2001–2002	*2002–2003*	*2003–2004*	*2004–2005*	*2005–2006*	*2006–2007*	*2007–2008*	*2008–2009*	*2009–2010*	*2010–2011*	*2011–2012*
RDR All ADCs	0.031	0.027	0.030	0.033	0.030	0.031	0.025	0.026	0.027	0.026	0.032
EDR All ADCs	0.024	0.025	0.026	0.026	0.027	0.020	0.022	0.028	0.021	0.019	0.025

Source: Author's compilation

represent the proportion of combined income and expenditure of the ADCs in a state to the total state government revenue and expenditure, and they are used here to show the importance of ADCs' finance with respect to that of the state government. We have used the fiscal decentralisation statistics of Meghalaya for the period 2000–2001 to 2010–2011 in Table 4.5.

The comparison of combined revenue and expenditure of the three councils in Meghalaya to the total revenue and expenditure of the state government is depicted by the revenue decentralisation ratio (RDR) and expenditure decentralisation ratio (EDR), respectively. The values of these two ratios measure the extent of financial decentralisation in the state. Both RDR and EDR fall within the range of 2–3 percent, thereby indicating the very limited financial decentralisation and negligible impact of the functions and activities of the ADCs in Meghalaya compared to functions of the state government, which are measured in terms amount of revenue generated as well as the spending by the state government.

Conclusion

This chapter argues that there are three factors responsible for the subdued development role of the ADCs, namely the limited development mandate as reflected in the legislative powers assigned to the ADCs and also the lack of effective devolution of powers to the ADCs by state governments as seen in case of Mizoram and Tripura. We have highlighted that the ADCs in Meghalaya, Mizoram, and Tripura have a very limited development role assigned to them by the Sixth Schedule, which is mainly limited to the management of primary school. In states like Tripura and Mizoram, the devolution of additional subjects to the councils has not been accompanied with transfers of finance and functionaries. In Meghalaya, the reverse of devolution of powers has taken place where even the assigned functions like primary education had to be taken over by the state government because of failure of then ADCs to run them properly. It is the recognition of these issues that has prompted the Union government to consider an amendment of the Sixth Schedule to provide more powers and a larger role to the ADCs to function as an effective institution to promote local development. The draft amendment of the Schedule proposes the assignment of more functions to the councils and also greater financial autonomy through more devolution of funds from Union government and state governments.

Another issue that affects the functioning of ADCs is the high revenue volatility in own revenue receipts of the councils. This points to the existence of loopholes and leakages in revenue collection. On the expenditure front, a huge chunk of financial resources goes towards current expenditure with very little left for supporting socio-economic activities. The lack of own source revenue is a crucial element which severely handicapped the ability of the ADCs to implement development works in the area under their jurisdiction. Much of the resources of the ADCs are in the form of grants from higher governments, which are routed through the state government. Very often, the flow of funds from state government to the councils is affected by political consideration, particularly in situations when opposing political parties are in power in the state government and in the councils. We find the political party controlling the state government often uses the release of funds as a lever to influence and install its own government in the councils. This has led to the demand for direct funding of ADCs by Union government.

Notes

1 Karbi Anglong Autonomous Council (KAAC), Dima Hasao Autonomous Council (DHAC), and Bodoland Territorial Council (BTC).
2 Khasi Hills Autonomous District Council (KHADC), Jaintia Hills Autonomous District Council (JHADC) and Garo Hills Autonomous District Council (GHADC).
3 Mara Autonomous District Council (MADC), Lai Autonomous District Council (LADC), and Chakma Autonomous District Council (CADC).
4 Tripura Area Autonomous District Council (TTAADC).

References

ActionAid India. 2016. *Functioning of Autonomous Councils in Sixth Schedule Areas of North Eastern States*. New Delhi: Natural Resource Hub and Democratisation Hub, ActionAid India.

GoI. 2006. *Planning for the Sixth Schedule Areas and those Areas Not Covered by Parts IX and IX-A of the Constitution*. Report of The Expert Committee, Ministry of Panchayati Raj. New Delhi: Government of India.

Goswami, P.J. 1996. The Sixth Schedule and Tribal Development in the Northeast: A Critical Appraisal. In L.S. Gassah (Ed.), *The Autonomous District Councils* (pp. 96–102). New Delhi: Omsons Publications.

Hansari, V. 2010. *Sixth Schedule to the Constitution* (3rd ed.). New Delhi: Universal Publishing Co.

Karlsson, B.G. 2005. 'Sovereignty Through Indigenous Governance: Revisiting Tradition Political Institutions in Northeast India.' *NEHU Journal*, 3(2): 1–16.

Kumar, C. 2008. *Institutional Dissonance in Forest Management in Meghalaya, India*. Available at: http://dlc.dlib.indiana.edu/dlc/bitstream/handle/10535/2146/Kumar_101901.pdf?sequence=1 (accessed on 17 April 2018)

Lok Sabha Constitutional Assembly Debates. 1949. *Draft Constitution – (Contd): Sixth Schedule- (Contd): Paragraph 2, Volume IX (30th July to 18th September*

1949), 6th September, 1949. Available at: Parliament of India Lok Sabha website, 164.100.47.194/Loksabha/Debates/cadebatefiles/C06091949.html (accessed on 18 April 2018).

Nongkynrih, A.K. 2008. 'Privatization of Communal Land of the Tribes of North East India: A Sociological Viewpoint.' In W. Fernandes and S. Barbora (Eds.), *Land, People and Politics: Contest Over Tribal Land in North East India* (pp. 16–37). North Eastern Social Research Centre, International Workgroup for Indigenous Affairs.

Rao, M.G. and Brunner, H.-P. 2010. 'Economic Governance in the North East.' In H.-P. Brunner (Ed.), *North East India: Local Economic Development and Global Markets* (pp. 83–105). India: Sage Publications.

Stuligross, D. 1999. 'Autonomous Councils in Northeast: Theory and Practice.' *Alternatives: Global, Local, Political*, 24(4): 497–526.

Syiem, S. 2007. 'Sixth Schedule of the Indian Constitution: A Boon or a Bane for Tribal Development?' In B.S. Nayak (Eds.), *Nationalizing Crises: The Political Economy of Public Policy in Contemporary India* (pp. 207–230). New Delhi: Atlantic Publishers and Distributors (P) Ltd.

Thomas, E.D. 2008. *Functioning of Autonomous Councils in the Sixth Schedule States of the North East of India*. New Delhi: Ministry of Tribal Affairs, Govt. of India.

Umdor, S. 2014. *Local Government Finances in Sixth Schedule Area*. New Delhi: ICSSR Major Research Project.

Umdor, S. and Syiem, B. 2014. 'State of Finances of Autonomous Councils in Northeast India: A Study of Khasi Hills Autonomous District Council in Meghalaya.' *Review of Development and Change*, 19(2): 77–96.

5 Instrumentalities of governance in a multi-ethnic nation-state

Sixth Scheduled Area governance

Chandra Bhushan Kumar and Sonali Ghosh

Introduction

The Sixth Schedule of the Indian Constitution was created as a bridge between a majority mode of governance and a traditional mode of governance. At the time of making of Constitution, the leaders were aware of the challenges of assimilation of those ethnic communities which were treated as backward and subsequently excluded during the colonial times. This Schedule creates space for a traditional mode of governance based on adult franchise within the state government. With time this institutional apparatus proved a successful one as it allowed the assimilation of various territories within the overall framework of nation.

The framers of the Constitution were aware of the ethnic sensitivities and the geo-political significance of the region while creating this specific Schedule. However, they didn't consider the concerns of those tribes which already inhabited the plain areas. The policy of the language-based reorganisation of states in 1950s didn't affect the Northeast region greatly. Bodos, which first sought the recognition of its language in the official discourse of Assam, gradually shifted their focus on migration-induced alienation from the resources (Vandekerckhove and Suykens 2008). Violence as a strategy of 1980s and 1990s finally led to accommodation of Bodoland within the Sixth Schedule in 2003, a departure from the original conception. The Memorandum of Settlement on Bodo Territorial Council was signed on 10 February 2003.

Scholars have debated the genesis of Bodoland in the context of migration concerns and further deliberated on the inherent flaws in the construct of Bodoland Territorial Areas District (BTAD henceforth) guaranteed under the Sixth Schedule. They have argued that in a multi-ethnic territory, the import of Sixth Schedule can never be successful as it not only alienates a larger section of the society, but also influences the use of violence to demonstrate the dominance in the territory (Saikia 2015). These arguments do seem convincing; however, these scholars fail to move away from the dominant narratives of 'politics' and 'election' to the 'devolution of power of administering the territory.' This chapter identifies this gap and, using Manas World Heritage Site, provides an alternate narrative that the concept of BTAD under the Sixth Schedule has been somewhat successful in arresting the depletion of resources as well as in showcasing the resolve of the local community to rejuvenate the natural resource base. It acknowledges that a considerable gap exists between the state governance and the local governance at the institutional level, which impacts the implementation process. The chapter is divided in five parts, including the introductory part. The second part discusses the genesis of Sixth Schedule and describes its specific intent. The third part traces the journey of Bodo movement, which culminated with its entry into the Sixth Schedule in 2003. The fourth part (encompassing several sections) focuses on the Manas World Heritage Site and its remarkable coincidence with the trajectory of Bodoland movement. This section allows us to delineate the connection between the protected natural resource, the question of local political autonomy and the possibilities of conflict resolutions. The final section concludes.

Autonomy within a nation-state: a case of the Sixth Schedule

In the making of a nation-state, the framers of the Indian Constitution were aware of the challenges of accommodating the aspirations of diverse territorial divisions and the colonial inheritance of political legacy (Brass 1996). In the new nation, there was an apparent tension between two divergent views on engaging with certain territories in Northeast India. The colonial power engaged with these territories for the specific purposes of protecting its resource, extracting machineries, as well as of avoiding the cost of overpowering these territories as against its usual method of expansion. This protectionist arrangement kept these territories excluded not only from the traditionally established system of contact with the outside world but also it led to creation of enclaves for hill tribes in the region. The framers of the Constitution took up the matter of administration of hill tribes. However, it didn't consider the matter of tribes inhabiting the plain territories (Gassah 2013). Among them were groups such as the Bodos, Misings, and Tiwas, which are described today as plains tribes to distinguish them from the hill tribes that came under the Sixth Schedule.

In the Constituent Assembly, the special needs of the plains tribes were the responsibility of a separate subcommittee, which was in charge of minority rights (Mazumder 1991).[1] Gassah (2013: 175) identifies three major considerations, which influenced the adoption of Sixth Schedule:

1 The necessity to maintain the distinct customs and socio-economic and political culture of the tribal people of the region and to ensure autonomy of the tribal people and to present their identities.
2 The necessity to prevent their economic and social exploitation by the more advanced neighbouring people of the plains.
3 To allow the tribal people to develop and administer themselves according to their own genius.

It seems that the Constituent Assembly decided to create two different approaches to create the nation-state. In the first approach, every individual citizen became a sovereign member of India; and in the second approach, certain communities were provided space within the scheme of the nation-state. The Sixth Schedule followed the second approach for specific considerations as discussed previously. It was a difficult but necessary option exercised by the framers of Constitution. However, as pointed out earlier, this debate left out the issues concerning plains tribes like the Bodos. By implication, the administration of Bodo-inhabited territory was like other territories, excluding Sixth Schedule territories, of the Assam state.

The design and purpose of the Sixth Schedule was political in nature. Its inherent flexibility in accommodating the local political aspirations allowed the state to assimilate the diverse and distinct ethnic communities in the common project of making a nation. The process has been gradual, which facilitated the accumulation of a type of 'capital' in these territories which was 'political' in nature and can be termed as 'political capital.' Distinct from 'social capital,'[2] this 'political capital' was achieved through the design of elections based on the concepts of universal adult franchise and secret voting.[3]

Bodoland's journey into the Sixth Schedule

Like other communities, the mobilisation of Bodos as a group was initiated during late 19th and early 20th centuries for social purposes including educational and cultural awareness mainly focused on Bodo language (Mahanta 2013). In the pre-independence era, the Simon Commission[4] (1927–1929) became the first forum to receive the demands of various communities, including tribals from Assam, in the consideration of schemes of governance at the national level. In existing elected bodies, they wanted a reservation of seats.[5] In 1933, the All Assam Plains Tribal League (AAPTL) was formed as a political party. It was to articulate the demand of protecting the interest and the identities of the tribal people inhabiting the plains areas of Assam. Subsequently, the Tribal League merged with the Assam Congress. This arrangement continued in the post-independence era. In northeast India, the decade of 1960 witnessed the political mobilisation of various communities, which led to the formation of new states and Union territories in hill areas. In this period, the plains tribes of Assam again formed a political organisation called the Plains Tribal Council of Assam (PTCA) on 27 February 1967 at the initiative of the All Bodo Students' Union leaders at Kokrajhar. Its focus was to achieve separation from the Assam state and, accordingly, it asked the central government to create a Union territory called 'Udayachal' in the Bodo-dominated areas. The PTCA along with the All Bodo Students Union (ABSU) and the Bodo Sahitya Sabha also jointly launched a peaceful non-violent movement from 28 February to 11 March 1968, demanding recognition of the Bodo language as a medium of instruction in the secondary stage of education, which was agreed upon. In post-emergency election, the leaders of PTCA were accommodated in the new council of ministers in Assam and in 1977, the PTCA gave up the demand for 'Udayachal': However, it didn't go down well with the young generation and this led to the formation of a new political party under the name and style of United Tribal Nationalist Liberation Front (UTNLF) in 1984. The emergence of ABSU as a main organisation led to the vociferous demand for a separate 'Homeland' in 1986 (Weiner 1978; Vandekerckhove 2009). The peaceful movement gave way to violent methods of protest. This led to the 1993 creation of the Bodoland Autonomous Council. However, it did not satisfy the aspirations of all the Bodos. In 1996, the formation of the Bodo Liberation Tigers (BLT) for the purposes of a separate state through violent methods witnessed another round of extreme violence (Baruah 2005; Barbora 2008; Mahanta 2013; Hazarika 1994, 2018).[6]

In its final report (2002), the Commission on consultation for the Indian Constitution recommended, '9.28 (1) the Sixth Schedule should be extended to the Bodoland Autonomous Council with protection for non-tribal, non-Bodo groups.'[7] This was agreed upon by the major stakeholders bringing an end to the violent period of Bodo struggle to some extent. Since its adoption in the Sixth Schedule, the Council has already witnessed its three successful elections.

The political struggle for Bodoland, though it seemed to be structured on the issue of identity and language, was primarily a result of the alienation of local tribals from their natural resources including land and forest (Horowitz 1985; Manor 1996; Stuligross 1999; Cordell and Wolff 2011; Vandekerckhove and Suykens 2008). The century-old transformation of the Bodo-inhabited territory with the expansion of tea gardens and the extraction of forest produce resulted in the influx of migration of outsiders. It outnumbered the local tribes, which gradually threatened their cultural existence. Their intent to preserve their culture and their territory at any cost led to their entry in the Sixth Schedule.

In this violent struggle, the protected forest territory became their hub of operations (Vigne and Martin 1991). It is surprising that the scholars of Bodo struggle largely gave this aspect very little attention in their scholarly works (Manor 1996; Goswami 2003, 2012; Baruah 2005; Barbora 2008). With more than two dozen of protected reserve forests within its territory, BTAD is one of the most protected territories in Northeast India. It may not be a mere coincidence that the militant groups found in these areas its safe heaven to demonstrate their demands. In the process, Manas, one of the World Heritage Sites, became a location of contested space during that period. The next section uses Manas as a contested space of governance during the period of turbulence and after to appreciate the transition in the area.

Manas as a World Heritage Site and Bodoland agitation and after

The dynamic political journey of BTAD in many ways is intertwined with the fate of the Manas World Heritage Site (Manas WHS henceforth, a UNESCO) designated World Heritage Site that has stood the ravages of time to emerge as '*invincible*' as nature can be.

Manas WHS is part of the core zone of the 283,700 hectares Manas Tiger Reserve, which lies alongside the shifting river channels of the Manas-Beki Rivers in Western Assam. It is bound in the North by the forests of Bhutan, River Sankosh and West Bengal in the West, and the administrative boundaries of BTAD/Assam in the East and South, respectively (Map 5.1). The recorded history of Manas dates back to late 15th century, when the renowned *Vaishnavaite* saint Shri Madhabdeb established the Barpeta *Satra* wherein the preserved sacred texts mention of a 'dense forest' beyond the boundaries of the Barpeta human settlement (Choudhury 2007). Since then, the land ownership changed hands from Indian royalty to British foresters to becoming a prized possession of the Assam Forest Department in the post-independence era. A chronological evolution of Manas is available as Annexure.

The historical evolution of Manas suggests a linkage between the resource (forest) alienation and the mobilisation of local tribals. With multiple methods, the then British government affected the Bodo-dominated territory in at least three ways: Using the forest as a revenue source, settling outside workers in the forest areas and in the process outnumbering the local tribals, and, as an unintended consequence, influenced the political mobilisation of Bodos as a group. In all this, Manas became a contested space for possession and dispossession for Bodos. By the time the nation hailed its inclusion in the UNESCO (United Nations Educational, Scientific and Cultural Organisation) World Heritage Site, Manas ended up being in the 'danger list' within a few years owing to struggle and unrest (Goswami and Ganesh 2014). Before discussing its downhill journey, it is appropriate to appreciate Manas in terms of its universal values for the world.

The site's scenic beauty includes a range of forested hills, alluvial grasslands, and tropical evergreen forests that provide a contiguous transnational landscape with critical and viable habitats for rare and endangered species, including the tiger, greater one-horned rhino, swamp deer, pygmy hog, and Bengal florican (Table 5.1). The presence of Manas also led to evolution of durable traditional ecosystem services (Saikia 2011; Das *et al.* 2014).

Such has been its exceptional biological importance within the Indian sub-continent's Protected Areas that the property has six national and international designations: *World Heritage Site, National Park, Tiger Reserve (core), Biosphere Reserve (national), Elephant Reserve (core)*, and *Important Bird Area* with the highest legal protection and strong legislative framework under the provisions of Indian Wildlife (Protection) Act, 1972, and Indian Forest Act, 1927/Assam Forest Regulation, 1891. All these values

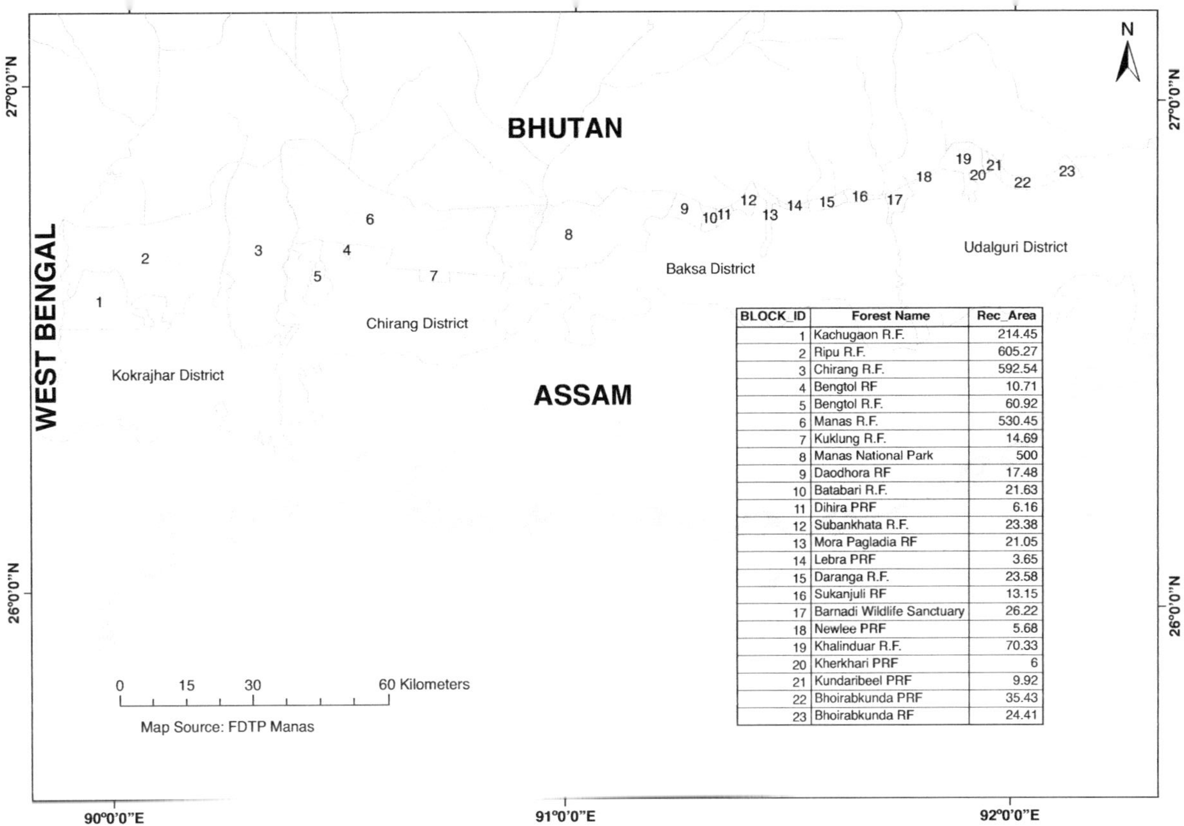

BLOCK_ID	Forest Name	Rec_Area
1	Kachugaon R.F.	214.45
2	Ripu R.F.	605.27
3	Chirang R.F.	592.54
4	Bengtol RF	10.71
5	Bengtol R.F.	60.92
6	Manas R.F.	530.45
7	Kuklung R.F.	14.69
8	Manas National Park	500
9	Daodhora RF	17.48
10	Batabari R.F.	21.63
11	Dihira PRF	6.16
12	Subankhata R.F.	23.38
13	Mora Pagladia RF	21.05
14	Lebra PRF	3.65
15	Daranga R.F.	23.58
16	Sukanjuli RF	13.15
17	Barnadi Wildlife Sanctuary	26.22
18	Newlee PRF	5.68
19	Khalinduar R.F.	70.33
20	Kherkhari PRF	6
21	Kundaribeel PRF	9.92
22	Bhoirabkunda PRF	35.43
23	Bhoirabkunda RF	24.41

Map 5.1 Map showing all protected forest areas under the Manas Tiger Reserve (Core zone being the Manas World Heritage Site)

Source: *Manas Tiger Conservation* Plan 2013

Table 5.1 Categories of socio-cultural values of the Manas World Heritage site

Sl. no.	*Value categories*	*Illustrative constituents*
1	Real/ Economic	• It produces timber, fuel wood, and non-timber forests produce for local people. • It provides fodder for domestic livestock • It provides water for irrigation • It generates mandays (a unit of one day's work by one person) for local people.
2	Biological	• It is located in the confluence of three major Bio-geographic Zones viz. Lower Gangetic plains (7B), Central Himalayas (2C), and Brahmaputra valley (8A). • It provides shelter to many endangered, threatened, and rare species of animals like the tiger, Asian elephant, pygmy hog, golden langur, hispid hare, Assam roofed turtle, Bengal florican, white bellied heron, great pied hornbill, etc. • It is a significant habitat for long-ranging species (elephant, tiger, and gaur) and provides habitat connectivity.
3	Ecological processes and functions	• Catchment conservation of several major rivers (Beki, Pahumara, Pata, Burisuti, and Basra) for downstream habitations and irrigation which sustain economic well-being of the region • Ecological security and environmental amelioration (pollution absorption) for the region • It acts as a carbon sink of the region
4	Conceptual	• It represents several elements of an Eastern Himalayan biodiversity hotspot
5	Scientific	• Significant scope of wildlife research and education • It has socio-economic issues, ethnic diversity, and many endangered and endemic species. Thus, it provides an excellent opportunity to scientists for improving understanding of the biological world
6	Physical attributes	• It represents the fragile Shiwalik and Himalayan landscape and rock features • It represents physical attributes of bhabar and terai eco-system
7	Recreational	• Potential for eco-tourism, aesthetic value, wilderness experience, close canopy and dense old forest, bird watching. Scenic beauty of Beki river near Mathanguri
8	Educational	• Significant scope for nature interpretation and conservation awareness
9	Religious	• Sacred rock carved of Bathao religion
	Historical	• Rock paintings and hunting records of the erstwhile royals of Gauripur
	Cultural	• Bodo, Assamese, and Tea tribe culture.

Source: Manas Tiger Conservation Plan 2013

led to the inscription of Manas as a UNESCO World Heritage Site in 1985 (Sarma *et al.* 2008; Das *et al.* 2014).

BOX 5.1 Criteria for inscription of Manas as a UNESCO World Heritage Site

UNESCO under the aegis of the World Heritage Convention 1972, links together in a single document the concepts of nature conservation and the preservation of cultural properties. The Convention recognises the way in which people interact with nature, and the fundamental need to preserve the balance between the two. More than 197 countries, including India, are signatory to the Convention and, since its inception, it has grown in popularity as one of the instruments for sustaining intergenerational peace. However, to be included on the World Heritage List, sites must be of Outstanding Universal Value (OUV) and meet at least one out of ten selection criteria. India currently has seven Natural World Heritage sites, and Manas has the distinction of being inscribed under three out of the total four selection criteria for natural World Heritage Sites. The criteria as applicable to Manas include the following:

Criterion (vii): Manas is recognised not only for its rich biodiversity but also for its spectacular scenery and natural landscape. Manas is located at the foothills of the Eastern Himalayas. The Northern boundary of the park is contiguous to the international border of Bhutan manifested by the imposing Bhutan hills. It spans on either side of the majestic Manas River flanked in the East and the West by reserved forests. The tumultuous river swirling down the rugged mountains in the backdrop of forested hills coupled with the serenity of the alluvial grasslands and tropical evergreen forests offers a unique wilderness experience.

Criterion (ix): The Manas-Beki system is the major river system flowing through the property and joining the Brahmaputra River further downstream. These and other rivers carry an enormous amount of silt and rock debris from the foothills resulting from the heavy rainfall, fragile nature of the rock, and steep gradients of the catchments. This leads to the formation of alluvial terraces, comprising deep layers of deposited rock and detritus overlain by sandy loam and a layer of humus represented by bhabar tracts in the north. The terai tract in the South consists of fine alluvial deposits with underlying pans where the water table lies near to the surface. The area contained by the Manas-Beki system gets inundated during the monsoons, but flooding does not last long due to the sloping relief. The monsoon and river system form four principal geological habitats: Bhabar savannah, Terai tract, marshlands, and riverine tracts. The dynamic ecosystem processes support broadly three types of vegetation: Semi-evergreen forests, mixed moist and dry deciduous forests, and alluvial grasslands. The dry deciduous forests represent an early stage in succession that is constantly renewed by floods and is replaced by moist deciduous forests away from water courses, which in turn are replaced by semi-evergreen climax forests. The vegetation of Manas has tremendous regenerating and self-sustaining capabilities due to its high fertility and response to natural grazing by herbivorous animals.

Criterion (x): The Manas Wildlife Sanctuary provides habitat for 22 of India's most threatened species of mammals. In total, there are nearly 60 mammal species, 42 reptile species, 7 amphibians, and 500 species of birds, of which 26 are globally threatened. Noteworthy among these are the elephant, tiger, greater one-horned rhino, clouded leopard, sloth bear, and other species. The wild buffalo population is probably the only pure strain of this species still found in India. It also harbours endemic species like the pygmy hog, hispid hare, and golden langur as well as the endangered Bengal florican. The range of habitats and vegetation also accounts for high plant diversity that includes 89 tree species, 49 shrubs, 37 under-shrubs, 172 herbs, and 36 climbers. Also occurring here are 15 species of orchids, 18 species of fern, and 43 species of grasses that provide vital forage to a range of ungulate species.

Source: https://whc.unesco.org/en/list/338 (accessed on 8 April 2018)

Manas in danger

Evident from the Box 5.1 is the fact that, in 1985, Manas Wildlife Sanctuary (391 sq kms) was inscribed in the list of World Heritage Site (UNESCO), a site of Outstanding Universal Value, under the criteria number (ii), (iii), and (iv) but in 1992 the UNESCO-IUCN reviewed the status of the Site and decided to tag it as a 'World Heritage Site in Danger' due to damages occurred to Park infrastructure and other properties during the Bodo agitation since 1988 (Vigne and Martin 1991; Goswami and Ganesh 2011). However, in June 2011, Manas regained its original status as a World Heritage Site (Ghosh and Kumar 2012).

This 20-year-long period of armed conflict had coincided with the period of civic unrest in which the Bodos fought for their community identity. As evident from worldwide studies (as in Africa and Afghanistan), several biodiversity hotspots in the world are currently in areas of great political volatility and armed conflicts (Hanson *et al.* 2009). Such conflicts often result in intentional and unintentional exploitation of wildlife and other natural resources such as forest timber by conflicting parties (Goswami and Ganesh 2011). With human security concerns taking priority, financial resources and international aids are diverted to peacekeeping, rehabilitation and humanitarian efforts, thereby marginalising conservation activities and priorities. Manas met the same fate during the insurgency period; it was left without paid staff, equipment or infrastructure, jeopardising short-term and long-term conservation goals. Reduced protection increased the presence of soldiers, refugees, and extremists, who relied on the forest for their sustenance, thereby increasing the burden on local natural resources.

A review of the literature available on similar natural World Heritage Sites in armed conflict zones (Hanson *et al.* 2009) from across the world (such as Virunga National Park, Garamba National Park, Okapi Wildlife Reserve, Kahuzi Biega National Park, and Salonga National Park in Central Africa, which continue to be on the World Heritage Site list in Danger since the mid-1990s) indicate that Manas had a remarkable turnaround in a comparatively short span of time of 19 years (1992–2011).

One of the authors served as a field functionary in Manas for intermittent periods between 2007 and 2014 and the period also coincided with the quick recovery path that ultimately helped the site regain its WHS status. The first-hand experience of working in the landscape formed the basis of the narrative put forth in the following section.

The revival: Manas model of community conservation

In 2005, when the first elected local government was formed, the Park infrastructure was in shambles and virtually there was no protection. The 100-odd rhino population had been completely decimated and more than 90 percent of the Park infrastructure was destroyed (Debonnet and Lethier 2008; TCP 2013). What emerged as a ray of hope was the evidence of persistent wildlife (camera trap studies yielded the signs of tigers present in the area; Goswami and Ganesh 2014), the international concern and support (the UNESCO Committee sent monitoring missions and called for annual status reports from the Government of India), and finally the local political will to take up the challenge to enable a turnaround.

First and foremost, protection to the site was of major concern. As the Forest Department was highly understaffed, a unique conservation model was adopted wherein the local youth from fringe villages were deployed to take up surveillance and anti-poaching activities inside the park. Such youth from forest fringe villages had experienced armed conflict in their lifetime and several were motivated to surrender their firearms and take up to conservation. In a way the alternative livelihood support provided immediately in the aftermath of a war was a major boost towards lasting peace in the area. At the same time, the sustained nudging from UNESCO, the international conservation agencies, and local NGOs helped in formulating a scientifically backed wildlife restoration plan including the highly ambitious 'wild-to-wild' rhino and swamp deer translocation and population augmentation programme at Manas. Funding from central and state governments was pumped into to rebuild Park infrastructure and regular manpower recruited and posted in the area.

A key component of the methods utilised was to catalyse empowered community institutions to protect forests and wildlife (Feeny *et al.* 1990; Horwich and Lyon 2007). Several governance models facilitated success, changing the situation from open access to an informal community co-managed system and subsequently into organised zones of wilderness and multiple-use zones in Manas WHS and forest fringe areas. It was a multi-pronged strategy that included the following:

1 Assurance of political will and support to administer newer models of governance: The formation of BTAD between 2003 and 2005 led to the transfer of executive, financial, and administrative powers transfer over 33 state subjects including forests that came under the jurisdiction of the autonomous council. Due to its historical British legacy, recorded forest area covered more than 40 percent of the total geographical area of BTAD. Therefore, one of the highest priorities was given to the natural resource management.[8] Funding, manpower, and reorganisation of forest working divisions were initiated. Before the formation of BTAD, the central share funds were routed through the state government, which led to a significant delay in sanctions and releases. This in turn impacted time-bound activities such as the clearance of forest roads, the cutting of fire lines, and the payment of casual wages. Infrastructure in Manas National Park was reconstructed on a priority basis; roads, vehicles, and communication channels were repaired and augmented. Important efforts were undertaken to rebuild anti-poaching camps destroyed during the insurgency. At least 40 anti-poaching camps were newly built or repaired with special focus on the construction of additional camps in the sector where the rhino reintroduction was planned, as part of the India Rhino Vision 2020 (IRV 2020) project. These camps were spread over the Park and regular forest frontline staff were posted full time, equipped with rifles, wireless handsets etc. Vehicles including jeeps, motorbikes, cycles, and boats were also procured for patrolling the areas. Approximately, 130 km of forest tracks and 100 km of foot trail were re-opened to allow surveillance activities by connecting all camps. Special management interventions were brought in to care for the existing number of captive elephants and their numbers augmented. More than 123 positions vacant in the forest frontline staff were filled up by fresh recruitments (Debonnet and Lethier 2008).
2 Involvement of the local authorities, NGO, and local communities in the management of the property: The acute staff shortage, besides the lack of confidence in forest surveillance by engaging in armed combat in a post-conflict war zone by the permanent field functionaries was

overcome by an ingenious method. To address the staffing problem, the park authorities in support from BTAD and local NGOs set up an interesting volunteer scheme. Under this scheme, more than 200 volunteers were hired to assist the park on a daily basis with conservation and management activities. Volunteers were recruited from local youth and included and erstwhile poachers/militants who had surrendered before law and hence were given a chance of gainful employment and rehabilitation. The volunteers received some basic training and allowed them to man the newly constructed or rehabilitated anti-poaching camps. The training included surveillance aspects such as handling GPS, field data recording on animal signs, and instances of human disturbance, animal and bird identification techniques, and the knowledge to handle camera traps for advanced animal monitoring. More than 200 conservation volunteers in at least six fringe locations of Manas National Park were trained by reputed NGOs such as Aaranyak, WWF, and WTI. They also received rations and a small subsistence allowance as funded by the BTAD budget. The volunteer scheme gained popularity as local semi-literate youth saw this as an immediate remedy towards their unemployment woes, it also helped wean them away from again taking up arms to carry out armed violence against the state and therefore indirectly helped in regaining peace. The local knowledge of the area combined with physical fitness and high motivation levels of these conservation volunteers ensured that poaching, illegal timber extraction, and grazing/encroachment for farming were drastically reduced. Several of these conservation volunteers also got recruited into regular positions through the basis of state-level exams, while many of them also branched out to take up community-based eco-tourism initiatives that brought back tourists to the Park and helped in generating revenue for the local economy.

3 Revival of scientific monitoring, reporting, and management of the Park: A systematic approach towards reviving the wildlife population of the Park was taken up. This included an ambitious never-tried-before wild-to-wild plan to reintroduce rhinos in the park. It also looked at newer population estimation methods (such as the camera trap mark recapture method for estimating tigers and other large mammals) and technology (such as satellite-based change detection techniques) to further gain the scientific evidence towards the health of the Park. Several international and national NGOs such as WWF (World Wildlife Fund) India, Ashoka Trust of Research on Ecology and Environment (ATREE), Aaranyak, and Wildlife Trust of India came up with important support programmes in research and monitoring, infrastructure development, providing field equipment, wildlife rehabilitation and reintroduction, capacity development, and community conservation and education. The Indian Rhino Vision 2020 plan was launched in 2006, and since then the population of rhinos in Manashas grown up to 34 rhinos in the wild.[9]

All these efforts helped in creating large-scale conservation awareness that reinstated the pride for Manas amongst Bodos and this community conservation model was lauded globally (Ghosh and Kumar 2012). Creation of a body politic often helps in raising the stakes and owning the particular subject.

Manas in the context of the Sixth Schedule

From the earlier narrative, it can be safely concluded that the study of revival of Manas World Heritage Site demonstrates the success of a community-based institutional model which allows the partnership and the ownership of ethnic groups in the process of governance. As it has been cited from global examples (Hanson *et al.* 2009), many of the world's biodiversity rich areas are also ravaged by armed conflict and war. Sixth Scheduled areas are largely dominated by forested landscapes with a dominance of tribal communities and a history of chequered governance. The Manas model wherein political will (emphasised through the formation of the Sixth Schedule) combined with local community support to bring about an expedited turnaround into the management of natural resources (thereby restoring democracy) is an example worth emulating in similar areas (Figure 5.1).

The case of Manas has shown that violent political conflict had an overall negative impact on the wildlife populations, particularly on economically valuable species. However, the cessation of conflicts and resumption of protection and management interventions appeared to have helped the recovery of depleted animal populations. The models for co-management (Figure 5.2),

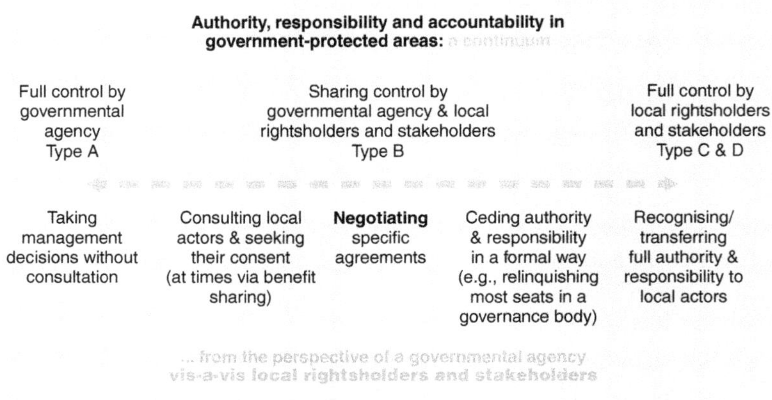

Figure 5.1 The governance continuum from the perspective of a government agency vis-à-vis local rights holders and stakeholders (e.g., local landowners or communities)

Source: Borrini-Feyerabend *et al.* 2013

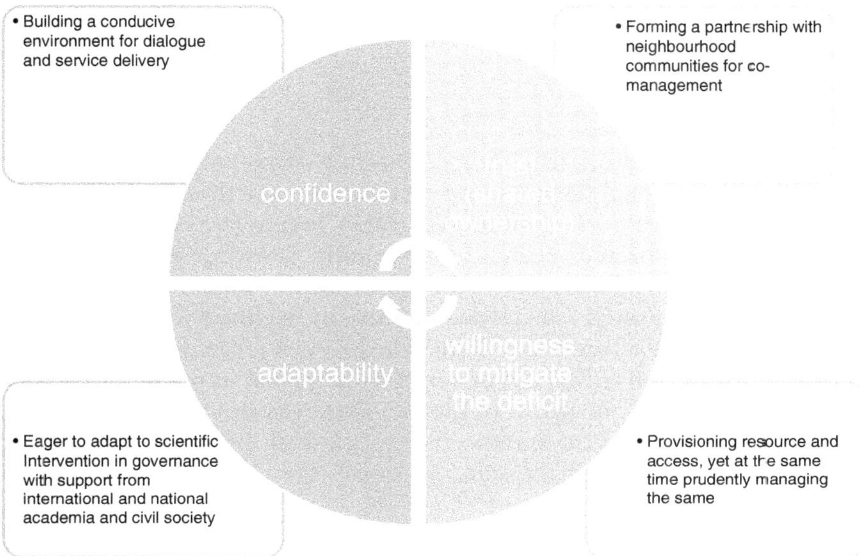

Figure 5.2 Pictorial depiction of Manas model of governance as applicable to Sixth Scheduled Areas

Source: Compiled by Author

especially when using local community approaches, have been particularly helpful for rebuilding the confidence, especially in a post-conflict Protected Area in areas dominated by tribal communities (as in the case of Sixth Scheduled Areas). Continued monitoring of the existing populations of wildlife species and protracted support for conservation will be critical for the future ecological health of the Park (Goswami and Ganesh 2014).

This case demonstrates the stakes and the ownership shaped by confidence and trust emerging from the political capital created by the sixth schedule in the territory. This can be elaborated in a simple diagram (Figure 5.2) indicating the cyclical nature of trust building, governance, and management of natural resources. Within a decade, the BTC has been able to create a conducive political environment, which facilitated shared ownership amongst the local stakeholders. Besides it, the council showed its eagerness to new ideas of scientific interventions and it allocated necessary resources.

It is debatable whether these attributes of political capital added value to the task of governance in all other sectors. As Manas WHS was not a contested space within the territory amongst various ethnic groups and it is easier to single out a protected territory, it was not a difficult exercise for the newly created political capital to nurture and guide the efforts of the revival of the WHS. This may not be the case in other sectors for at least three reasons:

Other sectors like land are more contested, it is too early to assess the outcome, and the accumulation of political capital for longer duration may lead to more mature governance.

Way forward

Each nation-state devises its own mechanism to accommodate the aspirations of its sub-national elements. During the framing of the Indian Constitution, the members of the Constituent Assembly were aware of the challenges of ethnic and territorial diversities of the country. Drawing lessons from the colonial legacy, the makers debated the methods of administering certain areas, earlier categorised as excluded or partially excluded territories in the Government of India Act, 1935. Sixth Schedule was created for the specific conditions of the hill tribes. It was not to be perpetual in nature. Nagaland and others gradually moved from the list. However, the application of the Sixth Schedule allowed the state to create a class of distinctiveness, within the territorial integrity of the state, to satisfy the political aspirations of certain ethnic groups.

Bodo, which initially mobilised for its language-based recognition, gradually witnessed the alienation of its resources by the other communities over a century. By 1986, Bodos became vociferous in their demand for a separate state. Use of arms and the availability of a vast forest area combined with the porous Bhutan border allowed the agitation to become deadly in its operations. The first attempt of settlement in 1993 failed, resulting in more violent attacks. After close to 30 rounds of talks, finally in 2003, the Bodo accord was agreed upon, with Bodoland becoming an entity within the Sixth Schedule.

The last 15 years have been a mixed bag for this institutional arrangement. Though it has brought peace to some extent, however, the political aspirations and its non-fulfilment has witnessed occasional but extreme violent responses. The scholars attribute it to the inherent problems in power-sharing arrangements which disfavour two-thirds of the population in the administered territory (Baruah 2005; Hazarika 2018). We argue that this tenuous relationship is but natural for a 'young democracy' and at best can be considered a transitory phase from a total lack of law and order to a gradual realisation and stabilisation of local self-governance. This chapter, while examining the inherent tension in the design of Sixth Schedule in the context of creation of BTAD, draws the attention towards 'forest,' an item of local as well as central governance. Manas, a World Heritage Site located in the territory of Bodoland presents an interesting and surprising coincidence with the Bodo movement. Declared a UNESCO WHS in 1985, the site was put on the 'Danger List' from 1989 to 2005, bearing the brunt of the agitation for homeland.

This protected reserve forest witnessed a number of conflict situations on the subject of land alienation which turned out violent. With the transition into the Sixth Schedule, this Heritage Site became a rallying point for the local tribe. Subsequently, local community governance under the new institutional arrangement facilitated the remarkable recovery of this Site in the UNESCO list.

The introduction of Sixth Schedule governance in the Bodo-dominated area brought a halt, though temporary, to the political contestation which had been affecting the governance in the area. It led to creation of a political capital which seems willing to invest and own a particular subject of governance in a sustainable manner. It brought an institutional framework derived from its own community, which facilitated a scientific approach to revive the Manas WHS.

The Sixth Schedule model was criticised at the[10] time of its inception for creating a distinctiveness and it was feared that it may lead to their alignment with neighbouring nations. The political history of last seven decades in the Northeast does not support this fear. In a large, diverse nation like India, the Sixth Schedule facilitated a political space that seemed more acceptable and assimilative to the project of nation making, which allowed it to extend its application in the case of plains tribes like Bodo in a particular territory. Though necessary, it may not be a sufficient condition to realise the aspiration of other communities in the enclaved territory. The challenge is to draw lessons from the experiences of revival of Manas WHS and bring more accommodative elements in the local governance to reduce the possibilities of conflict within the framework of Sixth Schedule.

Notes

1 Constituent Assembly debates on the incorporation of the Sixth Schedule illustrate divergent views on administering the tribal areas. A Bodo politician, Rupnath Brahma, was a member of the Minority Rights sub-committee. Members like Mr Kuladhar Chaliha and Mr Rohini Kumar Chaudhury opposed the move of separating the hill areas, fearing that this will lead to Tribastan on the lines of Pakistan. They considered it a separatist tendency of a British mindset. They feared that it might encourage those (hill tribes) people to side with the enemy states. Allaying these fears strongly, Mr Jaspal Singh and Mr Nicholas Ray argued in favour of specific provisions of governance for the hill tribes. They elaborated upon the tribal way of life and stressed the distinctiveness of their methods of administration of justice. In these two contrasting positions, Bordoloi committee (in the name of chairman of the committee, Gopinath Bordoloi) wanted to reconcile the aspirations of the hill people for political autonomy with the Assam government's drive to integrate them with the plains. (For details, may please see https://indiankanoon.org/doc/728063/ accessed on 25 April 2018.)

2 Bourdieu and Wacquant (1992) coins three distinct forms of capital, economic, cultural, and social, to appreciate the existing social order and its stratifications. Putnam (1993) in his seminal work 'Making Democracy Work' focuses on the creation of 'social capital' for the purposes of improving the efficiency of a society. In the works of both, the actors of 'social capital' are political in its character.

3 The creation of 'political capital' is an essential component of the design of devolution of power through local body election also. However it was different in

case of the Sixth Schedule for at least two reasons: (i) It provided more political space and therefore more power to specific ethnic class; and (ii) it acknowledged the cultural distinctiveness.

4 Led by John Simon and Clement Atlee, this Commission was tasked to report on the working of the Indian Constitution established by the Government of India Act, 1935.

5 Four different organisations of 'Primitive and Backward Tribes' submitted four different memoranda (Misra 1989; Choudhury 2007). The Bodo Committee of Goalpara district emphasised on the following points: (i) Since the Bodos have a distinct civilisation of their own, there should be a separate category, "the Bodos' in the census report. (ii) The Bodos should have separate representation in the state council. (iii) The Bodos should receive special treatment at the hands of the government in matters of education and employment. And (iv) the Bodos can, by no means, be called 'other than Assamese.' Subsequently, four seats were reserved for tribals in the Assam Provincial Assembly under the Government of India Act, 1935. For the first time, the plains tribes entered electoral politics.

6 After years of struggle, the BLT unilaterally decided to suspend its armed operations on 14 July 1999 and agreed to negotiate with the Government of India. This is an example to other underground groups in the region. Those seeking to improve the lives of their people through armed struggles should realise that this path cannot succeed. The conditions of people can be best improved in times of peace, leading to stability and development. The BLT gave up its demand for a separate state and settled for the extension of the Sixth Schedule Status to the Bodo areas, which empowers them with rights over land, ensures the protection of their traditions and ethnic identity, and also enables them to govern themselves. The BTAD is an outcome of a growing understanding that political goals must be realistic and that peace and development must take precedence over emotions

7 See http://lawmin.nic.in/ncrwc/finalreport/v1ch9.htm (accessed on 25 April 2018)

8 The Deputy Chief of the Council, Shri Kampa Borgayary, was entrusted with the task to revive the Department.

9 www.telegraphindia.com/states/north-east/manas-to-get-3-more-rhinos-198950 (accessed on 12 March 2018)

10 Please see the debates of the Constituent Assembly on sixth schedule at http://khadc.nic.in/acts_rules_regulations_bills/misc/Constituent%20Assembly%20Debate%20relating%20to%206th%20Schedule_excerpts_.pdf

References

Barbora, S. 2008. 'Autonomous Districts and/or Ethnic Homelands: An Ethnographic Account of the Genesis of Political Violence in Assam (Northeast India) Against the Normative Frame of the Indian Constitution.' *International Journal on Minority and Group Rights*, 15: 313–334.

Baruah, S. 2005. 'Citizens and Denizens: Ethnicity, Homelands and the Crisis of Displacement.' In S. Baruah (Ed.), *Durable Disorder: Understanding the Politics of Northeast India* (pp. 183–208). New Delhi: Oxford University Press.

Borrini-Feyerabend, G., Dudley, N., Jaeger, T., Lassen, B., Pathak Broome, N., Phillips, A. and Sandwith, T. 2013. *Governance of Protected Areas: From Understanding to Action*. Best Practice Protected Area Guidelines Series No. 20. Gland, Switzerland: IUCN. xvi + 124pp.

Bourdieu, P. and Wacquant, L.J. 1992. *An Invitation to Reflexive Sociology*. Chicago: University of Chicago Press.

Brass, Paul R. 1996. *The Politics of India Since Independence*. Cambridge: Cambridge University Press.
Choudhury, S. 2007. *The Bodos. Emergence and Assertion of an Ethnic Minority*. Shimla: IIAS.
Cordell, K. and Wolff, S. (Eds.). 2011. *Routledge Handbook of Ethnic Conflict*. New York: Routledge.
Das, B., Ghosh, S., Lahkar, B. and Kumar, C.B. 2014. 'Traditional knowledge, ecosystem services and disaster risk reduction in Manas World Heritage Site and Biosphere Reserve, India.' In *Safe Havens: Protected Areas for Disaster Risk Reduction and Climate Change Adaptation*. Gland, Switzerland: IUCN, p. 56.
Debonnet, G. and Lethier, H. 2008. *World Heritage Committee, United Nations Educational Scientific and Cultural Organization Mission Report – Manas Wildlife Sanctuary (India)*. Available at: http://whc.unesco.org/en/list/338/documents/ (accessed on 12 March 2018).
Feeny, D., Berkes, F., McCay, B.J. and Acheson, J.M. 1990. 'The Tragedy of the Commons: Twenty-Two Years Later.' *Human Ecology*, 18(1): 1–19.
Gassah, L.S. 2013. *The Sixth Schedule and the 73rd Amendment: An Analysis*. Available at: www.dspace.nehu.ac.in/bitstream/1/10608/1/The%20sixth%20schedule%20(LS%20Gassah).pdf (accessed on 12 March 2018).
Ghosh, S. and Kumar, C. 2012. 'Paradise Lost and Regained: Lessons From the National Parks of India.' *Solutions*, 3(4): 80–84.
Goswami, R. and Ganesh, T. 2011. 'Conservation Amidst Political Unrest: The Case of Manas National Park.' *India Current Science*, 100(4): 445–446.
Goswami, R. and Ganesh, T. 2014. 'Carnivore and Herbivore Densities in the Immediate Aftermath of Ethno-Political Conflict: The Case of Manas National Park, India.' *Tropical Conservation Science*, 7(3): 475–487.
Goswami, S. 2003. 'Assam: Multiple Realignments and Fragmentation of Party System.' *Journal of Indian School of Political Economy*, 15(1–2): 221–247.
Goswami, S. 2012. 'Changing Trends of Electoral Politics, Assam: Unstable Peace.' *Seminar. 640: Special Issue: Assam Unstable Peace*. Available at: https://northeastreview.wordpress.com/2012/12/03/seminar-special-issue-assam-unstable-peace/ (accessed on 30 May 2018).
Hanson, T., Brooks, T.M., Da Fonseca, G.A., Hoffmann, M., Lamoreux, J.F., Machlis, G., Mittermeier, C.G., Mittermeier, R.A. and Pilgrim, J.D. 2009. 'Warfare in Biodiversity Hotspots.' *Conservation Biology*, 23(3): 578–587.
Hazarika, S. 1994. *Strangers in the Mist: Tales of War and Peace in India's Northeast*. New Delhi: Penguin Books.
Hazarika, S. 2018. *Strangers No More*. New Delhi: Aleph.
Horowitz, D.L. 1985. *Ethnic Groups in Conflict*. Berkeley: University of California Press.
Horwich, R.H. and Lyon, J. 2007. 'Community Conservation: Practitioners' Answer to Critics.' *Oryx*, 41(3): 376–385.
Mahanta, N.G., 2013. 'Politics of Space and Violence in Bodoland.' *Economic and Political Weekly*, 48(23): 49–58.
Manor, J. 1996. '"Ethnicity" and Politics in India.' *International Affairs*, 72(3): 459–475.
Mazumder, K.A. 1991. Bodo Movement in Assam: A Constitutional Analysis (Doctoral dissertation, Aligarh Muslim University).

Memorandum of Settlement on Bodo Territorial Council. 2003. *Signed on February 10, 2003, New Delhi*. Available at: http://peacemaker.un.org/sites/peacemaker.un.org/files/IN_030210_Memorandum SettlementBodolandTerritorialCouncil.pdf (accessed on 24 March 2018).

Misra, U. 1989. 'Bodo Stir: Complex Issues and Unattainable Demands.' *Economic and Political Weekly*, 24(21): 1146–1149.

Putnam, R. 1993. 'The Prosperous Community: Social Capital and Public Life.' *The American Prospect*, 13(Spring), Vol. 4. Available at: http://www. prospect. org/print/vol/13 (accessed on 7 April 2003).

Saikia, A. 2011. *Forests and Ecological History of Assam, 1826–2000*. New Delhi: Oxford University Press.

Saikia, S. 2015. 'General Elections 2014: Ethnic Outbidding and Politics of "Homelands" in Assam's Bodoland.' *Contemporary South Asia*, 23(2): 211–222.

Sarma, P.K., Lahkar, B.P., Ghosh, S., Rabha, A., Das, J.P., Nath, N.K., Dey, S. and Brahma, N. 2008. 'Land-Use and Land-Cover Change and Future Implication Analysis in Manas National Park, India Using Multi-Temporal Satellite Data.' *Current Science*, 95(2): 223–227.

Stuligross, D. 1999. 'Autonomous Councils in Northeast India: Theory and Practice.' *Alternatives: Global, Local, Political*, 24(4): 497–525.

TCP Tiger Conservation Plan of Manas Tiger Reserve 2013 (draft). *Manas Tiger Project*. Government of Assam.

Vandekerckhove, N. 2009 'We Are Sons of This Soil.' *Critical Asian Studies*, 41(4): 523–548.

Vandekerckhove, N. and Suykens, B. 2008. '"The Liberation of Bodoland": Tea, Forestry and Tribal Entrapment in Western Assam.' *South Asia: Journal of South Asian Studies*, 31(3): 450–471.

Vigne, L. and Martin, E.B. 1991. 'Assam's Rhinos Face New Poaching Threats.' *Oryx*, 25(4): 215–221.

Weiner, M. 1978. *Sons of the Soil: Migration and Ethnic Conflict in India*. Princeton, NJ: Princeton University Press.

Annexure

Historical timeline of forest and wildlife conservation reconstructed especially for the Manas World Heritage Site, as an analogy to the evolution of democracy and governance under the Sixth Schedule

(Primary source: Tiger Conservation Plan (2013). Manas Tiger Reserve, Govt of Assam)

- AD 1853: Establishment of the Barpeta Satra, a seat for Vaishnavite religion. Ancient texts preserved here, mention the presence of a dense forest (Manas) in the vicinity of Barpeta.
- February 1826: The treaty of Yandaboo signed between British India and the princely state of Burma. The British foresters then started to look for revenue generation through agriculture and forestry expansion in the region, especially in Western Assam.
- 1857–1893: First survey of forest areas undertaken and large tracts of land in the buffer zone of Manas WHS declared as Reserved Forests. Local community rights abolished or ignored.
- 1871–1907: Game or hunting reserves declared in low productivity areas such as the flood-plain savannah areas of present day Manas WHS.
- 1893–1920: First working Plan written for forest areas implemented with special emphasis on silviculture management of highly priced Sal (*Shorea robusta*) tree.
- 1919: Introduction of the 'Line system' that demarcated between hills and plains tribe areas and prevented outsiders to settle in the hill tracts. Manas WHS region and its inhabitants (also termed as Bodo-Cacharis) come under the plains tribe areas.
- 1928: Declaration of Manas as a Wildlife Sanctuary and further expansion of the Protected Area.
- 1935: As armed rebellion continued among the hill tribes, more stringent laws in the form of excluded and partially excluded areas and the concept of tribal belt and blocks brought in to administer Northeast India.
- 1939: Grazing reserves opened up to settle immigrants under the 'grow food' campaign.

- 1955–1956: discovery of highly endemic Golden langur (*Trachypithecus geei*) primate by E.P. Gee in buffer of Manas WHS. The importance of Manas as a biodiversity cauldron is now known to the Western world.
- 1958–1973: Princely or Zamindari forests abolished and majority of private forests converted into state forests. Survey settlement and demarcation of rights for most of the forest areas other than Reserved Forests remain mostly unsettled.
- 1973–1985: Core area of Manas (the WHS region) recognised for its high biodiversity and its legal status strengthened by area expansion and declaring it as a National Park and a UNESCO World Natural Heritage.
- 1985: Signing of the Assam Accord between the government of India and the leaders of the Assam agitation thus paving the way for indigenous political parties. This also led to the formulation of policy that people entering Assam later than 25 March 1971 were to be considered illegal immigrants.
- 1987: Official Bodoland movement for an independent state started by the All Bodo Students Union (ABSU). Rise of two main factions of militant groups: The National Democratic Front of Bodoland (NDFB) and the Bodo Liberation Tiger Force (BLTF) in 1986 and 1996, respectively.
- 1989–1993: Availability of illegal sophisticated weapons with militant groups results in looting and marauding of forest resources and infrastructure. As a result of habitat destruction and heavy wildlife loss caused by civil unrest, UNESCO lists Manas World Heritage site 'in danger' zone.
- February 1993: First tripartite accord signed between government of India and ABSU and the Bodo People's Action Committee, paving the way for creation of Bodoland Autonomous Council (BAC). But the accord soon collapses due to factional splits and violence.
- 1992–1995: Manas closed to tourists due to presence of militant groups inside the Park.
- 1995: Local extinction of rhinos in Manas WHS and virtual collapse of all habitat management activities inside the National Park.
- 1999: Expiry of most forest working plans and a landmark court ruling banning extraction of timber and all forest-based industries from Northeast India.
- Feb 2003: Second tripartite agreement between Government of India, Assam, and representatives of BLT, along with laying down of arms by over 26,41 members of the militant wing. This paved the way for creation of BTAD (Bodoland Territorial Areas District), an autonomous self-governing body within the state of Assam.
- May 2005: The first general elections for BTAD held. Bodoland People's Front (BPF) voted into power with thumping majority. Forest transferred as a subject to BTAD and accorded highest priority and reorganised by the New Government. Forests and wildlife department directly reports to Deputy Chief of BTAD.

- June 2005: Ceasefire by NDFB militants under an agreement with the Government of India that stipulates laying down of arms and cessation of hostile action against security forces and civilians until further talks.
- 2006–2010: Massive forest infrastructure rebuilding and revival of forest administration. Critical tiger habitat of Manas expanded to square 840.04 km.
- April 2008: First 'wild to wild' translocation of adult rhinos from Kaziranga and Pabitora Protected Areas undertaken with much success. Program continued with international support from scientific agencies, civil society, and government departments under the ambitious India Rhino Vision 2020. A founder population of 20 plus adult rhinos established in record span of time.
- April 2010: Second general elections and BPF again voted to power.
- Jan 2011: First ever scientifically conducted survey (using camera-trap method) reveal the presence of nine tigers in Manas WHS. The tigers share their area with royal Manas in Bhutan, thereby emphasising the need to manage the landscape as a trans-boundary reserve.
- June 2011: Manas WHS removed from danger list and reinstated as a UNESCO World Heritage Site in recognition of the collective efforts of the state government, the Bodoland Territorial Council, the Park authorities, NGOs, and local communities including signs of recovery of the natural heritage values.
- April 2015: Third General Elections held in BTAD and BPF once again voted into power.
- August 2016: Formal issuance of a Final Gazette Notification for an addition of 350 sq. km. as a National Park adjoining the Manas WHS. Highest legal protection extended to 'Greater Manas.'
- February 2018: Trans-boundary tiger monitoring under TRAMCA (Trans-Boundary Manas Conservation Area) of Manas India and Bhutan enters into its third cycle with coordinated efforts to scientifically monitor and increase the number of tigers in the landscape.
- March 2019: Tiger numbers double in Royal Manas National Park, Bhutan. Evidence provided of at least 12 individuals using both sides of the border in the Transboundary Manas Conservation Area.

Part II

Rights, legalism, and politics

6 Mahua for Jharkhand's Ho?

An accountability analysis of minor forest product governance

Siddharth Sareen and Emma Jane Lord

Introduction: recognition as structural limits to resource governance and access

Accounts of governance in India's Scheduled Areas (SAs) often feature a focus on natural resources. Scheduled Tribes that inhabit these areas tend, more than other peoples, to rely on a combination of natural resources including minor forest produce (MFP). Leaves, flowers, and fruits supplement their subsistence, performing important functions for livelihoods. This dependence is especially evident during seasons when agricultural yield is meagre (e.g., summer under single-crop subsistence farming) and the extraction and sale of wood from the forest as an income source is particularly effort intensive (e.g., the monsoon season). For communities whose agricultural work load is seasonal (e.g., planting paddy during the monsoon and harvesting rice during the winter), supplemental means of food and income are a key resource during lean work seasons (e.g., spring) (see Gupta *et al.* 2017).

In existing accounts of governance within India's SAs, it is often resources such as forest, water, and land that receive the most attention. Their governance clearly plays an essential role in determining the lives of the Scheduled Tribes that inhabit these areas. Yet, natural resource governance scholarship has unfortunately accorded inadequate attention to how MFPs are governed (Shackleton and Pandey 2014). This remains the case despite acknowledgement that 'it is important to distinguish the central resources at stake, processes of domination, and the different categories of people with specific positions and interests' (Nuijten 1999: 5). The identification of a 'central' resource is a matter of perspective. Although minerals or timber, for instance, may generate more profit for powerful actors in terms of economic value, MFPs can be considered key to the intrinsic welfare of communities that subsist on the margins of a monetised economy and society.

In this chapter, we put forward a way to analyse the governance of MFPs, specifically in Fifth Scheduled Areas of India. We take up a case of the mahua (*Madhuca indica*) flower, or *matkam*, that is collected, dried, and sold by the Ho Adivasi/people in West Singhbhum district of Jharkhand state during the late spring season.[1] Through this case, our aim is to demonstrate how attention to the governance of MFPs can provide an additional, crucial lens onto the nature of governance in India's SAs. We interpret governance by deconstructing an assemblage of access to and authority over a single MFP. This builds upon previous scholarship examining patterns of access to natural resources and services in Jharkhand (Sareen 2017; Sareen and Nathan 2017), as outlined in the conceptual framework in the next section. Our analysis rests on the concept of 'accountability' as a relationship performed through practices of *legitimation* that produce and perpetuate institutional authority and particular configurations of resource allocation. This analytical approach helps direct our attention to how power is legitimated and enables us to unpack how legitimation produces institutional authority and cements resource access for actors. It leads to three contextualised definitions, each of which rests on the legitimation of underlying acts of formal recognition by the government at the national or regional level:

1 Specific natural resources are recognised as being MFPs (such as *matkam* in our case), and this recognition is instrumental in the legitimation of their allocation to various actors (such as the Ho but with limited 'use rights' in our case).
2 Specific communities are recognised as indigenous (alternatively 'tribal' or 'Adivasi') and as having associated traditional practices of natural resource governance within the territory they inhabit which is designated and territorialised as a SA, and this recognition is instrumental in the legitimation of their formal access to MFPs.
3 Specific areas are recognised as forest areas by law (and thereby as arenas for forestry schemes such as 'Compensatory Afforestation Fund Management and Planning Act' [henceforth CAMPA] and carbon forestry schemes such as 'Reducing Emissions from Deforestation and Forest Degradation with the added goals of Conserving and Enhancing Forest Carbon Stocks, and Sustainably Managing Forests' [henceforth REDD+]),[2] and this recognition is instrumental in the legitimation of both MFP governance and in the production of forest carbon as a new, abstract, and intangible commodity to govern.

Based on the conjuncture of this triple recognition, practices of legitimation perform relations of accountability between actors and institutions vis-à-vis MFPs in Fifth SAs of India. On the one hand, legitimation is normative and comprises input legitimacy (procedural), output legitimacy (measures), and outcome legitimacy (effects); on the other hand, legitimation is also sociological and comprises the public acceptance of institutional authority (Bäckstrand *et al.* 2018). This understanding of legitimation enables a non-linear articulation of accountability within an assemblage of networked actors trying to influence and secure access to resources: *matkam* in the case of the Ho. This moves beyond new institutionalist understandings of policy, to institutional processualist understandings of how situated interaction is influenced by stable context (Barzelay and Gallego 2006). It allows us to study not simply dynamics of the production and perpetuation of institutional authority, but the performance of accountability relations (cf. Komporozos-Athanasiou *et al.* 2017), understood as the recursive dialectic of the recognition and legitimation of access, in the governance of MFPs in India's Fifth SAs. The performance of accountability, whether substantiated or hollow, *de jure* or *de facto*, is described through attention to practices of legitimation of access to a single MFP (i.e., *matkam*) within a specific Fifth Scheduled Area, the West Singhbhum district of Jharkhand, and with reference to a particular set of communities, the Ho. This given context contributes to understanding the causal mechanisms highlighted in this case via interpretive methods (cf. Falleti and Lynch 2009).

The Ho subsist on a combination of single-crop farming (rice) and foraging, with many households having some modest cattle stock or poultry. They live in relatively homogenous rural communities, usually of one main Ho clan, with a few other clan members and non-Ho households in some villages, the latter being typically Hindu families that have been allowed in some generations ago and also speak the Ho language. Village populations range from a few dozen to over a hundred households, customarily centred around a *sarna* or sacred grove marked by old trees and featuring stones in front of houses to mark burial places of familial ancestors. Villages are organised in hamlets and led by a village chief (Munda) whose role is recognised under self-governance legislation, alongside the democratic institution of a Gram Sabha or village assembly comprising all adult inhabitants as members. Ho villages are in the forest, on the forest fringe, or on agricultural and scrub land (for details, see Sareen and Nathan 2017). Mahua trees grow in all of these landscapes, and customary Ho rights, recognised under Indian legislation, specify individual Ho households' access to mahua trees, including those on village forest land that is communally held. Besides the transaction-based uses of *matkam* as an MFP that are in focus here, it bears mention that mahua trees are of cultural importance to the Ho (see Sareen 2016a).

In this introductory section, we have explained the basis for our concern with the governance of MFPs, specified the triple acts of recognition pertaining to their governance in SAs, signalled a conceptual basis for an analytical focus on *accountability* as examined through practices of legitimation, and introduced the Ho people, as well as *matkam* as a key MFP they can access in the SA of the West Singhbhum district. In three subsequent sections, we proceed as follows. First, we detail our analytical framework, explicating its conceptual basis as well as its operationalisation for empirical study. Next, we apply it to the governance of the mahua flower in relation to the Ho people's access to it. In doing so, we empirically specify distinctions between hollow and substantive accountability. Finally, we discuss the conceptual import of our analysis in terms of the accountability relations it brings forward, and reflect upon what this implies for the governance of MFPs in SAs.

Recognition and legitimation of resource access: substantive and hollow accountability

Accountability is a means to render leaders answerable for their actions in order to hold their actions to public account and is as such distinct from responsibility, which refers to the obligation for leaders to act morally correctly (Braithwaite 2006). Therefore, transparency is closely connected to political processes of generating accountability. Whether it is feasible to achieve accountability without elections, beyond the boundaries of states, has been a key question within debates on globalisation and cosmopolitanism (Macdonald and Macdonald 2006). Civil society and non-governmental organisations (NGOs) have been shown to be instrumental in creating additional, non-electoral forms of accountability within natural resource governance globally: accountability can be vertical within structural hierarchies, horizontal between peers, or diagonal between leaders and citizens (Nuesiri 2016). Although the degree of resemblance of representatives to their constituent population (descriptive representation), their degree of acceptance within their constituent population (symbolic representation), or their particular forms of expertise are relevant criteria for leadership, elections are considered morally superior as they provide a means based on collective power for the removal of public figures who fail to perform over time. Such substantive political accountability in turn provides a basis for legal accountability, by enacting laws through legislative processes that render particular forms of recognition sticky and obdurate. Yet both political and legal accountability are limited in reach in contexts such as Jharkhand where formal processes are only part of the picture, and where historical state-community conflict over forest governance combines with long-running political instability and governmental welfare interventions, to present a complex and hybrid state-citizen relationship that informs local agency and access.

When the interplay of overlapping domains of authority and power relations blocks or circumvents substantive accountability, it generates hollow accountability. This relationship captures access that occurs without formal recognition (which would be *de facto* access) but also without local legitimation. Defining accountability as hollow or substantiated is a move to enrich the vocabulary available to understand the iterations of natural resource access. Describing the single case of mahua, geographically situated within Jharkhand, shows a sample of actors and reveals how they interact, rather than constituting a definitive portrait of the workings of accountability relations (Flyvbjerg 2006) – a worthy task for future research.

To make a case for accountability analysis of resource governance, we begin with a framework for analysing access that has proven influential in recent years and explain what our approach can add. The *theory of access* (Ribot and Peluso 2003) posits that access to resources must be understood as not only being rights-based, but also contingent on structural and relationship mechanisms (i.e., that access is partly premised on power that has not necessarily been legitimated). The former mechanisms address hybrid formal laws and customary rules-in-use, whereas the latter mechanisms concern trans-legal factors such as financial capital, social networks, epistemic politics, hierarchies based on intersectionality, and the very materiality of a specific resource. This sort of approach is particularly helpful in analysing natural resource governance in regions of conflict, in places where access often changes over time, and is held in place by a complex web of formal and informal governance. Their usefulness has been demonstrated in various contexts, including in relation to *matkam* in Jharkhand (Sareen 2016a).

The structural and relational mechanisms (access to technology, capital, markets, labour and labour opportunities, knowledge, authority, as well as through social identity and via the negotiation of other social relations) in this theorisation, called 'bundles of power,' are useful for understanding how power operates outside rights-based claim-making, but are rather static (Koch 2008). Consequentially, the treatment of rights-based mechanisms of access itself does not cut very deep in terms of explaining actors' agency. How does power exercised through these mechanisms translate into access to resources, and does it become legitimated or challenged over time through various locally grounded forms of contestation and wrestles over control? Sareen (2017) brings in such dynamism to access analysis by extending it to access to government services and demonstrating a recursive relation between access to services and local authority. This argument draws on the observation that privileged actors use structural and relational mechanisms not only to secure enlarged access to benefits from services, but also to enact institutional authority over these services. In order to address how bundles of power relate with legitimated claims over resources (entitlements) and with control over resources (*de facto* resource access, or endowments) (Koch 2008; Leach *et al.* 1999), such an approach holds promise. It treats the state as an assemblage of governmental recognition as well as non-governmental authority generated through the institutionalisation of emergent forms of recognising access claims. Whereas governmental recognition helps secure access to welfare and development at the same time as strengthening the role of the state in a politically unstable region (see Sanyal 2007), informal modes of recognising access claims hybridise the nature of local authority, complicating effects of formal recognition.

The sort of more dynamic, process-oriented approach described here must nonetheless operate within the structural limits that specific forms of recognition that are overarching and deeply entrenched make hard to reconfigure (such as the forms we delineate with respect to the governance of MFPs in SAs and their forests inhabited by the Ho). In the present context, for instance, the problem we have set up as a triple conjuncture of recognition is fairly well established in law and unlikely to change through local acts in peripheral settings. This is because it is safeguarded by a rather centralised, bureaucratic, and thereby obdurate legislative and policy framework, premised on social and legal conventions of expertise and authority. Even so, institutions that authorise actors' competing claims interact in multiple contested ways within the overarching structural limits set up by these specific acts of recognition – as we will show, the local level is rife with such agency, and our approach must reflect an attempt to theorise this as well. We therefore present an approach to analyse accountability that can treat rights-based and structural and relational mechanisms conjointly in order to contextualise MFP governance within the larger regional political economy of a SA.

In our approach, access claims are enacted by actors who draw on institutional authorisation. This conceptualisation is premised on recursive recognition: The institutional recognition of claims produces both resource access for actors and authority for institutions (Sareen 2017). This is a wider interpretation of Sikor and Lund's (2009) analysis of property and authority, extended as a continuum to access and power. To resolve the problem of how to treat power and authority (i.e., legitimated power) in a continuous way, we adopt a process orientation premised on the dialectic of recognition and legitimation of access that produces accountability relations. Thus, formal recognition is overarching and obdurate and primarily contestable at a higher level (e.g., state or national, where decision-making processes are often characterised by power differentials within the political economy at these levels beyond our present focus), whereas practices of legitimation are locally animated, observable in everyday resource governance, and a hybrid of formal and customary, embedded and emergent, established and contested over time. In essence, legitimation of access is ultimately recognition too, but its empirical specification as practices of legitimation is accurately represented when these are juxtaposed in dialectical relation with overarching forms of recognition that, locally, manifest primarily as boundary conditions (i.e., conditions that cannot be addressed through local agency alone and are relatively stable). Study can address the preliminary question: given entrenched forms of recognition that set up a specific structural logic, at least in the short run and for peripheral localities, what practices of legitimation represent the tussle to configure resource access in favour of particular actors?

Tracking practices of legitimation opens up a window on relations of accountability (and vice versa; see Kraft and Wolf 2016 on artefacts of accountability). If legitimation follows the form one would expect based on overarching forms of recognition, governance is enacted as per legislated accountability relations. This rarely bears up in practice. Practices of legitimation locally shape different accountability relations, thus reconstituting how the assemblage of power is legitimated to govern resources. This theoretical basis must be complemented by attention to the role of unlegitimated power in determining resource access. Since power that is not legitimated can still be exercised, it follows that the agency it exerts can be observed as a hollow performance of accountability. As opposed to a substantive performance of accountability that co-produces institutional authority and legitimates resource access, a hollow performance of accountability sets up

Table 6.1 Access-legitimation matrix characterising accountability relations under access

	Locally legitimated	*Locally unlegitimated*
Recognition grants access	1 Substantiated accountability (law exercised, access = yes)	3 *De jure* accountability (law ineffective, access = no)
Recognition denies access	2 *De facto* accountability (law altered, access = yes)	4 Hollow accountability (law bypassed, access = yes)

Source: Compiled by Author

neither *de facto* nor *de jure* legitimation; it simply secures access to resources for actors. This is possible because, even given a lack of formal recognition to enable access and without local legitimation, actors can nonetheless exercise power for theft or for disregard and defiance.

Thus, as Table 6.1 encapsulates, the dialectic of recognition and legitimation of access yields both kinds of accountability relations – hollow and substantiated. It also visualises how to distinguish these from access under *de facto* accountability (emergent institution authorising access) and access being denied despite *de jure* accountability (emergent authority preventing access). It allows us to answer the ultimate question pertaining to resource governance: What relations of accountability actually obtain, as evident from the nature of legitimated and unlegitimated access? In other words, is accountability hollow or substantiated? Unlegitimated power is instrumental in securing access within a specific overarching configuration of recognition (performance of hollow accountability), while legitimated power secures access through locally enacted practices of legitimation (institutional authority or substantiated accountability). Despite being qualitatively different, they can be applied as a single process-oriented, relational concept – accountability – to analyses of resource access. Moreover, the presence or absence of substantiated accountability has significant, potentially grave implications for the legitimacy associated with the government (i.e., the validity of the latter in the rural hinterland that SAs can be typically characterised as). In the next section, we approach the governance of mahua flowers based on this accountability analysis.

(Un)legitimated access to *matkam* as a dynamic resource governance analysis

Findings

Under India's federal system, mahua flowers are recognised as a minor forest product by the state analogue of the central Ministry of the Environment and Forests, which in Jharkhand is the Forest Department. This recognition is applicable both in village forests administered by village assemblies as well as in forests managed by the Forest Department (the latter under the Forest Rights Act, 2006), apart from on individually owned plots of land. The Panchayat (Extension to Scheduled Areas) Act, 1996 (PESA), which extends the 73rd Constitutional Amendment, 1992, to SAs such as the West Singhbhum district, also recognises the Ho Adivasis' right to govern this resource within their territory. Ho access rights are governed by a Munda or village chief system, usually passed on through patrilineal descent. The Munda adjudicates conflicts over resources within a Ho village, as captured in the colonial-era Wilkinson Rule stating that British colonists would allow the Ho to continue their system of local self-governance. This Ho customary law is backed by PESA (formalisation of customary practices), and in case conflicts prove hard to resolve by the Munda or the Manki, who is a paramount chief over a traditional cluster of villages called pir, a government official called the Kolhan Superintendent is available for recourse. The designation of this official harks back to the Kolhan Government Estate, the territory where the Ho have long lived and self-governed (for more details, see Sareen and Nathan 2017).

Under Ho customary law, ownership of mahua flowers is tree-specific. Ho households' land is typically scattered in parcels across village land. Mahua trees on individually owned land belong to that Ho household. Mahua flowers from trees on communally owned land belong to an individual Ho household based on who has laid a claim and subsequently had rights attributed to them. Although there is jurisdictional overlap with the village assembly as a decision-making forum based on a model of deliberative democracy also recognised under PESA, in practice this is typically a domain of decision for the Munda according to communally agreed principles. Yet despite these strong, relatively clear, well-established, and easily enforced and monitored ownership rights within villages, recognition of access to this minor forest product for the Ho is restricted to limited forms of use.[3] This limit concerns the main value associated with *matkam*, which comes from their use in distilling liquor. This potent mahua liquor is illegal to make in Jharkhand, even though according to PESA Scheduled Tribes have the right to democratically determine access to this minor forest product through the forum of the village assembly. The Ho do not have the resources (material and social capital) to run a licensed enterprise outside the state. This limits their extraction of value from *matkam* to two options: bootlegging liquor with its attendant risks including fines and imprisonment if caught by a historically hostile administration, or selling it at the local (and relatively low) going price in weekly village markets to middlemen from the district headquarters town Chaibasa who are better connected and trade it elsewhere (for more details, including gendered power differentials implicated in associated practices, see an ethnographic account in Sareen 2016a).

As Table 6.2 shows, the governance of *matkam* is characterised by multiple types of legitimation (or absence thereof) in relation to recognition of access rights along the value chain. In quadrant 3, even though recognition

Table 6.2 Access-legitimation matrix for mahua flowers accessed by Ho and local traders

	Locally legitimated	*Locally unlegitimated*
Recognition grants access	1 Substantiated accountability (law exercised, access = partial) *Ho can collect matkam and sell them to local traders based on laws but only at low prices*	3 *De jure* accountability (law ineffective, access = no) *Ho cannot gain much benefit from matkam despite ownership due to limited access*
Recognition denies access	2 *De facto* accountability (law altered, access = yes) *Local traders gain benefits as middlemen through trade of matkam out of state*	4 Hollow accountability (law bypassed, access = yes) *Bootlegging of liquor is done by actors using unlegitimated power to access benefits*

Source: Compiled by Author

grants access, it simultaneously imposes restrictions that limit local legitimation of access by the Ho, allowing better-off traders to gain access to uncaptured benefits. While access analysis would read this as Ho's lack of access to structural and relational mechanisms, accountability analysis explains it as a locally unlegitimated form of recognition (i.e., as *de jure* accountability). Traders, on the other hand, alter the law in practice, legitimating their access despite recognition giving ownership to the Ho. They legitimate their access to benefits through privileged roles in local practices, thus shaping minor resource product governance (quadrant 2).

Substantiated accountability (quadrant 1) is only present to the extent that the Ho gain partial benefits through accessing *matkam* premised on higher-level governmental recognition – they typically sell dried flowers ranging from Rs.18 to 25 per kilogram during the late spring. The few with no pressing need for income who are able to stockpile these dried flowers till the monsoon reported fetching up to three times higher prices (cf. Sareen 2016a), suggesting that traders capture a wide margin of benefits. Actors who bootleg liquor distilled from *matkam* within Jharkhand (typically men with some social and financial capital) can capture this benefit without legitimating their access by bypassing the law. This again requires drawing on various structural and relational mechanisms of access and is explained within accountability analysis as a performance of hollow accountability (quadrant 4).

Analysis

Accountability analysis thus addresses both contextually relevant questions evinced in the previous section:

1 Given entrenched forms of recognition that set up a specific structural logic for Ho villages as peripheral localities, what practices of

legitimation represent the tussle to configure access to *matkam* in favour of particular actors? (This is evident from Table 6.2.)

In addition to the practices of legitimation described earlier, we note that specific forms of recognition are important to identify in examining tensions over mahua flower governance. For instance, Ho Adivasis have the right to collect and sell it, but urban traders are the ones positioned to extract the most value from it through distillation and sale elsewhere. A similar exercise in terms of the current configuration for a different commodity such as bamboo (grass) in a different state or district might reveal an entirely different configuration of recognition under different state level operationalisation of the Forest Rights Act (FRA). This is due to overlapping domains of authority with various forms of recognition by government departments at the village level. The FRA has played a particularly important function in this regard since its enactment in 2006, due to historically troubled state-community relations. As we broach in the subsequent discussion section, a reconfiguration of the overarching recognition of forest rights is now imminent due to the recent advent of two large interventions, REDD+ and CAMPA, that introduce compensatory and carbon forestry.

Recognition under the Fifth Scheduled Area status is distinct from a Sixth Scheduled Area, which affords more extreme safeguards, and also from non-SAs. The latter leave much more scope for entry by non-Adivasis, while not espousing a totalising, land-bound definition of Adivasi identity as an approach to affirmative action (Oskarsson and Sareen 2019). Moreover, even despite territorial recognition as a Fifth Scheduled Area and the attendant safeguard that Adivasi land cannot be acquired by a non-Adivasi, exceptions due to land acquisition and coal extraction laws remain possible (cf. Sareen 2016b).

2 What relations of accountability are actually obtained, as evident from the nature of legitimated and unlegitimated access (i.e., is accountability hollow or substantiated?) (This is evident from explanation of the four quadrants from Table 6.2.)

Practices of legitimation of access comprise the second part of the dialectic of recognition and legitimation. Together, they constitute an account of the types of accountability relations performed. For instance, governmental recognition of rights accorded to Scheduled Tribes in SAs seems legitimated through Ho's sale of *matkam*, even though it leads to very limited benefits for this prioritised target group. By paying modest prices for *matkam*, traders obfuscate the rent capture enabled by their superior positioning within power structures through a market, a socially legitimate practice. These enactments respectively perform (i) a poor version of the access rights that formal recognition should secure, and (ii) local legitimation of access despite its lack of formal recognition. These examples demonstrate the effect of such legitimation and recognition in enabling types of accountability relations. These practices capture the totality of the legitimated forms of access to *matkam* by various actors, as encapsulated in Table 6.2. Conversely, the authorisation side of legitimation (as the recursive counterpart to access) reveals the relevant institutional authority involved in how mahua flowers are governed. Thus, whereas recognition in this dialectic affords window onto structural limits, legitimation opens up to capture *de facto* local authorisation of access.

Now we come to unlegitimated power and its implications for access to *matkam*. This involves performing hollow accountability relations by drawing on 'bundles of power' in a dynamic sense that has conceptual continuity with recognition (and the lack thereof) captured through attention to the nature of accountability being performed. Rent captured from the *matkam* in local village markets, in the district headquarters town of Chaibasa at a main trader's bungalow, further out during and after its transport out of Jharkhand where it becomes invisible to the Ho people, and finally in its sale as country liquor after distillation – the overall grabbing of rent by traders is not justified, nor is it held in place through performances of accountability, which is hollow in the sense that it cannot be observed as any practice of legitimation, yet does not result in a direct conflict (for details, refer to Sareen 2016a). These are the hollow accountability relations that make up access premised on 'unlegitimated power.' It operates within but despite overarching structural limits at the triple conjuncture of recognition, and in mutual exclusion from legitimated resource access. Where there is legitimation, this can be contested, but here it is 'managed' instead through the hollow performance of accountability in that there is no hue and cry that a large part of access to an MFP in a SA is being coopted by privileged actors at the expense of Scheduled Tribes. The forms that performances of accountability can take, then, include both practices of legitimation and hollow, unlegitimated practices (such as trade, including black markets) that maintain appearances of certain relations and thereby unlegitimated access to *matkam* for actors without attendant institutional authorisation. This constitutes a hollowing out of the state by privileged private actors (whose actions lack transparency in the public domain) and also of what governmental recognition is popularly perceived to stand for at the local level.

Discussion and conclusion: implications for MFP governance in SAs

Our accountability analysis of *matkam* has numerous implications for minor forest product governance in India's SAs. Recognition through legislation such as FRA and PESA has enabled limited gains and helped move access to this minor forest product towards legitimation, setting up substantive relations of accountability. Depending on the configuration of recognition of (i) specific characteristics of a minor forest product, (ii) the Adivasi identity of inhabitants, and (iii) forms of resource governance through overarching legislative framings, this legitimation sets up resource access for actors.

Yet, even for the single minor forest product we consider here, recognition and legitimation remain far from complete in providing an accurate picture of resource access. Moreover, there is likely to be significant variation across resources due to different operationalisations of recognition and legitimation based on the varying legal definitions applicable to each minor forest product and across different contexts (pertaining to both people and states, even within SAs across India). In other words, there is a need to also consider unlegitimated access, which as we have shown for *matkam* forms a significant part of the full resource access picture. This includes informal trade and the ability of privileged actors to take on positions of authority and extract benefits along the resource value chain.

The Ho people form a minority group of 1.1 million, within an overall state population of 32 million in Jharkhand, a young state formed in 2000 and a region in which macro-economic interests linked with resource extraction are at play. Resources such as iron ore generate powerful patterns of domination that necessitate careful consideration of appropriate institutional structures for decision-making over resource allocation between the electoral power of the state majority population and the Ho as a relative minority (Wolff and Yakinthou 2013). Access to *matkam* must be understood within this context of recent state formation amid insurgent struggles and counter repression by governmental authorities (Sareen 2016b). Such conflicts tend to undermine substantive accountability, as shown with respect to a village assembly case (Sareen 2017): despite inhabitants running their village assembly with considerable success during 2012–2014 to collectively manage natural resources and access developmental service schemes, subsequent crime led to the withdrawal of governmental support. By comparison, scholars in a context of civil conflict in Colombia have shown how violence can transform property rights regulatory institutions in a deeply anti-egalitarian sense, as paramilitary groups launder land to maintain the appearance of legality (Grajales 2015; Peña-Huertas *et al.* 2017). As threats of violence leading to discourses of securitisation in turn justify overrule of democratic procedures, such coercive patterns remain complex to resolve (Sareen 2016b; see also Lord 2018).

Interventions such as CAMPA and REDD+ must map on to such complex empirically informed understandings of forest governance in India in their scheme design in order to be able to live up to their stated ambitions. These ambitions seem to normalise a neat picture of access to forests and MFPs that is at a vast departure from the one that emerges in our analysis, both conceptually and empirically, upon taking on board both overarching structural limits and detailed local factors that jointly constitute natural resource governance. Attention to performances of accountability relations, both substantiated and hollow, approached as a dialectic of recognition and legitimation of resource access, enables evidence for our claims. The interactions between the three forms of recognition (1)–(3) indicated earlier may come to have future implications for the global democratic deficit, influencing the gap between communities such as the Ho and transnational rule-makers (Moravcsik 2004). Should the performance of accountability between the first two forms of recognition (1)–(2) become subjected to forest carbon offsetting schemes introduced via the third form of recognition (3), a noteworthy concern is that globalisation could introduce new steps in an ambiguous causal chain, enabling international bodies that can operate with locally unaccountable decision-making processes to reconstitute the Ho's standing as a people.

Thus, while we do not take up the important but demanding work of deconstructing the design of large forest governance-related schemes such as CAMPA and REDD+ itself in this particular chapter, we point to the danger of bringing these into a troubled context in terms of potentially undoing the limited gains secured with such difficulty under PESA and FRA over the past quarter century, especially in forest stretches of India's SAs. Further intervention requires detailed consideration and nuanced policy informed by these complexities and cognisant of the necessity to address them through sensitive scheme design. Rushing in without this detailed analysis and deliberation is likely to do more harm than good in terms of equity and justice impacts on resource access. It might also be detrimental in terms of moving towards more substantive accountability relations in forest governance, particularly in territories like India's SAs that have long suffered from poor governance in general. The accountability analysis we put forward constitutes a valuable, even necessary, tool for developing this conversation, and for ensuring the relevance of current debates on forest governance towards gains for democratic resource access.

Notes

1 The Ho are a Scheduled Tribe numbering 1.1 million people in all, concentrated predominantly in West Singhbhum district (district population: 1.5 million) in Jharkhand (state population: 32 million) and also present in two adjoining districts, one in Jharkhand and the other in the neighbouring state of Odisha.

2 We don't detail CAMPA or REDD+ within the scope of this chapter, only reflect in relation to them in the closing discussion. For a handy overview of forest governance concerns and REDD+ in India, see Balooni and Lund (2014), Kashwan (2015), and Vijge and Gupta (2014). This recognition has complex outcomes beyond the scope of empirical data currently available for Jharkhand; in other forestry case studies, it has led to recentralisation of power. Scholarship on CAMPA is still in its infancy, but for context see Lele (2017) and a piece in *The Wire*: https://thewire.in/environment/great-indian-land-grab-carried-name-compensatory-afforestation (accessed on 18 April 2018).

3 This is a hotly contested topic in Jharkhand and several neighbouring states. For some sense of recent developments, see: https://scroll.in/magazine/848690/as-toddy-tappers-and-mahua-pickers-struggle-country-liquor-in-assam-is-getting-a-new-lease-on-life (accessed on 18 April 2018).

References

Bäckstrand, K., Zelli, F. and Schleifer, P. 2018. 'Legitimacy and Accountability in Polycentric Climate Governance.' In A. Jordan, D. Huitema, J. Schoenefeld, H.V. Asselt and J. Forster (Eds.), *Governing Climate Change: Polycentricity in Action?* (pp. 338–356). Cambridge: Cambridge University Press.

Balooni, K. and Lund, J.F. 2014. 'Forest Rights: The Hard Currency of REDD+.' *Conservation Letters*, 7(3): 278–284.

Barzelay, M. and Gallego, R. 2006. 'From "New Institutionalism" to "Institutional Processualism": Advancing Knowledge About Public Management Policy Change.' *Governance*, 19(4): 531–557.

Braithwaite, J. 2006. 'Accountability and Responsibility Through Restorative Justice.' In M.W. Dowdle (Ed.), *Public Accountability: Designs, Dilemmas and Experiences* (pp. 33–51). Cambridge: Cambridge University Press.

Falleti, T.G. and Lynch, J.F. 2009. 'Context and Causal Mechanisms in Political Analysis.' *Comparative Political Studies*, 42(9): 1143–1166.

Flyvbjerg, B. 2006. 'Five Misunderstandings About Case-Study Research.' *Qualitative Inquiry*, 12(2): 219–245.

Grajales, J. 2015. 'Land Grabbing, Legal Contention and Institutional Change in Colombia.' *Journal of Peasant Studies*, 42(3–4): 541–560.

Gupta, A.K., Sharma, M.L. and Singh, L. 2017. 'Utilization Pattern of Non-Timber Forest Products (NTFPs) Among the Tribal Population of Chhattisgarh, India.' *International Journal of Bio-Resource & Stress Management*, 8(2): 327–333.

Kashwan, P. 2015. 'Forest Policy, Institutions, and REDD+ in India, Tanzania, and Mexico.' *Global Environmental Politics*, 15(3): 95–117.

Koch, J. 2008. 'Perspectives on Access to and Management of Natural Resources.' *Danish Institute for International Studies, Working Paper 8*. Copenhagen: DIIS.

Komporozos-Athanasiou, A., Thompson, M. and Fotaki, M. 2017. 'Performing Accountability in Health Research: A Socio-Spatial Framework.' *Human Relations*, 71(9). https://doi.org/10.1177/0018726717740410.

Kraft, B. and Wolf, S. 2016. 'Through the Lens of Accountability: Analyzing Legitimacy in Environmental Governance.' *Organization & Environment*, 31(1): 70–92.

Leach, M., Mearns, R. and Scoones, I. 1999. 'Environmental Entitlements: Dynamics and Institutions in Community-Based Natural Resource Management.' *World Development*, 27(2): 225–247.

Lele, S. 2017 'Forest Governance From Co-Option and Conflict to Multilayered Governance?' *Economic & Political Weekly*, 52(25–26): 55–58.

Lord, E.J. 2018. 'Displacement, Power and REDD+: A Forest History of Carbonized Exclusion.' In E.O. Nuesiri (Ed.), *Global Forest Governance and Climate Change: Interrogating Representation, Participation, and Decentralization* (pp. 115–143). Cham: Palgrave Macmillan.

Macdonald, T. and Macdonald, K. 2006. 'Non-Electoral Accountability in Global Politics: Strengthening Democratic Control Within the Global Garment Industry.' *European Journal of International Law*, 17(1): 89–119.

Moravcsik, A. 2004. 'Is There a 'Democratic Deficit' in World Politics? A Framework for Analysis.' *Government and Opposition*, 39(2): 336–363.

Nuesiri, E.O. 2016. 'Local Government Authority and Representation in REDD+: A Case Study From Nigeria.' *International Forestry Review*, 18(3): 306–318.

Nuijten, M. 1999. *Institutions and Organising Practices: Conceptual Discussion.* Rome: FAO.

Oskarsson, P. and Sareen, S. (forthcoming 2019) 'Understanding Adivasiness as Caste Expression and Land Rights Claim in Central-Eastern India.' *Journal of Contemporary Asia.*

Peña-Huertas, R., Ruiz, L.E., Parada, M.M., Zuleta, S. and Álvarez, R. 2017. 'Legal Dispossession and Civil War in Colombia.' *Journal of Agrarian Change*, 17(4): 759–769.

Ribot, J.C. and N.L. Peluso. 2003. 'A Theory of Access.' *Rural Sociology*, 68(2): 153–181.

Sanyal, K. 2007. *Rethinking Capitalist Development: Primitive Accumulation, Governmentality and Post-colonial Capitalism.* New Delhi: Routledge.

Sareen, S. 2016a. 'Whose Matkam? An Ethnographic Account of the Political Economy of Mahua Flowers.' *Journal of Adivasi and Indigenous Studies*, 3(1): 37–45.

Sareen, S. 2016b. 'Seeing Development as Security: Constructing Top-Down Authority and Inequitable Access in Jharkhand.' *South Asia Multidisciplinary Academic Journal*, [Online], 13, doi:10.4000/samaj.4146

Sareen, S. 2017. 'Who Governs Local Access in Jharkhand? Mechanisms of Access to Government Services.' *Forum for Development Studies*, 44(2): 249–274.

Sareen, S. and Nathan, I. 2017. 'Under What Conditions Can Local Government Nurture Indigenous People's Democratic Practice? A Case Study of Two Ho Village Assemblies in Jharkhand.' *The Journal of Development Studies*, 54(8): 1–20.

Shackleton, C.M. and Pandey, A.K. 2014. 'Positioning Non-Timber Forest Products on the Development Agenda.' *Forest Policy and Economics*, 38: 1–7.

Sikor, T. and Lund, C. 2009. 'Access and Property: A Question of Power and Authority.' *Development and Change*, 40(1): 1–22.

Vijge, M.J. and Gupta, A. 2014. 'Framing REDD+ in India: Carbonizing and Centralizing Indian Forest Governance?' *Environmental Science & Policy*, 38: 17–27.

Wolff, S. and Yakinthou, C. (Eds.). 2013. *Conflict Management in Divided Societies: Theories and Practice.* London: Routledge.

7 Politics of dispossession

Land, law, and protest in Jharkhand

Sujit Kumar

Introduction

The inhabitants of Scheduled Areas, primarily the Adivasis, do not *simply* subscribe to laws in asserting their rights above water, forest, and land (*jal, jungle aur jameen*). Protective laws on land – Chotanagpur Tenancy Act (CNTA), 1908, and Santhal Parganas Tenancy Act (SPTA), 1949 in the case of Jharkhand – evoke issues of history, culture, and landscape[1] when it comes to land acquisition. This convoluted legal discourse has often resulted in arbitrary judicial interpretations under different circumstances. Whereas the few successes in cases of litigation over land acquisition have inspired the Adivasi communities to ascribe to 'jury politics,'[2] their popular protest has deep historical and cultural meanings. Struggles of their forefathers in securing their rights over land and other resources are invoked as the part of historical imagination. Simultaneously, the cultural assertions are made on the basis of the *place of eminence* which nature enjoys in their worldview. Furthermore, claims based on indigeneity, communitarian, and egalitarian assumptions are also made. Thus, the vocabulary of resistance contains terms which derive as much from the modern lexicon of state as from pre-state social order.

This chapter attempts to understand the nature of laws governing land in Scheduled Areas, their judicial interpretations, and the form in which the Adivasi communities adopt the laws. The inferences for this study are drawn from the cases of land acquisition for Sponge Iron Projects (hereafter SIPs) in West Singhbhum district of Jharkhand. The approach followed for analysis subscribes to dynamic interpretation of inter and intra group relations, 'Adivasi' as a non-static notion acquiring varied meanings in a dialogue with political circumstances and 'state' as an institution enjoying limited and selective legitimacy. The chapter is arranged into five sections. The first section attempts to understand the land issue by providing a brief theoretical discussion on land dispossession followed by a description of the situation prevailing in Jharkhand. Here we attempt to arrive at an appropriate construct to extend the discussion. The third section deciphers the perception of law as an important factor in framing the common aspirations and imagination among the Adivasis. Attempts made by the companies to circumvent the issues of legality is analysed in the fourth section followed by an analysis of response of the community against land acquisition in the fifth section. Finally, the chapter concludes by arguing that the present legal ambiguities do not resolve the situation according to the popular aspirations of the Adivasis.

Understanding contemporary land dispossession in India

The global flow of capital through foreign direct investment (FDI) in addition to the domestic capital has emerged as the major sources of land dispossession in neoliberal India. Consequently, what has become important in the analysis of dispossession is not the origin of capital but its character which singularly requires forceful appropriation. Analysis of the present situation entails the use of either Marx's 'primitive accumulation'[3] or an innovation upon this construct in order to find answer to more complex situation. However, the major point of contention among the thinkers in accepting primitive accumulation for analysing the present form of land dispossession relates to its adoption either as a continuous phenomenon or as an historical event (Angelis 2001: 1). Supporting the continued relevance of primitive accumulation, Glassman (2006: 615) argues that the basic ontology of Marx's alienation 'links primitive accumulation and expanded reproduction and provides a basis for understanding primitive accumulation as more than merely historical.'

Building upon Marx's reticence to see primitive accumulation as a historical stage and his relegation of the accumulation based upon 'predation, fraud, and violence' to that stage, Harvey used the term 'accumulation by dispossession' (henceforth ABD) to emphasise the continuation of the process. He asserts that capitalism has made shrewd attempts to camouflage violence while its propensity to accumulate has increased manifold and the dispossession is now not only confined to the physical assets of the people but also to their hard-earned money through financial and credit institutions (Harvey 2003). Most of Harvey's analysis refers to the expansion of neo-imperialism through global capital flow in which he considers 'over-accumulation' as the chief phenomena over Luxemburg's 'under-consumption.'[4]

Levien is appreciative of ABD's ability to capture diverse contemporary dispossessions and uses this in analysing Special Economic Zones (SEZs) in India calculating the 'rate of accumulation by dispossession.'[5] Although an ingenious way of analysing the processes of ABD, this approach tends to ignore the fact that anti-dispossession movements rarely base themselves upon a prospective estimation of accumulation by the capitalists. Such movements are rather grounded in the sense of latent and manifest loss of resources upon which the people enjoy either legal or customary rights. Levien's approach, therefore, is useful to analyse a post-dispossession scenario for a rather objective assessment of loss-benefit incurred and generated by different social classes. However, the ongoing cases of dispossession solicit an approach which also captures the dispossession caused from the perspective of the 'dispossessed.'

Making yet another bid in search of a theoretical construct to identify the ongoing land dispossession in India, Levien (2015) comes up with his 'regimes of dispossession.' He argues that,

> A regime of dispossession is an institutionalized way of expropriating land from their current owners or users. It has two essential components: a state willing to dispossess for a particular set of economic purposes that are tied to particular class interests; and a way of generating compliance to this dispossession. These two aspects are intrinsically linked.
> (Michael Levien 2015:149–150)

But scholars like Bedi and Tillin (2015:195) have contested the claim of unbridled association of the state with certain classes and highlights the state-wise variation on the issue of land acquisition. Ostensibly, recognition of the state simply as a coercive institution in the discourse of land acquisition reduces the scope of capturing its variegated response. It is due to this reason that the present chapter attempts to capture the politics of land dispossession crafted as per the local realities, particularly the specific history and culture of the inhabitants.

Identifying land problematic in Jharkhand

The majority of the states in contemporary world are a part of neoliberal[6] regime with the underlying presumption that market forces will ensure better generation and distribution of resources. But several scholars (Escobar 1995; Harvey 2003; Vanaik 1990) find such ideas to be exhorted by the developed countries in favour of the metropolitan bourgeoisie and accepted by the developing countries in the interest of semi-peripheral bourgeoisie. Whereas the high growth rates of many developing countries is a testimony to the potential of private capital, the growing inequality and deteriorating employment conditions raises concern over the distributive aspects of neoliberal growth model.[7]

Notwithstanding this fact, rapid economic growth has attracted the attention of many regional states in India including newly formed Jharkhand which was carved out of Bihar on 15 November 2000. The Jharkhand government framed the New Industrial Policy in 2001 with the aim of pursuing development through rapid industrialisation and exploitation of huge mineral reserves. Several memorandum of understanding (MoU) were signed with private players for mining and industrialisation (through mega and small projects). But the majority of the projects are lingering due to protests organised around land issues. Land acquisition has remained a contentious issue in India and several scholars have explored its perplexed forms in different regions. However, a major lacuna in the studies on dispossession in India is its apparent silence over the differences characterising the process of land dispossession in a Scheduled Area from that of a non-Scheduled Area.[8] The present chapter attempts to fill this gap by analysing cases of land dispossession in the West Singhbhum district of Jharkhand, a Fifth Scheduled Area.

In their quest to understand land acquisition, scholars like Nilsen (2010), Bedi (2013), Levien (2012), and many others have built upon Harvey's construct of ABD. Coining the term ABD, Harvey (2003:156) accepts the centrality of state in facilitating the capitalist accumulation under advanced economies. But in the post-1973 scenario, he attributes primacy to the role of financialisation. Levien (2012:940) criticises Harvey for the ambiguities associated with the characterisation of ABD and considers insufficient the latter's assertion that 'the umbilical cord that ties together accumulation by dispossession and expanded reproduction is that given by finance capital and the institutions of credit, backed, as ever, by state powers' (Harvey 2003:152). In an attempt to better explain the state's role in land acquisition, Levien defines ABD as

> The use of extra-economic coercion to expropriate means of production, subsistence or common social wealth for capital accumulation. It is not simply an economic process of over-accumulated capital seizing hold of under-commodified assets, but fundamentally a political process in which states – or other coercion wielding entities – use extra-economic force to help capitalists overcome barriers to accumulation.
>
> (Michael Levien 2012:940)

Yet another notion related to land dispossession forwarded by Levien (2015: 150) is that 'dispossession cannot be mystified' and is pursued through three basic means (i.e., coercion, material compensation, and normative persuasion). In so arguing, Levien assumes the forcible acquisition of land which is either habituated or cultivated by people.[9] However, the nature of dispossession taking place due to 'dirty industries'[10] is mystified to the extent that it escapes protests even while violating the individual property rights of the land owners. Through the empirical analysis of the three Sponge Iron Projects (SIPs), this chapter will explain how 'dispossession' can be as much mystified. The mystification also takes place on count of 'displacement' which, though inevitable in the case of mega-projects, is not necessary in the case of small projects requiring lesser land parcels. Usually, dispossession associated with dirty industries is measured in terms of environmental degradation regarded as 'negative externalities.' However, reports have also established the losses incurred by the individual land owners due to such projects (CSE 2011).

Capable of evading the official attention – or say, ignored – dispossession is not neutral and is usually tilted in the favour of industrial section.

Moreover, dispossession also comprises of the strategies of land acquisition largely crafted in accordance with the social, political, and legal milieu in which it takes place. While using 'small independent methods' for some sort of 'decentralised accumulation,' SIPs raises questions –for example, whether the industrialisation of this nature fits in the state's scheme of pursuing high growth, increased output and employment generation? The analysis of dispossession in this chapter aims at a theoretical-empirical engaged research on the 'land grab' phenomenon and draws upon the eight months of fieldwork conducted between September 2012 and April 2013. In-depth and open-ended interviews were conducted with the landowners, company officials, middlemen, political representatives, and protest leaders in addition to the observation of events like protest meetings, *dharnas*, and marches.

Socio-legal discourse governing land in West Singhbhum

West Singhbhum is one of the most backward districts of Jharkhand. Despite being rich in mineral resources, distress migration – both seasonal and permanent – has remained a major problem. A report published by the World Bank in 2007 indicates that migration in Jharkhand has increased among all the social categories between 1995 and 2005. However, migration ensures upward mobility to only one-third of the rural migrant households (WB 2007: 46). The study also records that almost 60 percent of the entire migrant household migrated due to livelihood issues. Almost 70 percent of the migration is intra-district while inter-district and inter-state migration is around 10 and 20 percent, respectively (ibid.: 46). People find employment in the legal and illegal mining sites as well as crusher plants operating in the district apart from the cement factory at Jhinkpani and SIPs. Lack of governance can be widely witnessed in the studied areas due to the absence of irrigation facilities, poor implementation of rural employment schemes (MGNREGS), lack of proper health facilities, education, and so on. Although this act of non-governance cannot be called as deliberate due to a similar situation prevailing in other parts of Jharkhand, it still plays substantial role in reducing the bargaining power of the people vis-à-vis the companies, as discussed ahead in this chapter.

However, glorifying agriculture as the most appropriate vocation will be a sham because the rurban[11] thesis finds a reverberation also in West Singhbhum (Gupta 2008). Nevertheless, the emergence of this kind of labour regime is not inevitable but a product of politics (Bernstein 2010). In West Singhbhum, like many other places, the state plays an indirect role in land alienation by nurturing apathy among the owners for their land holdings. Even if we happen to differ from the opinion that this aspect of governance has anything to do with the greater design of capital, it will be very hard for us to deny that by internalising corruption, governance has played a covert role for the benefit of capitalism.

For understanding the process of dispossession, the socio-economic profile of West Singhbhum needs to be supplanted with the legal provisions governing land. Moreover, *jury politics* has emerged as a major strategy to protest land acquisition and, hence, it will be proper to discuss briefly the laws regulating land acquisition. For our purpose, we will briefly analyse certain provisions of the Chotanagpur Tenancy Act (CNTA) 1908, the Panchayat (Extension to Scheduled Areas) Act (PESA), 1996, and the Scheduled Tribes (and other Traditional Forest Dwellers) Act, 2006, which is popularly known as Forest Rights Act (henceforth FRA).

CNTA: law to protect land or culture?

It was largely due to the Birsa revolt of 1895–1900 that the colonial authorities were forced to bring the protective legislation of CNTA restricting the sale or transfer of tribal or non-tribal land to outsiders. While the colonial administrators never compromised on the revenue to be generated, they rather took steps in 1908 to deter the alienation of land. Against this fact, one can conclude whether the Britishers were concerned about the material *basis of life* or were sensible towards the cultural aspects of Adivasi *way of life*.

The CNTA is a protective legislation applicable in the Northern and Southern part of the Chotanagpur plateau and the protective provisions exists in Section 46. Clause (1) Proviso (a) of this section makes it mandatory for the Adivasi *raiyat*[12] to receive the prior sanction of the Deputy Commissioner for the transfer or lease or sale of Adivasi land (Jerai 2012: 30). Even then, the land cannot be transferred to an Adivasi who does not reside within the jurisdiction of the same police station to which the seller belongs. Against the much-held belief that the CNTA protects only Adivasi land, Proviso (b) of the same section makes it mandatory for the Scheduled Castes or Backward classes *raiyats* to receive prior sanction of the Deputy Commissioner in case they want to sell, transfer, or lease their land. In their case, however, the buyer needs to be a person of the same caste group to which the seller belongs and reside within the same district.

However, the CNTA could not be extended to Singhbhum before 1916 due to the protest from the Hos[13] owing to the fact that the CNTA recognised individual rights in land whereas the Hos believed in community ownership (DasGupta 2011). Kolhan (comprising of a major part of Singhbhum) was recognised as a British Government Estate and the land revenue was nominal. But due to prospect of mining the area was opened to the outsiders and, subsequently, the Hos realised the need to extend CNTA to Singhbhum. Power of the state to acquire land for industrial purposes under the principle of 'eminent domain' contravened the provisions of CNTA. Hence, section 49 of the Act was amended in 1995 expanding the domain of 'public purpose' by allowing land acquisition for industrial purposes. In post-independence India, the state happened to be the prime mover for land acquisition. But ever since the amendment of section 49, the private sector has taken upon this role giving rise to litigations. Even though the judiciary has remained inconsistent in dealing with cases of land acquisition, the litigants from Scheduled Areas are still guided by the *Samatha*[14] judgment of 1997. In addition to this, their claim has also been substantiated under the PESA, 1996, and FRA, 2006.

PESA, 1996, and FRA, 2006

Regarding the decisions on developmental projects, Clause (4) sub-clause (i) of PESA says that

> The Gram Sabha or the Panchayats at the appropriate level shall be *consulted* before making the acquisition of land in the Scheduled Areas for development projects and before re-settling or rehabilitating persons affected by such projects in the Scheduled Areas; the actual planning and implementation of the projects in the Scheduled Areas shall be coordinated at the State level.
>
> (MoTA 1996, author's emphasis)

The PESA merely gives consultation rights to the Gram Sabhas as far as cases of land acquisition are concerned. In context of Jharkhand, it is argued that in order to circumvent even this minimal provision on land acquisition the government has neglected the Panchayat elections, thus denying legal status to Gram Sabhas under PESA (Sundar 2005). In yet another account, Sharan (2009) provides the details on how land alienation of the tribals has continued unabated in Jharkhand despite the Special Area Regulation (SAR) courts taking up the issue of legality of land dispossession. Hence, while PESA fails to protect the interest of Adivasis due to several bottlenecks, the last rescue by the community was sought under the FRA.

Primarily dealing with the traditional rights of the tribals and other forest dwellers upon the forest resources, the FRA also aims at protecting their culture and habitat from being disturbed. The Act bestows power upon the Gram Sabha to take decisions on land and destructive practices which can affect the culture and natural heritage of the people (FRA 2006). In fact, the Supreme Court pronounced its verdict in the *Niyamgiri* case (2012) by interpreting the sub-clause (c) of clause 5, which says that 'the habitat of forest dwelling scheduled tribe and other traditional forest dwellers is preserved from any form of destructive practices affecting their culture and natural habitat.' On 18 April 2012 the Supreme Court instructed the Odisha government to seek consent of the villagers on the legal ground under the FRA (*OMC vs MoEF 2012*). The Supreme Court specifically mentioned that

> The villagers would decide whether the proposed mining would cause harm to their religious rights of worshipping Niyam Raja at Hundaljali

> hilltop, about 10 km from the identified mining site. FRA has been enacted conferring powers on the gram sabha constituted under the Act to protect community resources, individual rights, cultural and religious rights.
>
> (Manipadma Jena 2013: 14)

Whereas these things are happening in the legal domain of land acquisition, more crude examples of dispossession can be observed in society. In the succeeding sections, we will elaborate upon the politics of dispossession by citing examples wherein the companies do not simply apply arm-twisting and coercive measures like intimidating the people with the help of police and private goons but also use persuasive measures like alluring the people into the land deal with the active help of middlemen.

Circumventing legality: cases of Kotgarh, Petteta-Bahada, and Dimbuli

Politics of dispossession acquires a different form when the governed, which also happen to be the dispossessed, are not simply a part of 'political society'[15] but also electorally significant citizens. Even though land acquisition is pretty infamous for its use of 'eminent domain' and state repression in other parts of India, the state government in Jharkhand keeps its hands off acquisition, and the industries are required to acquire land through negotiations with individual *raiyats* (Chakravorti 2010). Consequence of the limited scope for the state to use repressive tactics is reflected in the process of land acquisition, which is stealthy, intricate, and persuasive in nature, though assisted with mild coercion (i.e., arm-twisting measures).

Almost all the villages in the West Singhbhum district comprises of both Adivasi and non-Adivasi population. The non-Adivasi population largely comprises of the Gopes, Tantis, Nayaks, and others who were allowed to settle down in the Adivasi villages to fulfil the non-agricultural requirements of the latter in an unequal but symbiotic relationship. As a part of their strategy to circumvent legal contestation the companies are mainly targeting hamlets or villages having substantial non-Adivasi land supplemented by '*gair mazarua*'[16] (GM) land. Only after considering factors like land ownership pattern and village demography do the companies approach the government to notify sites for industrial development under section 49 of CNTA.

Moreover, the non-Adivasis also seem to be averse to the social domination of the Adivasis and one of the non-Adivasi respondents[17] hesitatingly mentioned that

> A lot of our land was sold by our father and uncle to the Adivasis which resulted into further misery and only ensured the domination of these *politicking* Adivasis. After selling land to the company we have been able to receive some compensation and secure a job as well which ensures regular supply of money. It is good when compared to the non-profit

Table 7.1 List of companies, their current stages of operation, and the land acquired by them

Sl. no.	*Name of company*	*Date of MoU*	*Block*	*Village/s*	*Area acquired (in acres)*	*Protesting organisation/s*	*Present status*
1	V S Dempo	6–10–2005	Manoharpur	Dimbuli	110	Gram Ganhrajya Parishad	Still acquiring land
2	Sri Sai Shraddha Metallic Pvt. Ltd.	Non-MoU	Noamundi	Kotgarh	50	Jameen Bachao Samanway Samiti (JBSS), Oomon Mahila Sangathan	Under judicial consideration after case is filed by protesting organisation
3	Horizon Loha Udyog Ltd.	26–3–2004	Noamundi	Petteta and Bahada	105	JBSS	Still Acquiring land

Source: *Government of Jharkhand, Department of Industry (available at* http://jharkhandindustry.gov.in/ (accessed on 27 May 2013)

> and risky agriculture and has improved our condition. But the company has gone back on many of its promises and they require fulfilling them also.
>
> (Field Notes, January 2013)

This narrative speaks a lot about the attitude of the non-Adivasis towards their land as well as the fellow Adivasi villagers. Typically, the non-Adivasis who have a very small landholding size also stand little chance of sustaining exclusively through agriculture and this serves as the reason behind their readiness to sell the land. Besides this, the hope of ready cash in the form of compensation and some job ensuring regular monetary supply serves as the other reason. Thus, the non-Adivasi land is found be much more easily accessed by the companies in comparison to that of the Adivasi land.

As far as the Adivasi response to the issue of land acquisition is concerned there was no visible homogeneity. This can be said as several Adivasis, like their non-Adivasi counterparts, have also sold their land in Bahada-Petteta, Dimbuli, and Kotgarh. Nevertheless, in the case of Kotgarh as well as Bahada-Petteta where the companies had to acquire Adivasi land also, they are facing litigation. However, even in their selective approach of organising protests against Adivasi land acquisition, the protestors cannot be assumed to be simply driven by the exploitation of Adivasis. For example, even though acquisition was taking place in Petteta and Bahada at very low rates of compensation (see the Table 7.2) no protest was registered as late as the year 2012. Contrary to this, despite a high compensation (by local

Table 7.2 Compensation paid by different companies in the surveyed areas of West Singhbhum

Village(s) of acquisition	*Company*	*Market price (in Rs.)*	*Compensation paid (in Rs.)*	*Year*
Dimbuli	V S Dempo	100,000	120,000	2008
Kotgarh	Sri Sai Shraddha Metallic Pvt. Ltd.	120,000	500,000	2010
Petteta and Bahada	Horizon Loha Udyog Ltd.	55,000	55,000	2004

Source: Primary Survey (2012–2013)

standards) in Kotgarh, the protest was registered and the acquisition was legally challenged.

While the protesting organisations have dragged the companies to contest the legality of their actions, they have hardly succeeded in halting the land acquisition. They have also not been able to address the daily concerns of the people by targeting bureaucratic as well as political corruption. In fact, several instances can establish the issue of corruption within the ranks of the leaders. For instance, Antu Hembrom – President of the Manki-Munda Sangh – was suspected of assisting the companies in acquiring land around Chaibasa and was publicly humiliated by the protestors. This form of resistance though acting as a symbolic threat against the collaborators of companies offers little to counter the more nuanced and structured forces of dispossession. Failure of the protestors to apply the brakes on land acquisition can be explained by looking into the role of middlemen as well as analysing the local power structure and the balance of forces.

Popularly regarded as brokers, agents, and many more synonyms, the middlemen have emerged as an inevitable agency when it comes to land acquisition. In the present cases, the middlemen are either Adivasi or non-Adivasi and engage with the company right from the acquisition of land and remain associated even after the companies start functioning. Whereas in the case of Petteta-Bahada and Kotgarh they belonged to the non-tribal groups, in the case of Dimbuli and Barajamda, they were Adivasi. The significance of a middleman's role may be discerned from the fact[18] that a Delhi-based company has acquired a substantial amount of land at merely Rs.55,000 per acre. Surprisingly, the protesting organisations pitted against the Kotgarh plant claimed that they had no clue about this abysmally low compensation even though it was happening under their nose. The middlemen are quite influential, and the villagers rarely muster the courage to decline their offers made on behalf of the companies. In many cases, the land was found to be mortgaged to the middlemen in lieu of some money borrowed by the landowners. However, the inability to repay leaves limited options for the owners other than agreeing to the offer made by the agents. Application of an arm-twisting measure can be observed in instances where despite their unwillingness to sell land many people did so because of the apprehension that once the company starts operation on their neighbouring plot their land will become infertile and useless.

Moreover, a close nexus between the Munda[19] and the middleman was observed in Petteta and Kotgarh. Yet another group of village elites feel ridiculed for being kept or left out of this nexus between the company, middlemen, and the Munda. For such people, protest acts as the means to assert themselves socially and politically. Now this question arises: Are the protest movements exclusively based in the aspiration of the excluded group of elites to assert themselves? Or are they registered out of the concern over exploitation of people? An attempt was made to find an answer to this question by analysing certain facts in their local context and found the aspirations of the excluded leader to be a major reason behind the protests. Surendra Tubid (name changed), one of the protest leaders against Kotgarh plant, in order to assert his social and political status, participated in the Panchayat elections of 2010. In addition, he enjoys a close relationship with the ex-MLA of Jagannathpur, Mr Mangal Singh Bobonga, also pitted against the land acquisition. Nevertheless, the forces for land acquisition are also 'powerful but disguised' as there exists a probable link between the ruling MLA, the middlemen, and the companies acquiring land in Bahada-Petteta and Kotgarh. This brings to the fore a situation where one group of village elite in nexus with the companies are poised against another band of village elite. Thus, the companies play upon the social cleavages to procure land even though this strategy has left the people with poor compensation but regular monetary supply through employment. Incidentally, the areas where low compensation was paid also happen to be the areas where a complex power relation exists between the forces of acquisition and protest. Having anlaysed the socio-legal discourses in which the companies adopt different strategies to acquire land, we will now discuss the community response and its intricacies.

Deciphering community response

The Adivasis respond to the cases of land acquisition through protest movements by challenging the legality of such moves on the one hand and organising popular resistance through an articulation of history, culture, and landscape on the other. Jury politics has yielded inconsistent results in the cases of land acquisition. The judicial approach is itself contingent upon the juridical discourse as well as notion of 'public purpose' while the impetus for state-led development has guided judicial pronouncements in cases like the Narmada Bachao Andolan (NBA) movement of 2000, the *Samatha* case of 1997, and the *Niyamgiri* case of 2013, which has been considered from a more liberal viewpoint as recognising people's right over resources and the autonomy to choose preferred form of development and governance.

Scholars are divided in their views about jury politics with some scholars (Nilsen 2010) stating the futility of this method while others viewing it as strategic weapon to discourage 'regimes of dispossession' (explained ahead). Despite the mixed opinion on success and failure of jury politics Adivasis have consistently challenged the legality of land acquisition by premising their claims upon protective legislations as well as the constitutional commitment of the state towards Schedule V areas. However, the most dynamic form of these imaginations is visible in the popular resistance. In the subsequent part we will analyse the nature of movements by raising the issues of perceived legal discourse and culture and identity among the Ho Adivasis of West Singhbhum.

The Hos articulate CNTA from a historical and cultural standpoint wherein landscape is located at the core of the narrative. To understand the historical trajectory of this narrative we have to understand the provisions of the Wilkinson Rules (WR) of 1837 and as reiterated by PESA, 1996. The protracted struggle by the Hos against foreign domination culminated in the drafting of the WR, ensuring autonomy in customary self-governance while incorporating the Hos in a loose administrative linkage with the colonial government. However, the Birsa rebellion of 1895–1900 led to the assurance of their rights over land by restricting the 'outsiders' from acquiring land in Scheduled Areas. The CNTA itself was cautiously adopted for Singhbhum as a plausible measure to safeguard Adivasi culture and resources from encroachment by the state. Even though the Land Acquisition Act (LAA), 1894, was invoked to acquire land elsewhere in India the state never overlooked the provisions contained in CNTA to do the same in SAs. In fact, realising the handicap which the state faced on matters of land acquisition due to this duality several amendments were brought in the CNTA in post-independence India. These amendments sanctioned the land acquisition for industrial and other 'public purposes.' But the Adivasis have always contested such provisions on the ground that the protective legislations being a part of Article 39 B and under the Ninth Schedule are not open to amendments. Their position was also vindicated by the judiciary through *Samatha* judgment of 1997. Since then, the Adivasis have been uniformly and consistently citing this verdict to contest the legality of land acquisition in SAs. While the successes been limited it has convinced the community of the legitimacy, if not legality, of their claims and emboldened them to not only indulge in jury politics but simultaneously organise people's movements. Thus, we find that the Adivasis have been selectively reiterating law in its historical and cultural connotations as well as legality of state actions.

As clear from this discussion, the various notions of law are used to strengthen the movements. Moreover, the popular notions of Adivasi identity are also reconstructed to oppose land acquisition. It is in this context that we will understand the identity of *being Ho* which arises as a more concrete and plausible method in consolidating the community response. Ethnic identity serves as a basis for collective action in anti-globalisation movements.

But the generic notion of 'Adivasi' is not as appealing to the Adivasis of West Singhbhum as their belongingness to a particular Adivasi group. Such a construction of identity has the potential to incorporate the changes pervading the society, and 'culture' is reformulated both in order to constitute as well as resist 'power' (Damodaran 2006:179). Thus, the Ho identity in the present times is framed in a manner which is not only informed by the social changes pervading their societies but also by the rudimentary cultural practices which they have retained even now. Equally important is the public memory of the long history of struggles against predatory forces that did not simply target their land but the 'landscape.' Therefore, in a departure with the homogeneity of Adivasi identity the Hos identify themselves on the basis of their particular repertoire of history, culture, and landscape. At one point of time, the identity of being a Ho was so prominent that it resulted into a demand for the secession of Kolhan.[20] This dynamic construction of identity also results into formulating different modalities of protest.[21] Moreover, the act of serving petitions to the state Governor specifies the protestors' awareness of law and constitutionality of protests. Article 244 of the constitution endows upon the Governors powers to supersede any provisions made by state government in its application to Scheduled Areas. The Governor is considered the guardian of state's tribal population and is responsible for protecting their land, socio-cultural ethos, and also the people themselves from money-lenders.

Another noteworthy feature is the method of protest by the Adivasi community in most of the cases. The symbolic presence of traditional weapons like bow and arrows, battle axe, etc. during the protests is common. Even though not mandated by the constitutional means of protest which sanctions only unarmed gathering, the Adivasis consider this method to be a token of the Adivasi *way of life* and, hence, not be seen in contravention of the constitution. Mr Mukesh Birua, Vice-President of the *Akhil Bhartiya Adivasi Mahasabha*, stated that

> The carrying of traditional arms derives largely from the Adivasis' historical tendency to rebel against their exploiters. However, under the modern state this action has the token importance for their unique cultural practices. On the other hand, it also reminds the state of the disregard which has been meted out to them for being on the fringe of the greater Indian society.
>
> (Interview conducted on 4 January 2012 during pilot survey)

Thus, notwithstanding its presumed illegality, the Adivasis' engagement with the state is an attempt to test the state's sensibility to a section whose *way of life* transcends a few norms of modern citizenry. The Adivasi way of protest should be, hence, understood not as a threat to state's legitimacy but as a challenge which reinforces the need for the latter to revisit its commitment towards the former.

Conclusion

In the preceding sections, an analysis of the politics of dispossession shows how the companies apply different tactics to circumvent the legal provisions applicable in the scheduled area of West Singhbhum. In addition to this, they also play upon the political and economic cleavages in the social domain to access the land through persuasive measures. This persuasion, however, is not entirely based upon the legitimate portrayal of industrialisation as an alternative to agriculture. In fact, it is arm-twisting in nature as the owners are coerced to sell their land not only by capitalist manoeuvrings but also due to the non-governance of the state. One arrives at the conclusion based on the process of land acquisition that the Adivasi society has several fault lines which are available to the external forces for exploitation. In continuity with this narrative we also realise that a deep sense of local identity encompasses the discourse on people's protest against land acquisition. However, even the movements are not devoid of difficulties and many times serve as a tool for its leaders to create space for themselves in larger state politics. The local movements are better suited to identify the local actors assisting the forces of dispossession while keeping the immediate livelihood and welfare concern of the people alongside its core demands. But they simultaneously lack the ability to provide a broader framework within which the energy of the community can be tapped to challenge land acquisition at least at the district level. This chapter helps to analyse the process of land acquisition and provide a picture of the local politics, demographic realities, and the nature of protest movements.

Even though we have not discussed the issue from the state's perspective, the framework for the state to engage with the governance of SAs is not entirely absent. We have already discussed some of the laws which are applicable and tools of governance available to ensure the greater inclusion of the Adivasi communities in the SAs. In the post-liberalisation period, the Indian state cannot anymore camouflage the mass dispossession of the Adivasi population living in the SAs under the qualified moral terminology of 'public purpose.' The turf lays bare and the Adivasi community are directly posited against the private players while the former interrogate the Indian state's commitment to their culture and identity. As evident from the preceding discussion, the legal ambivalences have retained the possibility of misuse by the corporate forces. The inconsistent approach of the judiciary in dealing with cases of land acquisition in SAs has left the community confused. Even as the communities subscribe to the legal methods of protest, they are not quite sure about its outcome. This perplexed legal discourse shall be transformed, keeping in view the interest of the communities inhabiting the SAs. The demand of the time is to bring the laws dealing with land acquisition in conformity with laws like PESA and FRA. Further rights should be divulged to the communities to decide on the course of development by providing them autonomous self-governing institutions. Against this backdrop, the chapter proposes that Section 49 of CNTA should be done away with. Instead of it, a mechanism should be put in place which makes mandatory the consent of PESA Gram Sabhas for any industrial or mining projects. This is necessary not only to reduce the 'empty spaces' marked with confusion but also re-establish the faith of cultural minorities in the body politic called India.

Notes

1 Quoting D Cosgrove (1988) Vinita Damodaran (2006: 181) defines landscape as a 'socio-historical construct a way of seeing projected onto the land which has its own techniques and which articulates a particular way of experiencing a relationship with nature.'

2 Jury politics is the strategy adopted by protesting organisations to contest the legality of land acquisition by approaching the judiciary.

3 Karl Marx (1976: 874–875) argues that 'so-called primitive accumulation, therefore, is nothing else than the historical process of divorcing the producer from the means of production.' The usage of 'non-economic means' in this process is implicit in the word 'robbed' used by Marx.

4 Luxemburg (as quoted in de Angelis 2001) argues that the poor wage rates of the workers leave them with little surplus to purchase the commodities created by capitalists. This creates a situation of 'underconsumption' in the domestic market and forces the Capitalists to the find solution in an external market which can sustain the reproduction of capital by acting as a viable market. For Luxemburg, this market was non-capitalist and its sustenance as such was required by the colonising imperial power to ensure a safe market. Although Harvey accepts this argument, he relies upon the 'overaccumulation' theory to explain the present scenario. According to Harvey, after the optimum exploitation of domestic resources and exhausting the chances for profitable reinvestment, the capitalists look for avenues abroad for investing their accumulated wealth. However, he accepts that Britain in the context of India during the 19th century and earlier part of 20th century applied a 'underconsumption' method and it proved to be disastrous due to its reliance upon the 'territorial logic' instead of 'capital logic' which always asks for more accumulation.

5 Rate of accumulation by dispossession is calculated by subtracting the compensation given to the original owners of the land from the money which the capitalist receives after making the intended change in land use. Levien (2012) states that the rate is quite high and is highest when developed for real estate purposes.

6 The term 'neoliberalism' is used here to infer a regime where the state as an institution plays an active part by not only allowing market forces to freely produce and allocate goods and services but also facilitate them to overcome non-economic hindrances in performing this task.

7 This model emphasises upon the high rate of economic growth led by the private sector and the state's role is reduced to controlling the rate of inflation through financial decisions. This model is a direct replacement of import substitution model with increased impetus to export-led production scenario.

8 Scholars like Amita Baviskar (1995), Alf Gunvald Nilsen (2010) and several others are quite comprehensive in understanding the social, economic, and political niceties in the areas witnessing dispossession. But what has evaded their attention is the specific nature of laws governing land regime in Scheduled Areas. Up to a certain extent these vexed issues were addressed by Nandini Sundar (2009) through her edited work on Jharkhand, which explores the issue of legality of

land dispossession. Specific studies capturing the nuances of land alienation in a Scheduled Area as compared to that in a non-Scheduled Area are still awaited. Sujit Kumar (2016) 'People's response to Land Dispossession: Comparative analysis of Movements across India' in Varsha Bhagat-Ganguly (ed.) *Land Rights in India: Movements, Policies and Challenges* is an attempt in filling this void.

9 This explanation for using the 'demystified nature of dispossession' came up during my personal communication with the author.

10 'Dirty or Pollution-intensive' industries are regarded by Mani and Wheeler (1997:4) as those having 'low elasticities of substitution between the use of the environment and other productive factors.' The authors identify five sectors viz. iron and steel, non-ferrous metals, industrial chemicals, pulp and paper, and non-metallic mineral products, which 'have incurred high levels of abatement expenditure per unit of output' and are also intensive in capital, energy, and land (ibid.: 5). The operating of and proposed construction of Sponge Iron Industries in West Singhbhum fall within this definition.

11 According to Dipankar Gupta (2008) it is a misconceived notion that most of the people in rural areas are associated with agricultural works. He rather argues that a substantial workforce, maybe even majority, in rural areas are engaged in non-agricultural activities and this characteristic of rural areas is termed as 'rurban.'

12 A *raiyat* is a tenant who owns a right to land because he/she herself/himself, through family members or with help of labourers, cultivate a land.

13 Adivasi groups, primarily, residing in West Singhbhum, East Singhbhum, and Saraikela Kharsawan districts of Jharkhand. They can also be found in the neighbouring areas of Odisha, West Bengal, and Madhya Pradesh. The Hos claim to be drawing their lineage from the same ancestors as the Mundas.

14 Ruling out the prospect of land acquisition in the Scheduled Areas, the Supreme Court pronounced that even the private mining companies will be considered as a non-tribal person as far as land acquisition in the Scheduled Areas is concerned.

15 Partha Chatterjee (2005) uses this term to imply the people who, even though citizens, are not legally entitled to state benefits because of their illegal inhabitation. To ensure state benefits as well as their existence, the inhabitants of political society have to negotiate frequently with the political representatives resulting into a vote-benefit trade-off.

16 GM land is the common village land and is legally owned by the government. However, the inhabitants/occupants enjoy usufructuary rights which are temporary but customary in nature.

17 Bhuju Nayak (name changed) of Noangaon expressed satisfaction with the kind of employment which he got in lieu of selling land to the company. But he wants the company to arrange for things like village roads, drinking water, electricity, etc. which was promised as per the sale deed.

18 In the Petetta and Bahada villages of Noamundi, Block Horizon Loha Udyog, Global Primate Ltd, Prakash Industries, etc. have acquired both tribal and non-tribal raiyati land at a very low compensation.

19 A Munda is a customary village headman in a Ho Adivasi society. Usually hereditary in nature, a person from another family can also be appointed as village Munda by the District Collector. A *hukuk-nama* (record of rights) is issued mentioning the revenue and civil powers of the Munda.

20 The President of *Kolhan Raksha Sangh*, Mr K.C. Hembrom, who was earlier associated with Congress Party, later flouted the organisation during the 1980s. He demanded the secession of Kolhan from the Indian Union on the basis of the former being an autonomous British government estate which was never lawfully acceded to India.

21 In his essay 'Changing Modalities of Ho Social Protest in Colonial Singhbhum' in N K Das (ed.) *Adivasi Unrest and Rights of Tribes in Contemporary India*,

Asoka K Sen (2014) argues that the social response among the Hos, which varied from being 'silent to militant and finally legalism' during the entire span of colonial rule, 'was historically conditioned by shifting consciousness of collective self that forced them to surrender bow-arrow-battle axe and tread the path of peaceful protest.'

References

Angelis, M.D. 2001. 'Marx and Primitive Accumulation: The Continuous Character of Capital's "Enclosures".' *The Commoner*, 2: 1–22.

Baviskar, A. 1995. *In the Belly of the River: Tribal Conflicts Over Development in the Narmada Valley*. New Delhi: Oxford University Press.

Bedi, H.P. 2013. 'Special Economic Zones: National Land Challenges, Localized Protest.' *Contemporary South Asia*, 22(1): 619–647.

Bedi, H.P. and Tillin, L. 2015. 'Inter-State Competition, Land Conflicts and Resistance in India.' *Oxford Development Studies*, 43(2): 194–211.

Bernstein, H. 2010. *Class Dynamics of Agrarian Change*. Halifax: Fernwood Publishing.

Centre for Science and Environment. 2011. *Sponge Iron Industry: The Regulatory Challenge*. Available at: www.cseindia.org/

Chakravorti, T. 2010. 'No Land Acquisition by State Administration: Jharkhand.' *Business Standard*, Ranchi, August 24.

Chatterjee, P. 2005. *The Politics of the Governed: Reflections on Popular Politics in Most of the World*. New Delhi: Permanent Black.

Cosgrove, D. and Daniels, S. (eds.). 1988. *The Iconography of the Landscape* (pp. 1–8). Cambridge: Cambridge University Press.

Damodaran, V. 2006. 'The Politics of Marginality and the Construction of Indigeneity in Chotanagpur.' *Postcolonial Studies*, 9(2): 179–196.

DasGupta, S. 2011. *Adivasis and the Raj: Socio-Economic Transition of the Hos, 1820–1932*. Hyderabad: Orient Blackswan.

Escobar, A. 1995. *Encountering Development: The Making and Unmaking of the Third World*. Princeton: Princeton University Press.

FRA. 2006. MoTA, GoI. https://tribal.nic.in/FRA/data/FRARulesBook.pdf

Glassman, J. 2006. 'Primitive Accumulation, Accumulation by Dispossession, Accumulation by "Extra-Economic" Means.' *Progress in Human Geography*, 30(5): 608–625.

Government of India. 2013. *Right to Fair Compensation and Transparency in Land Acquisition, Rehabilitation and Resettlement*. New Delhi: Ministry of Law and Justice.

Gupta, D. 2008. 'The Changing Villager.' *Seminar*, 589: 47–50.

Harvey, D. 2003. *The New Imperialism*. Oxford: Oxford University Press.

Jena, M. 2013. 'Voices From Niyamgiri.' *Economic and Political Weekly*, 48(36): 14–16.

Jerai, R. 2012. *Adivasi Adhikar: Sambandhit Niyam, Adhiniyam tatha Ghosnaon ka Sankalan*. West Singhbhum: JOHAR.

Kumar, S. 2016. 'People's Response to Land Dispossession: Comparative Analysis of Movements Across India.' In V.B. Ganguly (Ed.), *Land Rights in India: Policies, Movements and Challenges* (pp. 215–229). New Delhi: Routledge.

Levien, M. 2012. 'The Land Question: Special Economic Zones and the Political Economy of Dispossession in India.' *The Journal of Peasant Studies*, 39(3–4): 933–969.

Levien, M. 2015. 'From Primitive Accumulation to Regimes of Dispossession: Six Theses on India's Land Question.' *Economic and Political Weekly*, 50(22): 146–157.
Mani, M. and Wheeler, D. 1997. 'In Search of Pollution Havens? Dirty Industries in the World Economy, 1960–1995.' OECD Workshop on *Pollution Havens and Pollution Halos*, PRDEI.
Marx, K. 1976. *Capital: A Critique of Political Economy*, Vol. I. London: Penguin Classics.
MoTA. 1996. *Government of India*. https://tribal.nic.in/actRules/PESA.pdf
Nilsen, A.G. 2010. *Dispossession and Resistance in India: The River and Its Rage*. London: Routledge.
Sen, A.K. 2014. 'Changing Modalities of Ho Social Protest in Colonial Singhbhum.' In K.K. Mishra and N. K. Das (Eds.), *Dissent, Discrimination and Dispossession: Tribal Movements in Contemporary India* (pp. 93–112). New Delhi: IGRMS and Manohar.
Sharan, R. 2009. 'Alienation and Restoration of Tribal Land in Jharkhand.' In N. Sundar (Ed.), *Legal Grounds: Natural Resources, Identity, and the Law in Jharkhand* (pp. 82–112). New Delhi: Oxford University Press.
Sundar, N. 2005. '"Custom" and "Democracy" in Jharkhand.' *Economic and Political Weekly*, 40(41): 4430–4434.
Sundar, N. 2009. 'Laws, Policies, and Practices in Jharkhand.' In N. Sundar (Ed.), *Legal Grounds: Natural Resources, Identity, and the Law in Jharkhand* (pp. 1–29). New Delhi: Oxford University Press.
Vanaik, A. 1990. *The Painful Transition: Bourgeois Democracy in India*. New York: Verso.
World Bank. 2007. *Jharkhand: Addressing the Challenges of Inclusive Development*. Available at: http://siteresources.worldbank.org/SOUTHASIAEXT/Resources/223546-1181699473021/3876782-1181699502708/fullreport.pdf (accessed on 16 April 2018).

8 Historical wrongs and forest rights

Nascent jurisprudence on FRA and participatory evidence making

Shomona Khanna

Introduction

That forests in India have for centuries been the abode of indigenous and forest-dwelling communities who have evolved methods of conservation, coexistence, and complex patterns of livelihood, is a well-documented fact. That the British colonial state, through a devious mix of legislation, centralised governance, coercion, and complicity established an architecture of forest laws across much of the country, taking over vast tracts of forests to provide timber and other raw material for its industrial machine, is also well known. The pre-existing rights and usages of forest dwelling communities remained unrecognised for a greater part, most of them continuing in blissful ignorance with life as usual until harsh contact with the colonial administration, for one reason or other, brought the *fait accompli* to their knowledge, often too late. Post-independence, one would have expected this clearly unjust legal regimen to shift. Far from it. The forest laws and administration thereof became even more stringent and centralised, while the existence of forest-dwelling communities in these forests became a 'problem' which needed to be solved through 'eviction' of 'encroachments.'

Recent studies point to the clear juxtaposition of the most dense forests in the country with the Scheduled Areas where Adivasi populations are concentrated. It is also well established that the Scheduled Tribes and other semi-tribal populations[1] outside the Scheduled Areas are found in close proximity to forest lands. Hence, the structures of forest governance and the recognition of forest rights of such populations is of integral importance to an understanding of how the law impacts the lives of Adivasi and forest-dwelling communities, both inside and outside the Scheduled Areas.

The present chapter[2] explores the legal remedies under colonial and post-independence forest laws available to such forest-dwelling communities, and their inadequacy in challenging the assault on traditional rights on such a massive scale. It examines how the approach to forest governance has seen a paradigm shift with the enactment of the Scheduled Tribes and Other Traditional Forest Dwellers (Recognition of Forest Rights) Act, 2006 (henceforth 'Forest Rights Act' or 'FRA'), with special attention to the procedures and processes established for the purpose of its implementation under the

Scheduled Tribes and Other Traditional Forest Dwellers (Recognition of Forest Rights) Rules, 2008 (henceforth 'Forest Rights Rules').

In particular, the chapter examines the nature of evidence and evidentiary rules which the FRA seeks to rely upon, the complexities arising out of operationalisation of such evidentiary rules in a system of forest administration based on colonial legal architectures, and the compounding of such complexity by the digital revolution. Through this examination, the chapter seeks to demonstrate the dramatic shift in the processes and procedures for recognition of forest rights by making such processes relevant and accessible to the Adivasi and forest-dwelling communities, resulting in a sea change in the administration of justice itself.

Forest laws in India: a snapshot

The unambiguous objective for declaration of forest lands, and the establishment of Forest Departments to administer these forests, was to ensure regular supply of timber for expansion of industrialisation both in England and India.

The Forest Act of 1865 (Act No. VII of 1865), the first forest legislation in India, provided that the notification by the Governor General of India of 'government forests' on 'land covered with trees, brushwood or jungle . . . shall not abridge or affect any existing rights of individuals and communities' (Section 2). It proceeded to proscribe all manner of such rights, including cultivation, extraction, use of grass and minor forest produce, grazing of cattle, use of water bodies, and so on. The focus of the statute was on the preservation and management of timber. While infringement of the prohibitions under the law invited search, seizure, and arrest, there was no statutory remedy for persons whose rights had been wrongfully proscribed. Clearly, such remedies were to be exercised in the domain of civil law *outside* of this statute.

This statute was replaced by the Indian Forest Act, 1878, providing the framework for the Indian Forest Act, 1927, which remains in force today. The 1878 Act was a more complex and comprehensive law, creating different categories of forests based upon their usefulness and productivity for the colonial state (reserve forests, protected forests, village forests, and private forests), and establishing its proprietary right over such forests. The Declaration of Reserve Forests (RF), over lands which were the most valuable to the state in terms of timber and therefore inviting the most stringent controls, involved a three-step process as under:

1 Issue of a *notification of intention* to declare a certain area as RF, giving its geographical boundaries.
2 A *Forest Settlement Officer* (FSO), specially appointed for the purpose, to receive, examine, and decide claims submitted by persons having pre-existing rights in the said area. Having arrived at a conclusion regarding

the nature of such rights, the FSO could either exclude the area on which such rights are claimed from the RF, or acquire these rights under the Land Acquisition Act, 1894, or award compensation. Under the 1878 statute, the FSO could also allow certain rights (such as grazing, easement, right of way, etc.) to continue to the extent recorded (Sections 13, 14, 15), but this power has been significantly curtailed under the 1927 Act.

3 *Final notification* of the RF by the local government, specifying the boundary marks and limits of the forest. This notification was issued only after the statutory period for appeal had expired. After the final notification was issued, any rights inside such RF which had not been specifically permitted, stood 'extinguished' (Section 9).

During this enquiry, the FSO determined 'the existence of any rights . . . so far as the same may be ascertainable from the records of Government and the evidence of any persons likely to be acquainted with the same'(Section 7). Towards this end, the officer was also vested with the powers of a civil court and the power to enter upon any land himself or through an authorised officer, for demarcating the land and making a map. In practice, however, the affected communities were expected to proactively seek out the FSO, rather than the other way around.

The declaration of Protected Forests (PF) was simpler. Although the law provided that 'no such notification shall be made unless the nature and extent of the rights of Government and private persons in or over the forest land or wasteland have been enquired into and recorded' it also allowed the local government to declare a PF without undertaking a settlement process, as long as existing rights of individuals and communities are not abridged. However, it was also provided that every such record shall be presumed to be correct until the contrary is proved (Section 28). Again, the burden was on the forest dwellers to assert their rights and challenge such presumptions.

Violations of proscribed activities in such forests were defined as 'forest offences,' inviting harsh punishments, including imprisonment, seizure of property, and monetary penalties. Scrutiny of the oppressive nature of the criminal law provisions under this law, and the existing 1927 Act, must await another opportunity. Suffice to say that the severity of these provisions violates a number of basic principles of criminal jurisprudence, including due process and presumption of innocence.

This same architecture of forest law has been adopted under the Indian Forest Act, 1927, and in the various state forest laws which emerged after independence. The three-step settlement process has also been adopted under the Wildlife Protection Act, 1972, for the declaration of National Parks and Wildlife Sanctuaries.

It is now an accepted fact that these high-minded provisions for 'settlement of pre-existing rights' were followed in the breach, barring a few exceptions such as in Uttarakhand,[3] Himachal Pradesh,[4] and Jharkhand.[5] Vast swathes of forests in the Central Indian tribal belts remained unsurveyed, with the terminology 'undemarcated protected forests' even entering official parlance. Indeed, the state legislatures of Orissa and Madhya Pradesh brought amendments to the central legislation permitting the declaration of 'deemed forests' where, by definition, no procedure for settlement or recognition of rights was necessary.[6] The initial optimism generated in the early 1990s by the government scheme of Joint Forest Management (JFM) quickly unravelled after it became clear that the state forest departments had no intention of including forest-dwelling communities in the process of decision-making, and were only interested in the subsidised labour they could provide (Lele 2014).

From time to time, forest dwellers found themselves punished by forest officials for going about their normal lives, but these practices did not result in any systematic displacement or dislocation, even becoming normalised over the years. The forest guard's visit to the village to feast on poultry and indigenous liquor has become part of the folklore and literature emerging from these regions,[7] while the periodic descent of such visits into torture and rape of the forest dwellers have also been well documented (CSD 2003). However, when these very forest lands were required for large development projects or mineral mining, the presence of traditional forest dwellers in these lands became more than a mere inconvenience. Tribals and forest dwellers who had been living in these lands for centuries suddenly found that their traditional rights had been 'extinguished' decades ago; labelled as 'encroachers' on government property, these forest dwellers were unceremoniously and often violently evicted to make room for the temples of modern India.

Courting justice: coming up empty

In one such scenario, forest dwellers in 433 villages within Dudhi and Robertsganj tehsils of Mirzapur district, Uttar Pradesh suddenly found themselves on the wrong side of the law as a result of a proposed NTPC[8] project. Several letter petitions were filed in the Indian Supreme Court by the Banwasi Seva Ashram, stating that the rights of Adivasis in the forests have not been settled, including their long-standing cultivations in and around their villages, as well their customary and traditional rights to forest produce.

The litigation has a long and chequered history, but it is useful to examine the detailed directions passed by the Supreme Court in 1986,[9] which proceeded within the existing legislative architecture under the Indian Forest Act, 1927. The approach of the otherwise well-meaning Supreme Court greatly restricted the nature of relief that it was capable of providing to the forest dwellers.

For one thing, the court categorically excluded from its protective orders those forest dwellers in forests where the final notification of the RF had been issued (under Section 20 of the 1927 Act), stating 'it is open to the claimants to establish their rights, if any, in any other appropriate proceeding.

We express no opinion about the maintainability of such claims' (ibid.at para 10(1)). Under the extant law there was simply no remedy at all, given that the 1927 Act 'extinguishes' rights of those who have not filed claims/ objections/appeals within the statutory period. Indeed, to expect forest dwellers, who have been unable to file claims before the FSO, to approach civil courts with suits under the Civil Procedure Code, was nothing short of cruelty. The inability of the Adivasi and forest-dwelling communities to even comprehend, leave alone navigate, the adversarial dispute resolution mechanisms entrenched in the colonial justice system remained unacknowledged, and hence unaddressed.

Be that as it may, detailed directions were issued by the Supreme Court regarding forest dwellers in forest lands where only the notification of intention (under Section 4) had been issued, including the following:

- Extension of time for filing of claims before the FSO (which had long expired under the statute).
- Wide publicity to be given, including through beat of drums, to the process and also to the geographical area involved, and also its demarcation on the ground with pillars/stone piles/markings on trees.
- Protection from dispossession of anyone until the process is complete.
- All decisions on claims taken by the FSO would be scrutinised as appeals, whether an appeal is filed or not.
- Appointment of five additional District Judges, who would be located in the five relevant locations to attend to appeals.
- Once the claim is approved, a title deed to be given to the claimant.
- Oversight of the process by a court-appointed high-powered committee.[10]

These directions demonstrated the court's obdurate, and quite misplaced, faith in the existing administrative structures as well as in the judiciary itself. Indeed, the court made no observation or direction regarding the nature of evidence which could be produced in support of claims, only making a concession towards the vulnerability of the forest dwellers within this system by directing that free legal aid will be provided by the state legal services authority.[11]

Even while these directions were being put into place, and while the writ petition was still pending, the NTPC started work on the proposed power project. Instead of acknowledging that these actions constitute an encroachment upon the rights of the forest dwellers bordering on contempt of court, the Court proceeded to make a compromise in the 'interest of the nation' as electricity is considered inevitable for national development – and exempted the forest land required by NTPC from the 'ban on dispossession.'[12] As a safeguard, it was merely required that dispossession will be done in the presence of the committee, and records would be maintained of the nature of rights exercised by the person dispossessed, for future reference.

This approach is a reflection of the failure of the Court to understand the symbiotic relationship of forest-dwelling communities to their lands. It is also contrary to the principle of 'free prior informed consent,' which forms part of numerous international agreements to which India is a party, such as the United Nations Declaration on the Rights of Indigenous Peoples (2007).

Information is not readily available on what happened to the settlement process in this particular case thereafter. However, the directions issued in this judgment clearly provided no encouragement to other Adivasi and forest-dwelling communities, who may have considered approaching the courts for the protection of their historical and traditional rights over the forest lands. The benevolent approach of the court towards 'laches' could not supplant the burden on forest dwellers to establish their claims for forest rights and their territorial domains through serpentine processes under the existing forest laws. As a result, in spite of the laborious efforts of the Supreme Court to establish these mechanisms for the benefit of the petitioners before it, the judgment did not create a judicial precedent sufficiently persuasive for the millions of other similarly placed forest dwellers to approach the justice system. Nor did it reduce the mistrust in the justice system borne out of decades of lived experience.

Early shifts in forest policy towards forest governance

The National Forest Policy 1988,[13] replacing the forest policy of 1952, marked the first shift in state policy towards Adivasis and forest dwellers. It acknowledged that these communities share a 'symbiotic relationship' with the forests, including their traditional and customary livelihood practices.[14]

In 1989, Dr B.D. Sharma, Commissioner for Scheduled Tribes and Scheduled Castes, presented his report to the President of India,[15] wherein he documented the myriad atrocities being committed against Adivasi and forest-dwelling communities across India as a result of the forest law regime. The report described the complete failure to settle rights during forest reservation in colonial and post-colonial India, and how the state governments have ignored the 'constitutional provisions for protection of tribal people as also their human rights.' It drew attention to the criminalisation of entire communities in the tribal areas, calling it the darkest blot on the liberal tradition of our country. The report also provided a detailed framework for the resolution of this historical wrong through a complete overhaul of the forest governance mechanisms in the country's forests and a paradigm shift in the mechanisms for the settlement of pre-existing forest rights, which would be participatory, transparent, accountable, and also accessible.

The central government, in an effort to address the concerns of forest-dwelling communities in a holistic manner, responded with a set of central circulars which have commonly come to be known as the '1990 guidelines.'[16] These guidelines made several important advancements towards the democratisation of forest governance, establishing the groundwork for the Forest Rights Act which came almost three decades later, including the following:

1 Enabling the state governments to re-open the process of settlement of rights, the first circular paved the way for hundreds of thousands of forest dwellers who were otherwise barred by myriad legal barriers under the 1878 and 1927 statutes, such as statutory limitation, the doctrine of laches, the legal extinguishment of their rights, and so on.[17]
2 Instead of relying upon the process delineated in the Indian Forest Act, as the Supreme Court had done in the *Banwasi Seva Ashram* case, the guidelines proposed a new mechanism for settlement of rights involving the Gram Sabhas as well as a multi-department committee at the local level.
3 New forms of evidence in support of claims were permitted, including 'preliminary offence reports'[18] recording forest offences under the extant forest laws.

Although these guidelines, in providing for participatory rights settlement mechanisms, marked progress in the right direction, they also paradoxically reflected a patronising approach of a benevolent state towards uplift of oppressed classes. The guidelines repeatedly describe forest dwellers as 'encroachers,' and the settlement of their legal rights as the 'regularisation of encroachments.' With use of such negative terminology at the outset, the initiative soon floundered in bureaucratic quagmires, such as the complete domination of the decision-making process by the state Forest Departments. Even where the state governments overcame these barriers to arrive at decisions to recognise rights, these decisions needed approval of the central government under the Forest Conservation Act, 1980, and were stymied by unconscionable demands for payments of 'compensatory afforestation,' and later 'net present value.' Despite the enthusiasm with which these guidelines were welcomed by social movements as a shift towards democratising forest governance, the rights recognition process under the 1990 guidelines made very little progress (*Pradip Prabhu and Ors. vs. State of Maharashtra and Ors.* 1995).[19]

With the judgments and orders passed by the Indian Supreme Court in the *Godavarman case*,[20] the process came to a complete standstill. Indeed, directions of the Supreme Court came to be misrepresented by the Union government as eviction orders in 2002, leading to violent eviction drives in many parts of the country, until social movements managed to get the evictions stopped (Khanna 2014). However, the grant of formal titles, as had been proposed by the Commissioner for SCs and STs in 1989, could not be resumed.

The Forest Rights Act

Much has been written about the processes and ideations which culminated in the enactment of the Forest Rights Act in 2006 (Sarin 2014). Since the

Act came into force, and until February 2019, about 1.88 million individual forest rights and 76,126 community rights extending over approximately 12.74 million acres of forest land have been granted (MoTA 2019). While many of these forest rights have been recognised in Scheduled Areas, it is important to state that the beneficial impact has been experienced by large numbers of Adivasi and non-Adivasi forest dwellers living outside of Scheduled Areas as well.

These results are unprecedented across the world, even while many estimates indicate that the rights recognition process is far from achieving its full potential (Rights and Resources Initiative 2015).[21] How did this happen? To fully understand the nature of this legislation, it is important to highlight some of its most critical features:

1 Enacted by the Union Parliament, with carefully crafted *non-obstante* clauses preceding the rights-vesting provision, the FRA is a 'special' legislation containing within it the necessary force of authority to invert the complex web of extant forest laws, both at the central and the state level. The statute, accordingly, has enabled the near total replacement of condescending terminology such as 'encroachers,' with the more accurate description of forest dwellers as 'right holders.' This reflection of the statutory paradigm shift in everyday perception of the relationship between forest dwellers and the forests has had far-reaching consequences.
2 A detailed Preamble foregrounds the foundational principles of the statute, which includes the acknowledgement that the forest dwellers in this country have suffered 'historical injustice,' that such forest dwellers are 'part of the forest ecosystem' and their relationship with the forest is necessary for the survival and preservation of the forests, while ensuring their traditional livelihoods.
3 The benefits of the statute are not restricted to the Scheduled Areas or to the Scheduled Tribes, in acknowledgement of the reality that there are significant Adivasi populations outside of the constitutionally designated Scheduled Areas. Other non-tribal and semi-tribal communities which have become integrated into the Adivasi culture, economy, and society through decades of integration as forest dwellers are also sought to be included. The governance framework grounded in constitutional and statutory provisions, which till now was restricted in geographical application exclusively to Scheduled Areas, is sought to be extended more realistically outside these areas to other Adivasi and forest-dwelling communities as well.[22]
4 The statute lists a variety of 'forest rights' which include the right to cultivation and habitation (often referred to as *individual rights*) as well as rights to minor forest produce, usufructuary rights, and rights to fishing, grazing, and so on (described as *community rights*). At the heart of the legislation is the right to protect, preserve, conserve, and manage the

'community forest resource' (CFR), for both livelihood and conservation, with the Gram Sabha actively spearheading this process.

5 A three-tier mechanism for decision-making is created, which is a judicious mix of community involvement and administrative oversight. As a first step, claims for forest rights are processed by the Gram Sabha at the village/hamlet level, and based upon inputs received from its Forest Rights Committee, the Gram Sabha passes resolutions. The definition of Gram Sabha as applicable to the Scheduled Areas under PESA, being the Gram Sabha at the hamlet level, is extended for the purpose of this Act to all areas where forest rights are to be recognised, thus extending the benefit of a governance model which was restricted to Scheduled Areas to other areas inhabited by tribals and forest dwellers. In the second stage, the resolutions of the Gram Sabha which are recommendatory in nature, are forwarded to a multi-department committee at the sub-division level, where they are consolidated. Finally, these are forwarded to the District Level Committee, which takes a final decision.

Both the SDLC and the DLC have officers from state revenue, forest and tribal departments, as well as members from the Panchayats at the sub-division and district level, respectively, thus ensuring that they are not dominated by any one stakeholder. Representation of women at all levels is another important requirement.

6 Finally, the statute and the rules framed under it provide a completely different approach to the evidentiary requirements for the recognition of forest rights through this three-tier process. These provisions will be examined in further detail in a later section.

Given its core characteristics described here, the Forest Rights Act is an unnatural fit with the existing forest law regime. In very fundamental ways, this statute displaces state monopoly on the governance of forest lands, over forest resources, their conservation and use for livelihood, and even over decision-making regarding who is eligible to thus displace it. Predictably, the law has been met with much hostility in the last eleven years since its implementation commenced, often from surprising loci.[23] Efforts to subvert the law in multiple mires of bureaucratic interpretation have also been unrelenting. However, through a combination of factors, which it is perhaps too early to fairly assess, the implementation of this law has continued to gain ground. As demonstrated by the analysis in the next section, the basic paradigm shift which this law embodies has resulted in a wealth of innovative approaches at the state level under the watchful eye of the central government through the nodal ministry.[24]

Innovations in evidence and evidence gathering under the Forest Rights Act

As the examination of the *Banwasi Seva Ashram* case demonstrates, while procedures for recognition and/or settlement of forest rights exist under the

1927 Act, these are unmistakably located within the mainstream paradigm of justice and its administration. This applies equally to the administrative processes undertaken by the FSO, and also the legal principles which permeate these processes. The 1927 Act placed an inordinate burden on forest dwellers to activate their rights or lose them forever, and it drew strict boundaries of limitation on the right to activate the redressal mechanism. Failure to activate such processes within the tight time frames provided under the law attracted onerous consequences. Those few who managed to approach the redressal mechanism found themselves further crushed under burden of proof standards drawn from the mainstream justice system, with a heavy reliance upon written documentation and records. The dice were loaded from the start against the Adivasis and forest dwellers within such an administrative and justice delivery mechanism.

In contrast to the Indian Forest Act of 1927, the principles and procedures under the Forest Rights Act and Rules surmount the restrictive parameters with regard to both procedures for determination of rights, as well as the evidence which may be relied upon to substantiate claims. While it may be difficult to describe the many departures made by the FRA from the dominant administration of justice approach, it would be useful to consider one such element in some detail, namely, the requirements relating to evidence in support of forest rights claims.

Types of evidence

The FRA consciously enables the claimants to produce diverse forms of evidence in support of their claims, taking into account the fact that forest-dwelling communities are primarily rural, and many of them have not transitioned to modern systems of written recordkeeping, relying heavily on customary traditions based on trust. It also acknowledges the historical processes through which even the records which may existed have been destroyed, damaged, or lost in over a century of oppressive forest management regimes.

A detailed list of such evidence is provided in Rule 13 of the Forest Rights Rules, and can be divided into the following categories:

- *Written/documentary evidence* such as a variety of government records like 'Gazetteers, Census, survey and settlement reports, maps, satellite imagery, working plans, management plans, micro-plans, forest enquiry reports, other forest records, record of rights by whatever name called, pattas or leases, reports of committees and commissions constituted by the Government, Government orders, notifications, circulars, resolutions.'
- *Physical evidence* which could include 'house, huts and permanent improvements made to land including levelling, bunds, check dams and the like,' which can be easily examined for age.
- *Oral evidence* is also permissible including 'statement of elders other than claimants, reduced in writing.'

In support of a forest rights claim, a claimant is required to produce any two pieces of evidence from the aforesaid list. This requirement applies equally to forest lands in Scheduled and non-Scheduled Areas, and also equally to Adivasi and non-Adivasi claimants, so long as they have established the preliminary requirement for their eligibility as 'forest-dwelling communities.'

Process of examining evidence

It is apparent that the procedure for determination of forest rights, in its effort to bring justice to the doorstep of those who have suffered a 'historical injustice,' makes a departure from the existing adversarial systems of administration of justice in general, and from the colonial forest law architecture in particular. The Gram Sabha at the hamlet level[25] as a community (through the Forest Rights Committee) takes responsibility for the receipt of claim forms, their examination and on-site verification. The preparation of maps in support of the claims before it, and also as a method to verify such claims, is an important part of the FRC's functions. Indeed, where community claims are concerned, the FRC takes the lead in the preparation of the claim form itself.

Under the FRA, the state administrative machinery is duty bound to proactively assist the process, attend the on-site verification conducted by the FRC,[26] and support the filing of claims by providing maps and records in advance to the FRC, especially where rights of pastoralists and particularly vulnerable tribal groups (PVTGs) are concerned. In some states, the district administration has made the fullest possible use of this space and has prepared 'tool kits' for each Gram Sabha in the area, which include cadastral and other maps, forest and revenue records, gazetteer reports, census reports, and so on. These tool kits are handed over to the FRCs along with detailed instructions on how to go about filing their claims, along with hands-on support for such processes.

Use of satellite imagery: the case of Gujarat

The FRA displaces a variety of entrenched interests, while re-arranging power hierarchies inside forests, and it has been met with different kinds of efforts to subvert it. In early 2009, monitoring data coming out of Gujarat revealed disturbing trends – approximately 90 percent of the claims filed had been rejected by the sub-division and district level committees, even after being approved by the Gram Sabhas. Such en masse rejection of claims was a cause for concern, since the post-recognition provisions relating to forest governance could not be accessed by the forest-dwelling communities.

Further examination revealed that the Gujarat government had issued a series of circulars imposing strict rules of evidence and burden of proof on the rights recognition process under the FRA, thereby perverting the object of the law. The circulars not only sought to restrict the eligibility of claims to those in possession on or before 30 October 1980[27] (as opposed to the date provided under the Forest Rights Act, which is 13 December 2005), but also required that every claim be supported by satellite imagery. At that time, the state government had made little or no provision to assist the claimants in accessing a technology which remains, even today, remote and expensive. It also insisted that such satellite images be sourced only from a specified source.[28]

The BISAG, which had been given the task of preparing 'maps' from the satellite imageries, juxtaposed the village map over the concerned satellite imageries of 2005, and earmarked as 'common plots' the areas where they found cultivation in that year. On the basis of these images, two-dimensional 'maps' were printed out for the purpose of rights recognition. Quite apart from the obvious fallacy of treating satellite imagery printouts as 'maps,' no effort at connecting these 'maps' with the actual ground reality was being made, yet these were being treated as gospel truth for the purpose of accepting or rejecting claims under the FRA. It seems incredible today that the state government adopted such an unreliable method for verification of claims.

Several rights-based organisations, who had been working for many decades with Adivasi communities to help them to assert their governance rights over their traditional forest lands, brought the matter before the Gujarat High Court by way of writ petitions. They argued that the state government was actively subverting the implementation of the FRA through these circulars, which were therefore *ultra vires*.

In a detailed judgment,[29] the court examined the objectives and purpose of the FRA with regard to correcting historical injustice against forest dwellers, thereby providing a comprehensive and participatory method for the recognition of rights which is geared towards meeting such objective. It took note of provisions under the Forest Rights Rules,[30] which categorically state that 'satellite imagery and other uses of technology may supplement other form of evidence and shall not be treated as a replacement' (at paragraph 36–37). Nor can the state insist upon any particular form of evidence in support of claims, being bound by law to accept the various kinds of evidence in the inclusive list in Rule 13 (supra). The court directed the state government to re-open all the rejected claims in the state and examine them afresh in light of its decision.

Recent developments in GIS technology and role of the nodal ministry MoTA

Meanwhile, taking their cue from the proactive approach of the FRA, local organisations had developed their own methods for using spatial technology. Satellite imageries were obtained from the National Remote Sensing Centre, Hyderabad. Thereafter, the physical survey of the land claimed was carried out using hand-held GPS-PDA devices, triangulating the coordinates of the corners of the lands. These images were then superimposed over the satellite imageries with an outline of the land claimed. This ground-truthing exercise produced highly reliable geo-referenced maps. Verification by the FRC on the ground would easily address anomalies which a desk-based exercise can never do.[31]

The judgment in the *ARCH Vahini* case (supra) came to be widely known across the country, and the use of stand-alone satellite images for the verification of forest rights claims has been all but abandoned. Even so, different states have come up with different technological innovations based on satellite imageries and invested considerable time and money into rolling out the use of these technologies.

The use of satellite imagery continues to require close scrutiny and monitoring. Recent evidence shows that notwithstanding the clear position of law that satellite imagery can be only a supplementary form of evidence, several states are rapidly moving towards use of satellite footage, often disregarding the validity and accuracy of other forms of documentary evidence.[32]

Concerns were being raised, both within the administration, as also by civil society organisations, that these technological innovations may yet again become a pretext for exclusion of eligible forest dwellers. Distrust of these technologies among social movements created another layer of resistance to their extensive use. It is no small task to undo the adversarial mindset of the colonial forest regime, where each individual claimant must establish his/her lawful right separately and on separate pieces of evidence before a benevolent bureaucrat.

In an attempt to challenge this mindset, the nodal ministry of the Union government, the Ministry of Tribal Affairs (MoTA), issued detailed guidelines[33] in July 2015, regarding the use of geo-referencing for assessment of potential areas and re-examination of rejected claims under the Forest Rights Act. The statutory requirement for the district administration to play a pro-active role by providing forest and revenue maps to the Gram Sabhas and FRCs was reiterated.[34] Thus the states were encouraged to prepare Geographic Information System (GIS) maps for each village, containing spatial information of physiographic features of that village, area of the forest land, and other relevant information, and make such maps available to the FRCs. The guidelines emphasised the requirement for the ground-truthing of these images, suggesting involvement of local youth or even the FRC itself after providing necessary training and GPS/android devices.[35]

Interestingly, the guidelines stress the importance of using such technologies in both the identification of potential forest areas for rights recognition as well as for the recognition of Community Forest Resource (CFR) rights. They also reiterate that the use of satellite technology must be supplementary in nature and cannot replace other forms of evidence submitted in support of a claim. In conflating the need to address the large number of rejected claims with the use of available GIS maps through modern technologies, the central government sent out a clear message that technology must be used to support the process of forest rights recognition, not subvert it.

The 2015 guidelines issued by MoTA, by re-affirming the proactive and people-centric governance approach of the FRA, provides the enabling environment for development of new technological innovations for forest-dwelling communities to realise their forest rights in spatial terms. Recognising the need to engage with technological advances, several civil society organisations have made concerted efforts to pioneer a more user-friendly interface amongst the forest-dwelling communities themselves.

Civil society organisations and grassroots NGOs in Gujarat have emerged as the pioneers of geo-referenced mapping in support of claims under the FRA, and the use of hand-held GPS/PDA devices for ground-truthing satellite imageries. Another collaborative pilot in Odisha[36] seeks to address the disconnect of GIS technology from the communities by building an android GIS application for the development of maps primarily for mapping CFR rights, an area of rights recognition under the FRA which is lagging behind. A unique alliance has emerged between the District Administration, local NGOs, community leaders and youth, and software developers.[37]

The GIS application, which can be used readily on an android mobile phone or tablet, has been piloted in four remote villages in Mayurbanj district which are primarily inhabited by Adivasis. Bridging the technology divide, this mapping tool has a number of empowering features, such as its ability to integrate with background maps, interfaces such as adding photos/text/voice recordings at landmarks, real-time validation and comparison with boundaries mapped by neighbouring villages, and so on. After the physical mapping process in the field is complete, the maps can be reviewed readily by village elders without the need to be physically present at the time of mapping.[38]

Transcending the exclusionary potential of such technology, the preparation of these spatial maps has become an opportunity for communities to coalesce and re-assert the traditional boundaries of their customary homelands. At the same time, it allows them to learn new technological skills which help re-knit community ties fragmented through decades of disuse, and also provides an opportunity to reconnect with their traditional role as stewards of the forest and its resources.

Other categories of evidence being used under the FRA

The use of GIS and spatial technology by Adivasi and forest-dwelling communities to advance their forest rights certainly debunks the stereotypical notion of the 'noble savage' which, unfortunately, permeates the attitudes of the state and its functionaries. At the same time, Rule 13 of the Forest Rights Rules has provided the legislative foundation for self-assessment of claims by Gram Sabhas based upon atypical evidentiary sources, which include physical evidence such as trees, structures, and wells, and oral evidence such as statements of village elders drawing upon their memories, ancient folklore, and customary practices. Cultural and spiritual practices have provided another vital source of 'evidence' outside the narrow framework confining the administrative machinery till now.

The bureaucracy has often found these innovations difficult to comprehend. To cite just one example, sometime in 2017 the Government of Karnataka approached the nodal ministry MoTA for a clarification regarding the types of physical evidence which may be presented by 'other traditional forest dwellers' to establish their dependence on forests for three generations.[39] The specific query of the state government was whether the physical evidence itself, such as a dwelling, should be 75 years old, and what method for determination of the age of such physical evidence can be used. In the ensuing discussions, the possible use of carbon-dating was proposed, only to be vehemently rejected by the central ministry. Eventually, a detailed clarification in this regard had to be issued, drawing attention to the open-ended nature of Rule 13, and to the fact that the Gram Sabha reaches a determination based upon an actual physical verification on-site.[40]

Conclusion

Before concluding the discussion on the use of evidence in recognition of forest rights in India, it would be useful to examine the landmark judgment of the Indian Supreme Court in the *Niyamgiri* case.[41] This decision came after a long and tortuous journey, which we must remit for examination another day. It is useful, however, to contrast the approach adopted by the court in this matter, with how the same court approached the *Banwasi Seva Ashram* case several decades earlier. In this case also, the customary lands of the tribal forest dwellers had been declared as government reserve forests decades ago, and the lands were now required for a large industrial enterprise (namely, mining of bauxite to provide raw material for an aluminium factory established nearby).

The project had obtained necessary permissions, such as a mining lease, environmental clearance and stage-1 forest clearance. Decisions of the Supreme Court itself, dating as far back as 2009, also expressed approval for grant of final forest clearance to the project. However, when the central government decided not to grant a final forest clearance on the ground that there were pre-existing rights under Forest Rights Act in the area, the matter came once again before the same court.

In the *Niyamgiri* case, the number of claims for individual forest rights were very few, and those related to the land in question had been granted titles over equivalent alternate sites. With regard to community rights, only six claims were received of which three claims were settled by granting an alternate site, and three remained pending. Under the previous legal regime relating to forests, the court could have taken a technical approach and refused to interfere, or at best permitted some leniency with regard to laches, as was done in the *Banwasi Seva Ashram* case. Indeed, the state government and the holder of the mining lease[42] had urged the court to do just that, pressing that the legal issues arising be scrutinised on the basis of the colonial forest law architecture alone. If the court had agreed, the Dongaria Kondhs, a primitive tribal group having a population of around 8,000, would most certainly have failed to establish their rights.

The court examined the historical processes which have resulted in widespread disenfranchisement of forest-dwelling communities, and how the FRA seeks to correct this historical wrong, through substantive provisions as well as procedures for vesting and recognition of forest rights. The integral relationship between the FRA and the Panchayats (Extension to Scheduled Areas) Act, 1996 (or PESA), was also explicated by the court. It further observed:

> Many of the STs and other TFDs are totally unaware of their rights. They also experience lot of difficulties in obtaining effective access to justice because of their distinct culture and limited contact with mainstream society. Many a times, they do not have the financial resources to engage in any legal actions against development projects undertaken in their abode or the forest in which they stay. *They have a vital role to play in the environmental management and development because of their knowledge and traditional practices. State has got a duty to recognize and duly support their identity, culture and interest so that they can effectively participate in achieving sustainable development.*[43]
>
> (Author's emphasis)

The *Niyamgiri* judgment is permeated with an acknowledgement of the people-centric approach of the FRA to governance and administration of justice. Stepping out from the narrow confines of legalism, the court linked the community rights under FRA to fundamental constitutional rights, such as freedom of religion and culture under Articles 25 and 26 of the Constitution. It reiterated the need to ensure that forest-dwelling communities are actively involved in decision-making regarding development initiatives which involve their customary forest resources, an approach the colonial era architecture of forest laws had completely erased. The Court concluded that it is the Gram Sabhas which must 'actively consider' and make a decision regarding whether they have religious rights over the Niyam Raja hilltop, and whether the proposed mining area would detrimentally impact their religious right to worship on the hilltop.

While issuing directions to ensure that these Gram Sabha meetings are held in a free and fair manner, the judgment required the attendance of a judicial officer of the rank of District Judge; such an officer would play no judicial or decision-making role on the substantive issues involved, attending only 'as an observer.' Apart from the three decades separating these directions from those issued in the *Banwasi Seva Ashram* case, they also represent a tectonic shift in the paradigm of forest rights recognition and governance in India.

This important shift in what was received as wisdom till recently, represents an evolving jurisprudence around indigenous peoples' rights in India, and is reflected in subsequent judgments emerging from other courts. Judicial officers have seized upon *Niyamgiri*'s expansive approach in order to address egregious violations of environmental and forest protection legislations, where a hyper-technical and legalistic approach would most certainly have failed.[44] The examination of these jurisprudential advances must wait for another day. Equally important is the permeation of the principles espoused in *Niyamgiri* in the everyday discourse and negotiation of space – taking place between forest-dwelling communities and the local administration at ground level.

It is also remarkable that these changes are visible not only in the Scheduled Areas, but the constitutional mandate regarding Adivasi homelands has overflowed outside such geographical exclusivity to Adivasis and forest dwellers outside such areas, who have hitherto been at a disadvantage by reason of their spatial location. By capturing the people-centric approach of the constitutional and statutory protections inside Scheduled Areas and taking them forward into a people-centric governance model for all Adivasis and forest dwellers in the country, the Forest Rights Act has provided an important framework for the undoing of historical injustice meted out to forest dwellers by a colonial dispensation.

Notes

1 It is important to note that the Scheduling of Tribes in India, under Article 342 of the Constitution of India, is a work in progress, and that there are numerous communities which have not been granted Scheduled Tribe status for a variety of reasons. The ILO Convention Concerning Indigenous and Tribal Populations (ILO Convention No. 107) to which India is a party, applies equally to 'indigenous and other tribal and semi-tribal populations,' and for this reason tribal communities which are in the process of being granted ST status would also fall under the protection of international law relating to indigenous populations.

2 An earlier version of this chapter was presented at the 4th International LASSnet Conference 'Thinking with Evidence: Seeking Certainty, Making Truth' held at New Delhi, 10–12 December, 2016. The author acknowledges the valuable research inputs provided by Ms Gayatri Raghunandan, Advocate.

3 The colonial government notified the Van Panchayat Rules of 1931 under the 'village forests' provision of the Indian Forest Act, 1927 (Section 28), providing the framework for creation and demarcation of forests governed by village communities in Kumaon and Garhwal.

4 The mountain regions of Himachal Pradesh, then a part of undivided Punjab, saw very detailed forest settlements in the early years of the 20th century, whose recorded rights continue to form the backbone of a highly complex forest-dependent citizenry till today.

5 The Santhal Parganas Tenancy Act, 1949, and the Chota Nagpur Tenancy Act, 1908, along with the recognition of the Wilkinson's Rules, have ensured a high degree of engagement of local tribal communities in the management of forests in present-day Jharkhand.

6 Section 81 of the Orissa Forest Act, 1972, makes provision for declaration of any forest land or waste land in the merged territories which had been administered

as a reserve forest under the erstwhile ruler as a 'deemed reserve forest', in which case the settlement procedure can be done away with. It further provides that those forests which were recognised as 'khasra forests, village forests or protected forests' under the merged territories, shall be 'deemed protected forests.' The requirement to undertake any exercise for settlement/enquiry/recording of rights exercise is done away with. Existing rights continue at the will of the government till they are altered, again at the will of the government.

7 See, for instance, Hansda Sowvendra Shekhar (2017) *The Adivasi Will Not Dance*, Delhi: Speaking Tiger.

8 National Thermal Power Corporation is a government owned company.

9 *Banwasi Seva Ashram vs. State of U.P. & Ors.* (1986) 4 SCC 753, (1987) 3 SCC 304.

10 This committee included well-known social activist, the late Dr. Vasudha Dhagamwar, and also a nominee of the Banwasi Seva Ashram.

11 The Legal Service Authorities Act, 1986 provides that free legal assistance and representation will be provided to the poor and marginalized, mentioning the Scheduled Tribes specifically.

12 The Court, in an attempt to balance the requirements of development while upholding the traditional rights of forest dwellers, held that

> Indisputably, forests are a much wanted national asset. On account of the depletion thereof ecology has been disturbed; climate has undergone a major change and rains have become scanty. These have long-term adverse effects on national economy as also on the living process. At the same time, we cannot lose sight of the fact that for industrial growth as also for provision of improved living facilities there is great demand in this country for energy such as electricity. In fact, for quite some time the entire country in general and specific parts thereof, in particular, have suffered a tremendous setback in industrial activity for want of energy. A scheme to generate electricity, therefore, is equally of national importance and cannot be deferred at paragraph 10.

13 Available at http://envfor.nic.in/legis/forest/forest1.html

14 The National Forest Policy 1988 contains numerous provisions recording the importance of tribal and forest dwelling communities to the survival of forests, including:

> **4.6 Tribal People and Forests**
>
> Having regard to the symbiotic relationship between the tribal people and forests, a primary task of all agencies responsible for forest management, including the forest development corporations should be to associate the tribal people closely in the protection, regeneration and development of forests as well as to provide gainful employment to people living in and around the forest.

15 29th Report of the Commissioner for Scheduled Castes and Scheduled Tribes, by the late Dr B.D. Sharma who was appointed under Article 338 of the Constitution of India.

16 For our purposes, the following four guidelines are relevant (Sharma 2003):

1. Encroachments on Forest Land – a Review thereof and measures for confinement (No.13–1/90/-FP (I)):This order provides for regularisation of encroachments predating the Forest Conservation Act, 1980, that is, those prior to 25 October 1980.
2. Review of Disputed Claims over Forest Land arising out of Forest Settlement (No.13–1/90/-FP (2)): This order provides for settlement of disputed claims over reserve forests where the Settlement of Rights has been faulty or has not been done.
3. Disputes regarding pattas/leases/grants involving forest lands (No.13–1/90/-FP (3): This order relates to pattas/leases/grants of forest land which

could not be renewed or have become 'illegal' due to the enactment of the 1980 Act.

4 Conversion of Forest Villages into Revenue Villages and Settlement of other Old Habitations(No.13–1/90/-FP): This order relates to the settlement of old habitations and dwelling sites, as well as de-reservation of forestland for conversion of forest villages into revenue villages.

Two other guidelines were also issued in the same batch, one relating to payment of wages to forest workers, and the other regarding compensation for loss of life due to predation by wild animals.

17 Under Section 6 of the 1927 Act, a claim for settlement of rights must be filed before the FSO within three months of the proclamation of intention. If such claim is not filed, Section 9 states that the rights 'shall be extinguished,' unless a satisfactory application explaining the delay is made before the final notification under Section 20 is issued, or alternately an appeal is filed under Section 17 within three months. The reality is that in vast swathes of forest lands, neither were any initial claims filed, nor were appeals filed, nor even any challenges filed before the High Courts in exercise of their writ jurisdiction, and the statutory limitations have been crossed not in months or years, but in decades.

18 Preliminary Offence Reports or PORs are similar to First Information Reports (FIRs) registered under the Criminal Procedure Code.

19 For a detailed examination of the administrative and legislative advancements made during this period, and their eventual failure, see *Unbroken History of Broken Promises: Indian State and the Tribal People*, by Dr B.D. Sharma, Sahyog Pustak Kuteer, 2010.

20 *T.N. Godavarman Thirumalpad vs. Union of India & Ors.* Writ Petition (Civil) No. 202 of 1995, Supreme Court of India, pending.

21 This study estimates that India has the potential to recognise 40 million hectares (about 100 million acres) of 'customarily-held forest land' through the formal legal recognition under the Forest Rights Act. Since this estimate is based on already existing government records, it is very likely that the actual potential area for such rights recognition is much higher.

22 An important example of such spillover of Scheduled Area principles to non-Scheduled Areas is the definition of 'Gram Sabha' and 'village' under the Forest Rights Act, which is based upon the definition contained in the Panchayats (Extension to Scheduled Areas) Act, 1997 (PESA). Drawing upon the PESA approach to governance, FRA defines the village at the smallest unit of habitation, which could be a hamlet, tola, pada, or revenue village, and the Gram Sabha as the body of all adult members of the village. This is a significant departure from several state panchayati raj legislations. It is also integral to the functioning of the FRA, since the Gram Sabha is at the heart of the democratic governance mechanisms the statute seeks to establish.

23 The earliest opposition to the Forest Rights Act came from associations of retired forest officials, who filed writ petitions in different high courts across the country challenging its constitutional validity. The initial vehemence of these challenges dissipated over the years. Surprisingly, the most hostile opposition to the Forest Rights Act has come from wildlife conservation groups, who have continued to argue with great conviction, both inside and outside the courtroom, that the statute needs to be struck down in the interest of conservation of the forests and wildlife. Since these matters are *sub judice*, they are not being discussed in any detail in the present chapter.

24 Section 11 of FRA states that the nodal ministry dealing with the implementation of the Act at the central government is the Ministry of Tribal Affairs.

25 The proper identification of Gram Sabhas is central to the effective implementation of the Forest Rights Act. As stated earlier, the definition of Gram Sabha is drawn from PESA, previously applicable only to the Scheduled Areas.

26 Rule 12 A of the Forest Rights Rules.

27 The date of 30 October 1980 as the cut-off for rights recognition first found mention in the 1990 Guidelines, becoming written in stone over years of discourse within the administration and also in the Courts. The date is traceable to the Forest Conservation Act, 1980, which was brought into force on 30 October 1980. Needless to say, it has no relevance under the Forest Rights Act, which makes no mention of it, and also exempts the recognition of forest rights from the operation of the 1980 Act.

28 The approved source for satellite imagery in support of claims under the Forest Rights Act was stated to be the Bhaskaracharya Institute for Space Applications and Geo-Informatics (BISAG), Gujarat.

29 *Action Research in Community Health & Development (ARCH) & Ors. vs. State of Gujarat & Ors.* Judgment dt.3.5.2013 in Writ Petition (PIL) No. 100 of 2011. 2013 SCC OnLine Guj 2583.

30 One such provisions is Rule 12-A(11) of the Forest Rights Rules, which states:

> **12A. Process of Recognition of Rights:**
>
> XXX
>
> (11) The Sub-Divisional Level Committee or the District Level Committee shall consider the evidence specified in rule 13 while deciding the claims and shall not insist upon any particular form of documentary evidence for consideration of a claim.

31 A ground-truthing exercise, for instance, would be able to determine whether lands which are otherwise showing up 'green' in satellite images are actually under self-cultivation within the larger definition contained in Rule 12-A (8) of the Forest Rights Rules, which states:

> **12A. Process of Recognition of Rights:**
>
> XXX
>
> (8) The land rights for self-cultivation recognised under clause (a) of sub-section (1) of section 3 shall be, within the specified limit, including the forest lands used for allied activities ancillary to cultivation, such as, for keeping cattle, for winnowing and other post-harvest activities, rotational fallows, tree crops and storage of produce.
>
> Explanation: 1. Fine receipts, encroacher lists, primary offence reports, forest settlement reports, and similar documentation by whatever name called, arisen during prior official exercise, or the lack thereof, shall not be the sole basis for rejection of any claim.
>
> 2. The satellite imagery and other uses of technology may supplement other form of evidence and shall not be treated as a replacement.

32 In Maharashtra, for instance, the stated rationale behind adoption of satellite technology was described by one study as under:

> The use of GPS technology assists in improving the traditional process of land measurement and helps responsible authorities to make **objective verifiable decisions** in allocating land rights under the FRA. This technology is also providing information to make plane table survey of forest land plots more cost effective and less laborious.
>
> (Goswami 2016).

The reliance on satellite images to make 'objective verifiable decisions' regarding forest rights militates against the law at multiple levels, and could potentially defeat its historical purpose entirely.

33 Circular dated 27 July 2015 bearing F. No. 23011/18/2015-FRA issued by the Ministry of Tribal Affairs, Government of India to the Chief Secretaries of All States, available at https://tribal.nic.in/FRA/declarationsClarifications/3Guidelinesforgeo-referencing.pdf (accessed on 22 May 2018).

34 Rule 6 of the Forest Rights Rules, where, while delineating the Functions of the Sub-Divisional Level Committee, states '(b) provide forest and revenue maps and electoral rolls to the Gram Sabha or the Forest Rights Committee.'

35 The July 2015 Guideline issued by MoTA also stated that training support on how to use these technologies can be obtained from BISAG, Gujarat, National Resource Centre Tribal Research Institute, Odisha, the BHUVAN portal of Department of Space, and other State Remote Sensing Agencies.

36 Chaudhury, Pranab, *et al. Community Mapping through An Android OS based mobile GIS application: An attempt towards Inclusive, Transparent & Participatory mapping of Community Forest Rights in India,* unpublished paper presented at 2016 World Bank Conference on Land and Poverty, Washington DC, March 2016, at page 4.

37 The various collaborators in this pilot are *Vasundhara* (Odisha), *Centre for Land Governance* (NRMC) (Delhi), *Rights and Resources Initiative* (Washington DC), and a GIS start up *Geolysis*.

38 The simple and easy to use Android App is supported by a web portal, to which the information collected is transmitted through the server network. Although the App is still in its testing stage, the initial results are positive, with several villages having actually submitted claims for CFR rights based on the maps generated through this innovation.

39 Section 2(o) of the Forest Rights Act requires that OTFDs establish primary residence and dependence on forests for at least three generations or 75 years.

40 Clarification dated 7 March 2017 bearing F. No. 23011/02/2013-FRA issued by the Ministry of Tribal Affairs, Government of India to the Secretary, Social Welfare Department, Karnataka government. Available at https://tribal.nic.in/FRA/declarationsClarifications/OTFDClarificationtoGovtofKarnataka.pdf (accessed on May 22, 2018).

41 *Orissa Mining Corporation vs. Ministry of Environment and Forests & Ors.* (2013) 6 SCC 476.

42 It is important to clarify that the mining lease had been granted to Orissa Mining Corporation, a state-owned mining company, and that the actual mining of bauxite was to be done by the UK-based multinational corporation Vedanta Resources through its Indian subsidiary, Sterlite Industries Pvt. Ltd.

43 *Ibid* at para 47.

44 See, for instance, *Paryawaran Sanrakshan Sangarsh Samiti Lippa vs. Union of India & Ors.* Judgment dt. 4.5.2016 in Appeal No. 28 of 2013, National Green Tribunal. The judgment has also been relied upon in the *ARCH Vahini* judgment (supra) of the Gujarat High Court which specifically relates to evidence and the meaning of Rule 13 of the Forest Rights Rules.

References

Action Research in Community Health & Development (ARCH) & Ors. vs. State of Gujarat & Ors. Judgment dt.3.5.2013 in Writ Petition (PIL) No. 100 of 2011. 2013 SCC OnLine Guj 2583.

Banwasi Seva Ashram vs. State of U.P. & Ors. (1986) 4 SCC 753, (1987) 3 SCC 304.

Campaign for Survival and Dignity (CSD). 2003. 'Endangered Symbiosis: Evictions and India's Forest Communities.' *Report of the Jan Sunwai Public Hearing*, July 19–20. New Delhi: Delhi Forum and The Other Media.

Chaudhury, P.R., Rao, G.V., Kumar, K., Deo, B. and Dash, T. 2016. 'Community Mapping Through an Android OS Based Mobile GIS Application: An Attempt Towards Inclusive, Transparent & Participatory Mapping of Community Forest Rights in India.' Paper presented at *2016 World Bank Conference on Land and Poverty*, Washington, DC.

Goswami, B. 2016. *Geo-informatics for Forest Rights: Harnessing Technology for Better livelihood Support and Access to Forest Rights* (20 November 2016). Available at: http://negd.gov.in/writereaddata/files/Case%20Study%20-%20Geoinformatics%20for%20Forest%20Rights%2C%20Maharashtra.pdf (accessed on 22 May 2018)

Hansda, S.S. 2017. *The Adivasi Will Not Dance*. New Delhi: Speaking Tiger.

Khanna, S. 2014. 'Boundaries of Forest Land: The Godavarman Case and Beyond.' In S. Lele and A. Menon (Eds.), *Democratizing Forest Governance in India* (pp. 225–260). New Delhi: Oxford University Press.

Lele, S. 2014. 'What Is Wrong With Joint Forest Management.' In S. Lele and A. Menon (Eds.), *Democratizing Forest Governance in India* (pp. 25–62). New Delhi: Oxford University Press.

Lele, S. and Menon, A. (Eds.). 2014. *Democratizing Forest Governance in India*. New Delhi: Oxford University Press.

Ministry of Tribal Affairs (MoTA). 2019. 'Status Report on Implementation of the Scheduled Tribes and Other Traditional Forest Dwellers (Recognition of Forest Rights) Act, 2006 [for the period ending 28.2.2019].' *M/o Tribal Affairs of India, I.D. No.23011/3/2016-FRA dated 28.5.2019*. Available at: https://tribal.nic.in/FRA/data/MPRFeb2019.pdf (accessed on 11 June 2019).

Orissa Mining Corporation vs. Ministry of Environment and Forests & Ors. (2013) 6 SCC 476.

Paryawaran Sanrakshan Sangarsh Samiti Lippa vs. Union of India & Ors. Judgment dt. 4.5.2016 in Appeal No. 28 of 2013, National Green Tribunal.

Pradip Prabhu and Ors. vs. State of Maharashtra and Ors. 1995 Supp (3) SCC 450.

Rights and Resources Initiative. 2015. *Potential for Recognition of Community Forest Resource Rights Under India's Forest Rights Act: A Preliminary Assessment*. Washington, DC: Rights and Resources Initiative.

Sarin, M. 2014. 'Undoing Historical Injustice: Reclaiming Citizenship Rights and Democratic Forest Governance Through the Forest Rights Act.' In S. Lele and A. Menon (Eds.), *Democratizing Forest Governance in India* (pp. 100–146). New Delhi: Oxford University Press.

Sharma, Dr. B.D. 1989. *29th Report of the Commissioner for Scheduled Castes and Scheduled Tribes*. Commissioner for Scheduled Castes and Scheduled Tribes under Article 338 of the Constitution of India.

Sharma, Dr. B.D. 2003. *Forest Lands: Tribals Struggle for Survival*. New Delhi: Sahyog Pustak Kuteer.

Sharma, Dr. B.D. 2010. *Unbroken History of Broken Promises: Indian State and the Tribal People*. New Delhi: Sahyog Pustak Kuteer.

T.N. Godavarman Thirumalpad vs. Union of India & Ors. Writ Petition (Civil) No. 202 of 1995, Supreme Court of India, pending.

United Nations Declaration on Rights of Indigenous Peoples, Resolution adopted by the United Nations General Assembly on 13 September 2007, 61/295; available at https://www.un.org/development/desa/indigenouspeoples/declaration-on-the-rights-of-indigenous-peoples.html (accessed on 11 June 6 2019).

9 Left wing extremism

Re-examining challenges for development and governance in the Scheduled Areas

Richard Hemraj Toppo

Introduction

This chapter is concerned with the Scheduled Areas (SAs)[1] in the Eastern and Central parts of the country that are largely, if not wholly, 'affected' by the ongoing *Naxalite* Movement, a term broadly used in reference to the multiple left-leaning armed insurgencies currently limited to peninsular regions. The chapter makes a critical reading of the Statist discourse on the challenges of development and governance in these 'affected' areas towards re-examining the bounded-ness of relevant entities, that of *Adivasis*,[2] Naxalites,[3] and State. It attempts to situate the development-governance practices within the fluidity of relations between these actors; thereby, going against the popular readings, be it on the left or right side of the spectrum, of fixated roles and functioning of State, society and insurgents. The discussion, then, moves beyond the identification of problems in these regions and a prescriptive to-do list; it rather explores the workings of 'development and governance' as co-constitutive of different actors involved.

The linkages between development and governance, though ostensibly have an outward appearance of an end-means relationship, respectively, is equally confusing. Development as a relational project, aimed at enhancing the livelihood of people (Sen 1988), had traditionally subsumed the processes of governance in a centralised fashion, which often related to State practices of administering or controlling resources in the developmental context (Pierre 2002; Peters 2002). With an increased role of civil society and non-governmental organisations, this paradigm of state-centrism took a more nuanced turn towards understanding governance as a poly-centred and coordinated efforts of multiple stakeholders, beyond the erstwhile monopoly of state, towards addressing the societal problems (Pierre 2002). However, this congruency in the dynamics of development and governance, which is largely situated within the state and defined norms and boundaries despite the multiplicity of actors, stands contested in the Adivasi areas that are LWE affected. In these regions, the workings of governance are predominantly collapsed into security establishment, to the extent of going against the betterment of the very people whom these practices seek to empower.

But before declaring governance in these areas 'problematic' and antithetical to the idea of development, it might be of interest to historically and contemporarily explore the notions of 'development' itself, which have been inherent in the policy making process and which have rather imposed their vision of future on the Adivasi communities. In this regard, such state-led development-governance practices in the Adivasi areas might well be in congruence, though in opposition to the development of Adivasis (in a literal sense).

The notions of development amongst the policy makers, pertaining to Adivasis and SAs, have historically been entwined with disparaging perceptions of the socio-cultural-economic positioning of the Adivasis. During the Constituent Assembly debates in the year 1949, when the issue of Fifth Schedule was put up for discussion, several members of the assembly colligated Scheduled Areas with notions of backwardness and inferiority (Constituent Assembly Debates 1949). Fifth Schedule provisions for a different governance in the SAs of the country were aimed at ameliorating the conditions of Adivasis in these regions, who were considered to be less-advanced than the 'mainstream' society in the evolutionary schema of socio-cultural life. Several of the Constituent Assembly members, in their discussions of the Fifth Schedule, ignored issues of Adivasi cultural idiosyncrasies, and rather emphasised on the need for abridging the gap between Adivasis and non-Adivasis.[4] The comment of one Prof Shibban Lal Saksena during the assembly debate is illustrative:

> the existence of the scheduled tribes and the Scheduled areas are a stigma on our nation just as the existence of untouchability is a stigma on the Hindu religion. That these brethren of ours are still in such a sub-human state of existence is something, for which we should be ashamed . . . that these scheduled tribes and areas must as soon as possible become a thing of the past. They must come up to the level of the rest of the population and must be developed to the fullest extent. I only want that these scheduled tribes and scheduled areas should be developed so quickly that they may become indistinguishable from the rest of the Indian population.
>
> (Constituent Assembly Debates 1949)

These opinions were grounded in the assimilationist tradition[5] that sought policy interventions in the SAs, aiming to alleviate the socio-economic conditions of Adivasis in these areas. A year before, a prominent advocate from the assimilationist camp, A.V. Thakkar, who chaired the sub-committee on 'Excluded and Partially Excluded Areas (Other than Assam),' submitted in the committee's report to Constituent Assembly about the impoverished conditions of Adivasis across the partially excluded regions, and blamed social evils like alcoholism and contemptuous attitude towards education as reasons for their backwardness (Constituent Assembly Debate 1948). It is important to note that, throughout this conversation, the Adivasis were projected as the backward 'other' in socio-economic-cultural terms, in dire need of intervention, forceful or otherwise. The eventuality of Scheduled Areas, thus, was imagined in the processes of development and governance that would, perhaps, homogenise the entire population, Adivasis and non-Adivasis alike. One might argue for a nuanced perspective on policy orientation, especially in regard to India's first Prime Minister, Jawaharlal Nehru's concept of *Panchsheel* – 'five pillars of tribal development.'[6] However, the economic policies pursued thereafter in the SAs were telling of a contrary position adopted by the government that disregarded any bottom-up perspectives or participatory approaches (De 2014).

Implicit in such top-down notions of development, the idea of 'processes' took prominence over the intended 'outcome.' There was a seeming disparity between the policies and policy makers on the one hand, and policy outcomes and subjects on the other. Several policies that resulted in displacement and exploitation of Adivasis were carried out on the pretext of improving their socio-economic conditions.[7] Policies like industrialisation and urbanisation, aimed at building dams and setting up of industries, translated into large-scale land acquisition and massive displacement of the Adivasis.[8] In a high-level committee report on the 'Socio-Economic, Health and Educational Status of Tribal Communities from India,' under the chairmanship of Virginius Xaxa, published by the Ministry of Tribal Affairs (2014), the total number of displaced population since independence until 1990 was estimated at 60 million people, with Adivasis constituting 47 percent of the displaced.

It was in this context of increased Adivasi dispossession and exploitation as well as an un-concerned or complicit state that one needs to understand the Naxalite movement which established its stronghold amongst Adivasis in the SAs. Whilst several of the state-led developmental policies appeared distanced from the welfare of Adivasis, the governance practices further aggrieved the masses through their oppressive functioning. In such Adivasi areas of Peninsular India, the Naxalites projected themselves as an Adivasi manifestation of defiance against the exploitative policies of the state or the oppressive functioning of the state agents. In an expert-committee report titled 'Development Challenges in Extremist Affected Areas,' under the chairmanship of D. Bandopadhyay, submitted to the Planning Commission of India in the year 2008, it was argued that the state-led development-induced displacement, in addition to the ongoing social oppression and ineffective judiciary and policing, had caused severe grievances to the Adivasi communities, thereby, creating fertile grounds for the spread of the Naxalite movement (Planning Commission 2008). To give a brief overview, the Naxalite Movement can be traced back to 23 May 1967, when a group of Adivasi peasants in the Naxalbari village of Darjeeling district, West Bengal, attacked a police convoy with bows and arrows, killing one of the Police Inspectors, Sonam Wangdi (Mukherji 1979; Banerjee 1980, 1984; Gupta 2007). The police convoy had come to the village in response to the peasants' activities against landlords in the region that included forcibly taking over their [landlord's] lands, burning the land records and debt documents, looting guns from the landlords, and pronouncing death sentences to oppressive landlords (Banerjee 1984: 87). These peasants were reportedly being led by a rather radical group within the Communist Party of India (Marxist), that called for a violent struggle against the big landlord and comprador-bureaucrat bourgeoisie to bring in social-political changes; this group was inspired by Mao's ideology of an armed rebellion (Chandra 1990). This violent Adivasi uprising against the state and landlords, though, was severely repressed by the state in the following days, its implications traversed across other parts of West Bengal and in the States of Bihar, Orissa, and Andhra Pradesh, where 'similar peasant movements found a new inspiration in the ideology of armed rebellion' (Basu 2011: 374). One of the most prominent Naxalite organisations, the Communist Party of India (Maoists), formed in the year 2004 after the merger of People's War (PW) and Maoist Communist Center (MCC), aim at overthrowing the state and bringing in a genuine people's democracy. The movement is currently spread, by the government's own admission, across 106 districts in ten states[9] (Press Information Bureau 2016) and has claimed the lives of 7,844 people between 2005 and 2018, of which 1,959 were security personnel, 3,106 were civilians, and 2,779 were Naxalites (SATP 2018).

The apparent State's domination and Naxalite confrontation seem to posit the two entities in absolute opposition, where the presence and legitimacy of one is predicated on the demise of the other. However, many of the recent scholarly works in LWE-affected Adivasi areas have shown the co-existence of the two, where 'symbiotic relationship' rather than 'competition' define the dynamics of state-Naxalite interaction (Suykens 2010; Shah 2006, 2010; Sareen 2016). This might seem in contradiction to the hegemony that the state seeks to establish through the absolute control of legitimacy-generating practices; such control is not to be confused or contradicted with the workings of independent Non-Governmental Organisations (NGOs) or civil society. The NGOs or civil society are based within the premise of state structure, legalised and regulated, if not controlled, by the state agencies. These organisations, unlike the Naxalites who challenge state's authority to the extent of creating parallel administration, work with the state agencies and agents, thereby increasing the fluidity between the state and the society. In several states of Peninsular India, NGOs like PRADAN are contracted by the state to perform and deliver state-like governance practices in the field of water conservation and managing natural resources, amongst several others. The seemingly contradictory position in regard to the state's dealings with the Naxalites, at the street-level functioning of governance, where a hegemonic project seems to have come to terms with counter-hegemonic forces, needs to be differentiated from the public narrations of state. Such practices are often not acknowledged by the state or the Naxalites, but rather exhibit their subtle presence in the everyday sightings and activities of Adivasis in the LWE affected SAs. In line with such observations, the chapter proposes that the presence of Naxalites, instead of posing a challenge to development and governance, has paved way for an intimacy of processes between the three actors – Adivasis, Naxalites, and the state. To illustrate this, the chapter begins with a critical examining of discourses, that of the state and the Naxalites, to showcase the non-fixity of relations and roles in regard to the processes of development. It is further argued that the intimacy of relations and fluidity of boundaries has led to a re-conceptualisation of the traditional notions of state-controlled governance and development.

Challenges for development and governance: questioning state's narrative

In questioning state's narrative, it is important, first, to clarify if the state has a singular narrative. Or, are there divergent voices within the state that are not necessarily coherent? Is the state to be considered a singular entity? Such questions acquire importance especially when analysing the pronounced challenges to development and governance, in considering who gets to speak for and whose voices are being heard as the state. Several scholars have critiqued the idea of a singular monolithic state based on the (non-)interactions between people and the different state agents and agencies. Lipsky (1980) talks about the variances between the policy making level and how differently the said policies are interpreted and adapted at the street level. Migdal (1994, 2001), Fuller and Harris (2001) and Corbridge *et al.* (2005), amongst others, have expressed similar opinions on the plural reading of Indian state at different levels. However, the idea has not been uncontested, as scholars the likes of Chatterjee (1997, 1998, 2004, 2008), Kaviraj (2010) and Acharya (1993) have made a detailed enquiry on the mechanisms and trajectory of state as a homogenous entity. Extending such readings of a uniform state, from a more nuanced perspective, Nilsen (2013) talks about the variant workings of the state agents, from responsive to repressive, in different contexts, but only to conclude that the state remains as a uniform oppressive collective in face of structural challenges.

This chapter argues against any fixated understanding of the State, much in conformity to the pluralist readings. However, in what might seem as a contradiction, it is also proposed that the evident dis-aggregation of state practices, as showcased later, does not imply a lack of coherent ideology at the policy making level. The political-bureaucratic elite do not frame policies in complete abstraction from the context, but the policies are also not simply an outcome of context 'only.' The policy makers' positioning of privilege is contingent on the legitimacy of the policy making institution, that is, the State; hence, their voices are in uniformity when projecting a narrative or framing a policy that embeds and entrenches the idea of state within the society. The dialectical relationship between the state and society, then, is played out at the local levels of policy implementation or lack thereof, where the society reacts and responds to the state's activities, opening up possibilities for fluid relations and blurry boundaries between the state and the society. This emerging relationship, in turn, informs the policy makers, who re-frame their narratives and policies to suit their political interest, nevertheless, their narratives remain uniform to the extent that it privileges the status quo between State and society.

This uniformity of narration, spelt in regard to challenges for the development and governance in LWE-affected areas, is exemplified in the articulation of Ministry of Home Affairs, the principal state agency tasked with internal security. The MHA (2017) identifies the Naxalites as the primary challenge to the functioning of state in LWE-affected areas. It claims that the Naxalites through terrorist activities have destroyed any and all of the state infrastructures in Adivasi areas and have threatened the presence of any state agents in the area, thus creating a governance vacuum. MHA further claims that the Naxalites have not allowed any of the development works to be carried out in these regions, thereby alienating Adivasis from government's welfare schemes, and mobilising them against such perceived state's apathy towards the Adivasis. As described on MHA website (2017), the Naxalites resort to:

> guerrilla warfare, which primarily aims at creating a vacuum at the grass-roots level of the existing governance structures. This is achieved by killing lower-level government officials, police-personnel of the local police stations, the workers of mainstream political parties and the people's representatives of the Panchayati Raj system. After creating a political and governance vacuum, they coerce the local population to join the movement. A strident propaganda is also carried out against the purported and real inadequacies of the existing state structure.

This uniformity against Naxalites, projecting them as anti-development, was most evident in the speech of former Prime Minister, Manmohan Singh, when he famously referred to Naxalites as the biggest internal security threat the country has ever faced (Press Information Bureau 2006). In the subsequent years, several of the state officials, including Union ministers, made similar charges, attributing Adivasi impoverishment in LWE-affected areas to the Maoists (The Indian Express 2009; Joshi 2010; Singh 2014; Deogharial 2016). The current Home Minister, adding to the chorus, has remarked that the Naxalites want people to remain poor, as they 'thrive at the cost of poor people' (The Economic Times 2018). Within this narrative, whilst the armed Naxal guerrillas are projected as primary impediments to the development processes, the over-ground cohort of activists and academicians who tend to oppose the 'developmental' projects or supposedly romanticise the Naxal movement are also framed as 'problems' or 'challenges' to the workings of the state. It is claimed that the Naxalite organisations use many of these well-educated intellectuals as their 'frontal' agents to facilitate mass mobilisation against the state-led development, and 'provide short-term democratic subterfuge to cover-up the totalitarian and oppressive nature of the Maoist ideology' (Ministry of Home Affairs 2018). The role of these intellectuals, then, as presumed by the state, is to de-stabilise and de-legitimise the foundations of State-organised governance, working against the 'stable' binary relations of state and society.

In a critical reading of this narrative, the State seems to have discovered the Naxalite 'challenge' only recently. It was only in the early 2000s, with the exponential increase of Naxalites in the Adivasi areas of Eastern and Central India that the state took cognisance of the socio-economic dimension when countering the Naxalites (Ministry of Home Affairs 2004), who were previously dealt with from a 'security-only-perspective.' It is important to note that the relative condition of Adivasis vis-à-vis non-Adivasi communities have remained unequal and impoverished throughout the six decades of independence; the Adivasis still constitute the highest number of illiterates in the country (58.96 percent literates against a country average of 72.99 percent), they also constitute the highest levels of school dropouts (Ministry of Tribal Affairs 2013), and on health indicators, they have the maximum number of malnourished children under five and the highest levels of child mortality rate (Ministry of Health and Family Welfare 2017). The sudden emergence of Naxalite as the primary challenge to development evades the question on state's intentions and efficiency towards governing and developing the SAs. The State's framing of Adivasi discontent as a mere Naxalite construct ignores the several ongoing Adivasi protests against mining and industrialisation policies that have resulted in massive displacement; it rather implicates a top-down perspective of Adivasis and development, where Adivasis are seen as victims who need to be rescued from Naxalites through means of securitised development, as mentioned by Basu (2011). The state projects securitised development as a holistic response to the Naxalite problem, where the state, in principle, follows a dual strategy of development and counter-insurgency; however, in practice, the security measures seem to have enveloped the developmental concerns (Basu 2011). As a result, the Adivasis in the LWE areas are doubly repressed, first, in facing the onslaught of development-displacement policies, and second, through violent suppression in the name of counter-insurgency. Gladson Dungdung (2015: 131, 136–137), author activist from Jharkhand, vividly pens down the atrocities that Adivasis face in the name of countering the Naxalites:

> It is a regular practice of the armed police to enter any village without warning, rob the houses, catch innocent villagers, torture them, exploit women, shoot people, and finally hand over the dead bodies to family members after a couple of days, telling them that the person was killed in crossfire. These are the kind of inhuman acts the security forces have perpetrated in Saranda Forest. . . . A series of anti-Naxal operations were carried out by the security forces since 2001. However, 'Operation

> Bravo Boy', 'Operation Monsoon' and 'Operation Anaconda', carried out jointly by the Jharkhand police and the paramilitary force during June-August 2011, were the worst. During these operations, 35 villages were seized by the security forces. . . . The security personnel frequently destroyed harvests, and ate and spoiled huge quantities of food grains stored in Adivasi houses. . . . They destroyed many houses, and broke doors and windows in countless others.

Challenging development and governance: a view from the 'other' side

As mentioned previously, if the State's narration of challenges is a recent construct, what has prevented the state from carrying out developmental and governance projects in the SAs of eastern and central India? In a monolithic reading of the state, several authors have argued that the state acts as an instrument of the bourgeoisie elite; that the state formulates policies only to serve the interests of the big businesses (Roy 2010b; Satnam 2010; Navlakha 2012). The discussion, then, shifts from examining the challenges, to projecting state-led 'development and governance' as a challenge to Adivasis' welfare.

Supporting this proposition, scholars have repeatedly cited various legislations that have come to destroy the Adivasi livelihoods, and yet had been enacted to serve the interests of few elites. Legislations like the National Mineral Policy of 1993, Special Economic Zone Act of 2005, and the former Land Acquisition Act of 1894 (which has recently been amended), amongst several others, have had immense adverse effects on the livelihoods of millions of Adivasis. Bhengra *et al.* (1998) remarks that the state-led economic policies have resulted in massive displacement of the Adivasis. Since independence, India's development policies, much to the dismay of Adivasis, were geared towards industrialisation – building of dams, mining activities and government-run industrial estates took centre stage (Baviskar 2004). In pursuit of such projects, the state displaced millions of Adivasis to acquire their lands (Fernandes and Thukral 1989). As early as the 1960s, the Elwin Committee Report and the Dhebar Committee Report had identified displacement as one of the major causes for the deprivation of Adivasis (Sahay 1968: 234). Yet, the State, until present times, has continued such policies of displacing Adivasis. Chakrabarty and Kujur (2010: 113), in their case study on LWE in Orissa, claim that such problems of land alienation have resulted in the consolidation of Maoists amongst the Adivasis in the region. This is further ascertained in the popular Maoist sloganeering of 'land to the tiller,' which implicitly reveals the primacy of land within the Adivasi-insurgent relations.

Based on such readings of the State, where development and governance are themselves a challenge to the Adivasi empowerment, authors have projected Naxalite Movement as a rightful dissent against the State-led exploitation (Roy

2010a, 2010b; Satnam 2010; Navlakha 2012). One of the prominent writings to shape this perspective is Arundhati Roy's 'Walking with the Comrades' (2010a). The writing vividly details the plight of poor Adivasis in Dantewada, marginalised at the hands of a neoliberal State and further pushed into violence through brutal counter-insurgency measures. Roy (2010a) portrays the Naxalite armed struggle as a brave resistance put forth by the Adivasis, as a last resort, to defend their livelihoods. Satnam (2010) too, like Roy, vividly describes the hardships of Naxalites, and their fight against the exploitative State for a better society. Several other writings, including Choudhary's *Let's Call Him Vasu: With the Maoists in Chhattisgarh* (2012), Navlakha's *Days and Nights in the Heartland of Rebellion* (2012), and Pandita's *Hello, Bastar* (2011), have followed a similar trend in exploring the Naxalite lives and their motivations towards joining the armed struggle. Within the academic circles, Kunnath (2009, 2012) has done extensive work on situating the blame with the state, though his research focuses on the dalit[10] lives. He contradicts the notion of people 'caught between two fires' and claims that the oppressed masses have consciously decided to take up weapons against the semi-feudal, semi-colonial state. Basu (2011) gives a discourse analysis of how the government has securitised development, paving way for brutal counter-insurgency measures that have further aggrieved the Adivasis and led to the spread of the Naxalite Movement. Garg (2008), too, reaches at a similar conclusion on the causal relationship between state-led atrocities and the spread of Naxalite Movement amongst Adivasis. Sundar (2016b) vividly describes the counter-insurgency measures carried out in Chhattisgarh, where the state had recruited the local Adivasi villagers and former Naxalite cadres as part of the vigilante group, *Salwa Judum*,[11] to fight the insurgents. The group, in cahoots with the paramilitary forces, would burn down villages, forcefully displace the villagers to police camps, rape local women, and kill anyone whom they presumed as supporters of the Maoists (ibid.). Sundar narrates the incident of one Jogi from the village Koruthguda in Chhattisgarh. Jogi had her house shielded from the groves of mango and tamarind trees, so when the *Salwa Judum* forces came to her village, little did she and her father know about it. The other villagers had already fled to the nearby forest, but Jogi and her father, unaware and un-prepared, were at home. As the forces made their way to Jogi's house, her father, sitting outside the house, was attacked by the Judum members un-provoked. When Jogi ran in to save her father, she was raped by the forces and later shot dead. The next day, the forces displayed her corpse dressed in a Maoist uniform, declaring her as the guerrilla squad commander (ibid.). Such instances, not uncommon in the LWE-affected Adivasi areas, are exemplary of the governance practices that have come to define the state and its practices amongst the Adivasis. In this regard, the challenges, then, towards Adivasi welfare (avoiding the use of words like 'development' and 'governance,' which have inherent state linkages in the popular imaginations) comes from the State practices of development and governance.

In a critique to this narrative, where the blame is singularly pinned on State's developmental and governance practices, authors have pointed out the 'dual violence' faced by Adivasis at the hands of both, the State and the Naxalites. This goes against the revolutionary imagery of the Naxalites fighting for the rights of Adivasis. The Independent Citizens' Initiative came out with a report in the year 2006 that examined the ongoing conflict in Chhattisgarh between the state-backed *Salwa Judum* and the Naxalites (Guha *et al.* 2006). The report claimed that the Adivasis were doubly repressed by both of the armed forces. Guha (2007), who was also part of this report, remarked that the Adivasis were marginalised at the hands of state-led developmental policies, and were subsequently caught in the revolutionary calls of the Naxalites against the state; eventually, the Adivasis find themselves locked into a lasting violence between Naxalite insurgency and state counter-insurgency. Several Adivasi rights activists have acknowledged such narratives of double repression. Adivasi activist Gladson Dungdung, in a report titled 'Jharkhand Human Rights Report 2001–2011,' has detailed the various atrocities caused by both the state and the Naxalites (Jharkhand Human Rights Movement 2011). Bela Bhatia (2005, 2006), an academic-activist, whilst critiquing the State for its policies against the Adivasis also remarked about the 'troubling aspects' of the Naxalite Movement; she argued that in several of the strategic decisions made by the Naxalite party, the party had taken precedence over people. She further criticised the Movement for engaging in the killing of suspected informers who might well be innocents (Bhatia 2006). Nandini Sundar, also an academic activist, has directed much of her criticism against the state violence towards Adivasis, whilst also making critical remarks against the Movement. She claimed that the Naxalite movement had 'resisted even genuine government initiatives' and had resulted in the prominence of violence in these Adivasi areas (Sundar 2006: 3190).

During the fieldwork in Jharkhand, conducted between May 2014 to January 2015 across four districts (Khunti, Simdega, Latehar, and Gumla) where the author selectively interviewed 35 participants, similar instances of Naxalite's objection to construction of roads and dams were observed, besides noting the high-handedness of security officials in their interactions with the locals. In one instance, when the Naxalites had called for a party meeting, the interviewee had requested during the meet that Naxalites allow a nearby bridge to be constructed for the convenience of villagers, who otherwise had to travel a long distance to reach the local markets. The Naxalites responded to the interviewee in a somewhat threatening tone, saying that he should perhaps live on the other side of river if he was so troubled. In other similar situations, the villagers often remained silent listening to the Naxal justification of blocking the construction works, fearing that any dissenting voice would not be taken lightly by the Naxalites. However, it is to be noted that the Naxalites' objection to development is only limited to the construction of roads and bridges, as they provide easy accessibility to security forces inside the insurgent strongholds. Erstwhile, one of the most common tactic to prevent security forces from accessing these areas was the use of land mines, which could easily be planted on mud tracks and camouflaged. However, with the construction of roads and increased patrolling of security forces in such areas, the Naxalites have been left with limited options. Banerjee and Saha (2010) record a similar instance of Naxalite objection to road construction 'only,' and also remark that no other works, like land development providing irrigational facilities and afforestation, have been blocked by the Naxalites.

In a further critique to the narrative of a monolithic understanding of State, the state-instituted legislations (which define the developmental policies and governance practices), here, are understood in passivity, oriented inherently against the Adivasis. However, the everyday tensions between the state and the citizens in interpreting the policies and laws and ensuring the rights is revealing of the 'politics' that goes beyond the 'passive' dynamics or top-down order. Citizens as subjects actively pursuing, interpreting, and re-defining the policies and rights vis-à-vis the state require an understanding of laws (legislations) as an evolving engagement between the citizenry and the state. Such engagements also highlight the often-contradictory positions of various state agencies against each other (Harris 2006), and the variance in understanding and interpreting the laws at various levels within any state agency (Migdal 2001; Lipsky 1980). Such variations, however, are different from the uniformity of narratives, as mentioned earlier, as the former poses no direct threat to the legitimacy of the state institution. Instead, the variation could rather be seen as a nuanced functioning of the State, which also has legislated policies to safeguard the interests of the Adivasis. Legislations like the Scheduled Tribes and Other Traditional Dwellers (Recognition of Forests) Act, 2006, which recognises the rights of Adivasis to live in the forests (The Gazette of India 2007: 3); the Panchayat Extension to Scheduled Areas (PESA) Act, 1996, which empowers Gram Sabha (village assembly) as the primary decision maker in SAs; and the Mahatma Gandhi National Rural Employment Guarantee Act (MGNREGA), 2005, which is directed at employing Adivasis in Naxalite-influenced areas (Planning Commission 2008; Pawar 2012) can be read as state enactments in the interest of Adivasis.[12]

However, such readings do not absolve the State from charges of pursuing exploitative 'developmental' policies against the Adivasis or indulging in practices of Adivasi repression. Rather, it points to the limitations of the state in directing and controlling 'development and governance' projects in the SAs of Eastern and Central India. The State, as a complex assemblage of different institutions and interests, though articulating homogeneity when furthering the legitimacy of the state, however, stands diversified in undertaking development and governance amongst the Adivasis at the local level. The Naxalites, on the other hand, do not pit themselves as the 'solution' in face of an inefficient or exploitative state functioning. Their fight, even though against the injustices meted out by the state, is not necessarily aimed at alleviating the conditions of Adivasis.

Practicing development and governance: intimacy of processes between Naxalites, the state and Adivasis

The previous sections have illustrated the non-fixated roles of the State and Naxalites, occupying varying positions, from friends to foes, in their engagement with the Adivasis. However, it is important to note that their roles and functions do not occur in abstraction, and that their relations with the 'other' sovereign are not necessarily oppositional. A prominent voice within this discourse, that seeks to go beyond the traditional fixated readings of the state and Naxalites, is that of Alpa Shah. In her initial writings, she had analysed the workings of Naxalites in some of the Adivasi areas in Jharkhand (2006; 2010). Shah claimed that the Naxalites, in contrast to their imagery of anti-state and anti-bourgeoisie, were in fact colluding with the village elites and the state officials and were strengthening their presence by offering 'protection' to these elites, which Shah termed as 'markets of protection' (2006; 2010).

Observing a similar fluidity of relations in the Telangana province, Suykens (2010) talked about the Naxalite engagement with the Beedi[13] industry, and their role in raising the prices of tendu leaves sold by the Adivasis in the region, thereby earning local support amongst the Adivasi population. The Movement, Suykens claimed, had clear linkages with the state in what appears to be a 'joint extraction regime.' Sareen (2016) recorded a similar instance in Jharkhand, where access to certain government services – like that of fixing the prices of tendu leaf or the regulation of the tendu contract – was within the domain of Naxalites as well; thus, hinting a complex linkage of the state, Naxalites, and Adivasis, beyond the narratives of 'victim-perpetrator' or oppositional binaries. During my fieldwork, in conversation with an administrative official posted in a LWE-affected district in Jharkhand, the author was given a similar account of the fluidity of relations between the three entities. The following is an excerpt from the conversation:

Q. What kind of relationship do the Maoists have with the police and administrative officials? What kind of problems do the state officials face in implementing government programs like MGNREGA or PDS [Public Distribution System]?

A: Maoists would target the police officials irrespective of their individual background [Adivasi or non-Adivasi]. However, it's not the same with administrative officials. A dedicated officer, in my knowledge, faces no problem from the Maoists. It is rather easier to implement MGNREGA and other government programs in affected areas. On PDS, the Maoist interaction is not with the officials, but the local PDS dealer. They collect their food supplies directly from the local PDS dealers.[14]

Another high-ranking administrative official, from the Madhya Pradesh cadre, who was primarily tasked with the functioning of MGNREGA in Jharkhand, made similar observations:

> MGNREGA is not something that is wholly run by the government; the projects are planned and implemented by the villagers themselves – the government only supervises and pays for the work done. In rural villages, mostly in tribal areas, people are ignorant about the functioning of MGNREGA or how it is to be implemented. Especially works that involve paper-work or gathering of raw materials for construction works. Maoists help to smoothen up the process. They can easily get the raw materials and provide help in several other things.[15]

Banerjee and Saha (2010), in their study of the functioning of NREGA in Naxalite-affected areas, put forth a similar proposition, concluding that performance in several of the 'affected' areas were better than the 'normal' areas. Such instances, which are not sporadic accounts and are widely observed across the LWE-affected Adivasi areas, necessitates a re-orientation of perceptions on development and governance, which are traditionally seen under the exclusive domain of the state. It is in this context that Christian Lund's (2006a, 2006b) reading of 'public authority' assumes importance. For Lund (2006a, 2006b), the idea of state is grounded in the idea of 'public authority,' which draws legitimacy from people's consent and their recognition of authority. However, it's not necessary that the government has a monopoly on the institutions of public authority. Several institutions, especially at the times of crisis, outside the purview of government, have assumed the role of public authority, thus exhibiting twilight characteristics, that of being a public and a private institution. In the Adivasi context, the Maoists in several of the SAs of the Eastern and Central parts of India, have come to assume the role of the state or have become 'public authorities' ('mimetic sovereignties' as Nandini Sundar [2014] calls it). Lund's concept, though it might not seamlessly flow into the idea of fluid entities, however, is important in regard to displacing the imagination of the state as the only legitimate actor to provide governance and development. The state is only one of the many actors in the workings of the state. Nevertheless, Lund's idea can be problematised on the account of fixating binaries of 'authority' and 'commoners.' The implied power structure, though not focused on the State, yet remains centred on twilight institutions who assume the role of public authority. Perhaps, an extended understanding of such institutions would be to include the Adivasis as a co-constituent in the re-defining, re-designing, and re-interpreting the templates of development and governance.

But why is there a need to re-conceptualise the orientation and workings of development and governance, besides it being a mere academic exercise? Numerous committees[16] at the central and state level have been formed and countless reports submitted on the issues of Adivasi deprivation and impoverishment, and yet the Adivasi situation remains the same. The reports, papers, and committees have, on several occasions, pointed at the Adivasi grievances and the causal factors, and yet the reasons have persisted. The problem, as the chapter implicitly argues, is in the fallacious imagination of the state as a solution to all the problems. The workings of the state in the Scheduled Areas that are Naxalite affected are severely limited not only by the constraints imposed by Naxalites, but also in its multiplicity of intentions and institutions that remain highly fractured on issues of Adivasi development. In this regard, understanding development and governance as a co-constitutive practice by the state, Naxalites, and Adivasis alters the previously internalised hegemony of the state as the only route to ameliorating Adivasi conditions, and rather opens up the venue to multiple actors and institutions, thereby bringing back the focus to the empowerment of Adivasis, instead of legitimacy struggles.

Conclusion

This chapter has critically examined the narratives of the state and oppositional voices on the challenges to development and governance in the SAs that are LWE affected. The state puts forth a narrative blaming the Naxalites for the lack of development and governance in the regions, however, a critical reading of the state and the narrative reveals that 'Naxalite problem' is only a recent construct, and that the state has engaged in several policies and practices that have gone against the interests of Adivasis, leading to their dispossession and displacement. On the other hand, the 'other' narrative that alleges the state to be an instrument in the hands of bourgeoisie and claims that the Naxalites are only a manifestation the state-created problem, and that they are rightly challenging the exploitative practices of the state, seems equally flawed. The violence committed by the Naxalites, and their prioritising of self-interests over the Adivasis, is telling of the fact that Naxalites are no revolutionaries. The chapter, then, moves beyond these oppositional narratives to understand the processes of 'development and governance' as a co-constitutive of the Adivasis, Naxalites, and the state, and that these entities have equal, if not symmetric, stakes in these processes. The chapter has attempted to dislodge the idea that the processes of 'development and governance' are under the exclusive domain of the state, and that the state or the Naxalites only (separately) can work towards alleviating the impoverished conditions of the Adivasis. In terms of limitations, the chapter has projected Adivasis as a homogenous collective. It acknowledges the multiplicity of voices within the Adivasi communities, and the fallacy of declaring one single notion as 'Adivasi interest.' However, the chapter is limited in its space and content to bring forth all the issues that are pertinent to the discussions of SAs and LWE.

Acknowledgement

I would like to thank the editors for the opportunity to publish this chapter. I would also like to thank Prof Lawrence King for having funded my fieldwork in Jharkhand.

Notes

1 The Scheduled Areas, as provided by the Indian Constitution, Article 244(1), refer to the areas listed under Fifth and Sixth Schedule of the Constitution. These areas, traditionally, have a preponderance of Adivasi population, and are economically backward than other areas (Ministry of Tribal Affairs 2018). The Constitution provides that these areas be governed differently, to ensure that the Adivasis are gradually integrated into the mainstream society. The historical origin of SAs could be traced back to the British Government's Order of 1936 to create Excluded Areas and Partially Excluded Areas, or even earlier, to the British Government's legislation of Scheduled Districts Act in 1874, when the British demarcated areas that constituted groups (Adivasis) whose cultures and way of life were not in accordance with the mainstream traditions. In principle, it aimed at protecting and preserving these different cultures, and also prevent their exploitation from the 'outsiders.'

2 Adivasis, meaning original inhabitants, refer to the indigenous population of India. The term was first used in the 1930s with the formation of the political party 'Adivasi Mahasabha' in the Chotanagpur region (Dasgupta 2016; Banerjee 2016; Munda and Mullick 2003; Aaron 2005; Sengupta 1988; Sundar 2016). The Adivasi communities are commonly identified with the government-designated category of 'Scheduled Tribes' (STs), and Adivasis are popularly referred to as tribals. However, against this popular typology, the term 'Adivasi' does not extend to the entire category of STs and is rather largely confined to the peninsular tribals; the Northeastern tribes do not associate themselves with the term 'Adivasi.' In this chapter, the term 'Adivasi' has been used throughout.

3 The chapter acknowledges the differences in the various terminologies like Naxalites, Maoists, and Left wing extremists. However, not to dwell on the differences and largely perceiving them as part of left-leaning insurgency movements, the chapter uses these terms interchangeably.

4 One of the lone voices in Constituent Assembly to have raised the issue of Adivasi culture was that of Jaipal Singh Munda. He cautioned against the binaries of 'backward and advanced' between Adivasis and non-Adivasis, criticising the latter's assumption of superiority. He emphasised the necessity of a genuine respect for Adivasis, especially when working towards ameliorating their conditions (Constituent Assembly Debates 1949). What Munda attempted, if one were to interpret his speeches, was to disassociate cultural underpinnings of Adivasis with their material realities, thereby, implying a concerted effort in improving their conditions without sacrificing the cultural preserve. However, much of assembly's orientation was ostensibly guided through imaginations of a singular evolutionary trajectory, in which the Adivasis were yet to climb up to the level of mainstream society, and that an interventionist course was essential to bring about changes.

5 At the time of independence, and even before, scholars and policy makers working on the Adivasi issues were largely divided into two camps – isolationists and assimilationists. The isolationists projected Adivasis as a separate entity if not

exclusionary (Elwin 1939, 1943, 1947) and argued that their deprivation was a result of the 'outsider' interference in their economic and social ways of living. They argued for the autonomy of Adivasi areas in order to minimise the external interference. The assimilationists, on the other hand, re-examined the essentialist and distinct projection of the Adivasis, emerging from the isolationist writings, to highlight the fallacy of Adivasis as a separate category, which in their opinion was no different than the peasant or the 'lower caste Hindu' (Bose 1941; Ghurye 1959; Burman 1983). These arguments were situated in the nationalist discourse of independence struggle, which argued for integration and assimilation of varying identities into a singular Indian identity, against the perceived divisive project of colonial segregation of Indian communities; as a collective, this strand was referred to as 'assimilationist' that argued for a cultural non-differentiation between Adivasis and mainstream.

6 The five principles were these: '1. People should develop along the lines of their own genius and we should avoid imposing anything on them. . . . 2. Tribal rights in land and forests should be respected. 3. We should try to train and build up a team of their own people to do the work of administration and development. . . . 4. We should not over-administer these areas or overwhelm them with a multiplicity of schemes. . . . 5. We should judge results, not by statistics or the amount of money spent, but by the quality of human character, that is evolved' (Bedi 1992: 248).

7 Such a pretext was evident when P. Chidambaram, the former Home Minister of India, in an interview with Shoma Chaudhury talked about tribals as 'hunters and gatherers,' and to develop them would require the state to mine the resources buried beneath their lands (Chaudhury 2009).

8 Singh (2006) explains that a 'large part of our natural resources lies in the hilly and forest areas, mostly inhabited by the tribals,' and for the state to pursue its development plans, it required the acquisition of such lands.

9 LWE affected states: Andhra Pradesh, Telangana, Bihar, Chhattisgarh, Jharkhand, Madhya Pradesh, Maharashtra, Orissa, Uttar Pradesh, West Bengal.

10 The term 'Dalit', literally meaning depressed class, refers to the so called 'lower castes' that constitute the lowest strata of Indian societal hierarchy. Against the official terminology of Scheduled Castes (SC), erstwhile untouchables or as Gandhi would call them, the *Harijans*, the term 'dalit' signifies a political consciousness used for mobilising a certain group of people against caste-based discrimination. Scheduled Castes is a constitutionally defined term that has several qualifying criteria like religion, geography etc., however, dalit captures a much wider population who have had faced the brunt of caste oppression. For more information on caste hierarchy, see Dumont (1970), Appadurai (1986), Sharma (1999), and Gupta (2000).

11 Salwa Judum roughly translates into purification hunt. Salwa Judum was initially claimed as civilian initiative in Chhattisgarh to fight against Maoist oppression. This state government popularly supported this initiative, claiming it to be a citizen-led movement. However, it soon emerged that the members of Salwa Judum were armed militia, backed by the state, to wield terror tactics against the Maoists or any of their perceived supporters (Sundar 2016a; Basu 2011; Guha *et al.* 2006; Guha 2007; Roy 2010).

12 In a critical reading of these policies, their implementation has failed to deliver on the promises. For example, in regard to PESA, as noted by Ramakrishnan and Mahaprashasta (2013), the state that has often and brazenly violated the provisions of PESA. In many cases, the state has acquired lands and displaced people without consulting the Gram Sabha. MGNREGA, similarly, though largely credited for improving the livelihood of Adivasis in terms of employment opportunities and female participation (Khera 2008), is also riddled with several flaws.

Bhatia and Dreze (2006) have detailed the various faults, in relation to wage payment, role of mediators, lack of worksite facilities, amongst others, in implementation of MGNREGA. In several interviews with the villagers in Jharkhand, conducted by the author, the popular perception on MGNREGA was captured in their oft-articulated quote 'NREGA Marega' (roughly translates into 'NREGA will die'). Several of the villagers had not been paid their due wages for over six months. The Naxalites in the area, though articulate in the describing the failings of the State, did little to ameliorate the conditions of the Adivasis in this case. The Naxalites seemed concerned only when someone falsely used the Naxalite influence to get their work done, thereby, bringing a 'bad name' to the organisation.

13 Beedis are cheap hand-rolled cigarettes made of dry tendu leaves.

14 Fieldwork Notes.

15 Fieldwork Notes.

16 Committees like Dhebar Commission 1961, Bhuria Committee 1991, Bhuria Commission 2004, Bandopadhyay Committee 2008, and Xaxa Committee 2014 have consistently mentioned the importance of land and forests in the Adivasi livelihood, and that their alienation would have disastrous consequences. However, despite the recommendations, the state has legislated several economic policies that have resulted in the displacement of tribals.

References

Aaron, S.J. 2005. 'Contrarian Lives: Christians and Contemporary Protest in Jharkhand.' *Asia Research Centre Working Paper 18*. London School of Economics and Political.

Acharya, J. 1993. *Nehru Socialism: Colonialism, Capitalism and Ideology in the Making of State Policy*. New Delhi: Indian Publishers Distributors.

Appadurai, A. 1986. 'Is Homo Hierarchicus?' *American Ethnologist*, 13(4): 745–761.

Banerjee, K. and Saha, P. 2010. 'The NREGA, the Maoists and the Developmental Woes of the Indian State.' *Economic and Political Weekly*, 45(28): 42–47.

Banerjee, P. 2016. 'Writing the Adivasi: Some Historiographical Notes.' *The Indian Economic and Social History Review*, 53(1): 131–153.

Banerjee, S. 1980. *In the Wake of Naxalbari: A History of the Naxalite Movement in India*. Calcutta: Subarnarekha.

Banerjee, S. 1984. *India's Simmering Revolution: The Naxalite Uprising*. London: Zed Press.

Basu, I. 2011. 'Security and Development – Are They Two Sides of the Same Coin? Investigating India's Two-Pronged Policy Towards Left Wing Extremism.' *Contemporary South Asia*, 19(4): 373–393.

Baviskar, A. 2004. *In the Belly of the River: Tribal Conflicts Over Development in the Narmada Valley*. New Delhi: Oxford University Press.

Bedi, M.S. 1992. 'Nehru and Tribal Development Policy.' In R. Malhotra (Ed.), *Anthropology of Development: Commemoration Volume in Honour of Professor I P Singh* (pp. 244–255). New Delhi: Mittal Publications.

Bhatia, B. 2005. 'The Naxalite Movement in Central Bihar.' *Economic and Political Weekly*, 40(15): 1536–1549.

Bhatia, B. 2006 'On Armed Resistance.' *Economic and Political Weekly*, 41(29): 3179–3183.

Bhatia, B. and Dreze, J. 2006. 'Employment Guarantee in Jharkhand: Ground Realities.' *Economic and Political Weeekly*, 41(29): 3198–3202.

Bhengra, R., Bijoy, C.R. and Luithui, S. 1998. *The Adivasis of India*. Minority Rights Group International Report.

Bose, N.K. 1941. 'The Hindu Method of Tribal Absorption.' *Science and Culture*, 7(2): 188–194.

Burman, B.K. Roy. 1983. 'Transformation of Tribes and Analogous Social Formations.' *Economic and Political Weekly*, 18(27): 1172–1174.

Chakrabarty, B. and Kujur, R.K. 2010. *Maoism in India: Reincarnation of Ultra-Left Wing Extremism in the Twenty-First Century*. Oxon: Routledge.

Chandra, A. 1990. 'The Naxalbari Movement.' *The Indian Journal of Political Science*, 51(1): 22–45.

Chatterjee, P. 1997. 'Development Planning and the Indian State.' In P. Chatterjee (Ed.), *State and Politics in India* (pp. 271–297). New Delhi: Oxford University Press.

Chatterjee, P. 1998. 'Beyond the Nation? Or Within?' *Social Text*, 16(3): 57–69.

Chatterjee, P. 2004. *The Politics of the Governed: Reflections on Popular Politics in Most of the World*. New York: Columbia University Press.

Chatterjee, P. 2008. 'Democracy and Economic Transformation in India.' *Economic and Political Weekly*, 43(16): 53–62.

Chaudhury, S. 2009. 'Halt the Violence! Give Me 72 Hours.' *Tehelka*. Available at: www.tehelka.com/story_main43.asp?filename=Ne211109coverstory.asp (accessed on 6 May 2013).

Choudhary, S. 2012. *Let's Call Him Vasu: With the Maoists in Chhattisgarh*. New Delhi: Penguin Books.

Constituent Assembly Debates. 1948. *Appendix D: Annexure I to XIV, Vol. VII*. Available at: http://164.100.47.194/Loksabha/Debates/Result_Nw_15.aspx?dbsl=148 (accessed on 25 April 2018).

Constituent Assembly Debates. 1949. 'Paragraph 3.' *Parliament of India*, Vol. IX. Available at: http://164.100.47.194/Loksabha/Debates/Result_Nw_15.aspx?dbsl=1047 (accessed on 25 April 2018).

Corbridge, S., Williams, G., Srivastava, M. and Veron, R. 2005. *Seeing the State: Governance and Governmentality in India*. Cambridge: Cambridge University Press.

Dasgupta, S. 2016. '"Heathen Aboriginals", "Christian Tribes", and "Animistic Races": Missionary Narratives on the Oraons of Chhotanagpur in Colonial India.' *Modern Asian Studies*, 50(2): 437–478.

De, D. 2014. 'Nehruvian Vision of Sustainable Development for Tribals in India: A Critique.' *South Asia Research*, 34(1): 1–18.

Deogharial, J. 2016. 'MoS Home Blames Maoists for Tribal's Underdevelopment.' *The Times of India*. Available at: https://timesofindia.indiatimes.com/india/mos-home-blames-maoists-for-tribals-underdevelopment/articleshow/56026902.cms (accessed on 10 May 2017).

Dumont, L. 1970. *Homo Hierarchicus: An Essay on the Caste System*. Chicago: University of Chicago Press.

Dungdung, G. 2015. *Mission Saranda: A War for Natural Resources in India*. Ranchi: Deshaj Prakashan.

The Economic Times. 2018. 'Naxalism Will be Wiped Out From the Country: Rajnath Singh.' Available at: https://economictimes.indiatimes.com/news/politics-and-nation/naxalism-will-be-wiped-out-from-the-country-rajnath-singh/articleshow/63870310.cms (accessed on 28 April 2018).

Elwin, V. 1939. *The Baiga*. London: Wyman & Sons.

Elwin, V. 1943. *Maria Murder and Suicide*. London: Oxford University Press.

Elwin, V. 1947. *The Muria and Their Ghotul*. London: Oxford University Press.

Fernandes, W. and Thukral, E.G. 1989. *Development, Displacement, and Rehabilitation*. New Delhi: Indian Social Institute.
Fuller, C.J. and Harris, J. 2001. 'For an Anthropology of the Modern Indian State.' In C.J. Fuller and V. Benei (Eds.), *The Everyday State and Society in Modern India* (pp. 1–30). London: Hurst & Company.
Garg, R. 2008. 'Roots and Causes: The Case of Dandakaranya.' In P.V. Ramana (Ed.), *The Naxal Challenge: Causes, Linkages and Policy Options* (pp. 25–38). Delhi: Pearson Longman.
The Gazette of India. 2007. 'REGISTERED NO. DL-(N)04/0007/2006–08.' *Government of India*. Available at: http://tribal.nic.in/writereaddata/mainlinkFile/File1033.pdf (accessed on 5 May 2013).
Ghurye, G.S. 1959. *The Scheduled Tribes*. Bombay: Popular Book Depot.
Guha, R. 2007. 'Adivasis, Naxalites and Indian Democracy.' *Economic and Political Weekly*, 42(32): 3305–3312.
Guha, R., Harivansh, Naqvi, F., Sarma, E.A.S., Sundar, N. and Verghese, B.G. 2006. 'Salwa Judum: War in the Heart of India: Excerpts From the Report by the Independent Citizens Initiative.' *Social Scientist*, 34(7–8): 47–61.
Gupta, D.K. 2000. *Interrogating Caste: Understanding Hierarchy and Difference in Indian Society*. New Delhi: Penguin Books.
Gupta, D.K. 2007. 'The Naxalites and the Maoist Movement in India: Birth, Demise, and Reincarnation.' *Democracy and Security*, 3(2): 157–188.
Harris, J. 2006. *Power Matters: Essays on Institutions, Politics, and Society in India*. New Delhi: Oxford University Press.
The Indian Express. 2009. 'Maoists Are Terrorists: Home Secy Pillai.' Available at: http://archive.indianexpress.com/news/maoists-are-terrorists-home-secy-pillai/544202/ (accessed on 12 February 2017).
Jharkhand Human Rights Movement. 2011. *Jharkhand Human Rights Report 2001–2011*. Ranchi: JHRM.
Joshi, S. 2010. 'Chidambaram: None Should Support the Maoists.' *The Hindu*. Available at: www.thehindu.com/news/national/Chidambaram-none-should-support-the-Maoists/article16128040.ece (accessed on 12 February 2017).
Kaviraj, S. 2010. *The Trajectories of the Indian State*. Ranikhet: Permanent Black.
Khera, R. 2008. 'Empowerment Guarantee Act.' *Economic and Political Weekly*, 43(35): 8–10.
Kunnath, G.J. 2009. 'Smouldering Dalit Fires in Bihar, India.' *Dialectical Anthropology*, 33(3–4): 309–325.
Kunnath, G.J. 2012. *Rebels From the Mud Houses: Dalits and the Making of the Maoist Revolution in Bihar*. New Delhi: Social Science Press.
Lipsky, M. 1980. *Street-Level Bureaucracy: Dilemmas of the Individual in the Public Services*. New York: Russell Sage Foundation.
Lund, C. 2006a. 'Twilight Institutions: Public Authority and Local Politics in Africa.' *Development and Change*, 37(4): 685–705.
Lund, C. 2006b. 'Twilight Institutions: An Introduction.' *Development and Change*, 37(4): 673–684.
Migdal, J.S. 1994. 'The State in Society: An Approach to Struggles for Domination.' In J.S. Migdal, A. Kohli and V. Shue (Eds.), *State Power and Social Forces: Domination and Transformation in the Third World* (pp. 7–35). Cambridge: Cambridge University Press.
Migdal, J.S. 2001. *State in Society: Studying How States and Societies Transform and Constitute One Another*. Cambridge: Cambridge University Press.

Ministry of Health and Family Welfare. 2017. 'National Family Health Survey (NFHS-4) 2015–16.' *Government of India*. Available at: http://rchiips.org/NFHS/NFHS-4Reports/India.pdf (accessed on 20 January 2018).
Ministry of Home Affairs. 2004. 'Annual Report 2003–2004.' *Government of India*. Available at: http://mha.nic.in/pdfs/ar0304-Eng.pdf (accessed on 5 May 2013).
Ministry of Home Affairs. 2017. 'Left Wing Extremism Division.' *Government of India*, Available at: http://mha.nic.in/naxal_new (accessed on 20 March 2017).
Ministry of Home Affairs. 2018. 'Left Wing Extremism Division.' *Government of India*. Available at: https://mha.gov.in/division_of_mha/left-wing-extremism-division (accessed on 20 April 2018).
Ministry of Tribal Affairs. 2013. 'Statistical Profile of Scheduled Tribes in India 2013', *Government of India*. Available at: https://tribal.nic.in/ST/StatisticalProfileofSTs2013.pdf (accessed on 10 June 2017).
Ministry of Tribal Affairs. 2014. 'Report of the High Level Committee on Socio-Economic, Health and Educational Status of Tribal Communities in India.' *Government of India*. Available at: www.indiaenvironmentportal.org.in/files/file/Tribalpercent20Committeeper cent20Report,per cent20May-Juneper cent202014.pdf (accessed on 23 May 2017).
Ministry of Tribal Affairs. 2018. 'Declaration of 5th Schedule.' *Government of India*. Available at: https://tribal.nic.in/declarationof5thSchedule.aspx (accessed on 3 May 2018).
Mukherji, P.N. 1979. 'Naxalbari Movement and the Peasant Revolt in North Bengal.' In M.S.A. Rao (Ed.), *Social Movements in India: Volume One* (pp. 17–90). New Delhi: Manohar Publications.
Munda, R.D. and Mullick, S.B. (Eds.). 2003. *The Jharkhand Movement: Indigenous People's Struggle for Autonomy in India*. Copenhagen: IWGIA.
Navlakha, G. 2012. *Days and Nights in the Heartland of Rebellion*. New Delhi: Penguin Books.
Nilsen, A.G. 2013. 'Contesting the Postcolonial Development Project: A Marxist Perspective on Popular Resistance in the Narmada Valley.' In C. Barker, L. Cox, J. Krinsky and A.G. Nilsen (Eds.), *Marxism and Social Movements* (pp. 167–185). Leiden: Brill.
Pandita, R. 2011. *Hello, Bastar: The Untold Story of India's Maoist Movement*. Chennai: Tranquebar Press.
Pawar, M. 2012. 'The Adoption of a Rights-Based Approach to Welfare in India.' *Journal of Comparative Social Welfare*, 28(1): 35–47.
Peters, B.G. 2002. 'Governance and Comparative Politics.' In J. Pierre (Ed.), *Debating Governance: Authority, Steering, and Democracy* (pp. 36–53). Oxford: Oxford University Press.
Pierre, J. 2002. 'Introduction: Understanding Governance.' In J. Pierre (Ed.), *Debating Governance: Authority, Steering, and Democracy* (pp. 1–10). Oxford: Oxford University Press.
Planning Commission. 2008. 'Development Challenges in Extremist Affected Areas: Report of an Expert Group to Planning Commission.' *Government of India*. New Delhi: Planning Commission, Government of India.
Press Information Bureau. 2006. 'Text of Prime Minister's Independence Day Address.' *Government of India*. Available at: http://pib.nic.in/newsite/erelease.aspx?relid=29937 (accessed on 4 May 2013).

Press Information Bureau. 2016. 'LWE affected Districts.' *Government of India*. Available at: http://pib.nic.in/newsite/PrintRelease.aspx?relid=136706, (accessed on 10 August 2017).

Ramakrishnan, V. and Mahaprashasta, A.A. 2013. 'Illusory Rights.' *Frontline*. Available at: www.frontline.in/social-issues/social-justice/illusory-rights/article 4613760.ece (accessed 3 May 2015).

Roy, A. 2010a. 'Walking with the Comrades.' *Outlook*. Available at: www.outlookindia.com/magazine/story/walking-with-the-comrades/264738 (accessed on 5 May 2013).

Roy, A. 2010b. *Listening to Grasshoppers: Field Notes on Democracy*. London: Hamish Hamilton.

Sahay, B.N. 1968. 'Tribal in the Recent Reports: A Summary and Appraisal of Reports of Elwin Committee and Dhebar Commission.' In L.P. Vidyarthi (Ed.), *Applied Anthropology in India: Principles, Problems and Case Studies* (pp. 222–241). Allahabad: Kitab Mahal.

Sareen, S. 2016. 'Who Governs Local Access in Jharkhand? Mechanisms of Access to Government Services.' *Forum for Development Studies*, 44(2): 249–274.

Satnam. 2010. *Jangalnama: Inside the Maoist Guerrilla Zone*. New Delhi: Penguin Books.

SATP. 2018. *Fatalities in Left-Wing Extremism: 2018*. Available at: www.satp.org/Maoistdatasheets (accessed on 10 May 2018).

Sen, A. 1988. 'The Concept of Development.' In H. Chenery and T.N. Srinivasan (Eds.), *Handbook of Development Economic*, Vol. I (pp. 10–26). North-Holland: Elsevier

Sengupta, N. 1988. 'Reappraising Tribal Movements – II: Legitimisation and Spread.' *Economic and Political Weekly*, 23(20): 1003–1005.

Shah, A. 2006. 'Markets of Protection: The "Terrorist" Maoist Movement and the State in Jharkhand, India.' *Critique of Anthropology*, 26(3): 297–314.

Shah, A. 2010. *In the Shadows of the State: Indigenous Politics, Environmentalism, and Insurgency in Jharkhand, India*. London: Duke University Press.

Sharma, U. 1999. *Caste*. Buckingham: Open University Press.

Singh, A.K. 2006. 'Tribal Ecology in India: The Ugly Face of Development.' In S.K. Chaudhury (Ed.), *Culture, Ecology and Sustainable Development* (pp. 111–122). New Delhi: Mittal Publications.

Singh, V. 2014. 'Maoists Should be Treated as Terrorists: Chattisgarh to MHA.' *The Indian Express*. Available at: http://indianexpress.com/article/india/india-others/maoists-should-be-treated-as-terrorists-chattisgarh-to-mha/ (accessed on 11 May 2017).

Sundar, N. 2006. 'Bastar, Maoism and Salwa Judum.' *Economic and Political Weekly*, 41(29): 3187–3192.

Sundar, N. 2014. 'Mimetic Sovereignties, Precarious Citizenship: State Effects in a Looking-Glass World.' *The Journal of Peasant Studies*, 41(4): 469–490.

Sundar, N. 2016a. 'Introduction: Of the Scheduled Tribes, States and Sociology.' In N. Sundar (Ed.), *The Scheduled Tribes and Their India: Politics, Identities, Policies and Work* (pp. 1–45). New Delhi: Oxford University Press.

Sundar, N. 2016b. *The Burning Forest: India's War in Bastar*. New Delhi: Juggernaut Books.

Suykens, B. 2010. 'Diffuse Authority in the Beedi Commodity Chain: Naxalite and State Governance in Tribal Telangana, India.' *Development and Change*, 41(1): 153–178.

10 *Pathalgadi* movement and conflicting ideologies of tribal village governance

Anjana Singh

Introduction

On 21 February 2018, Khunti district police forces entered the Kurunga village, 51 kilometres away from the district headquarters at Khunti, and arrested the *Gram Pradhan*(Village Headman) Sagar Munda. He was charged for doing *Pathalgadi* (erection of stone slabs) on the boundary of village on which a 'misleading' interpretation of constitutional rights of *Gram Sabha*(GS)(village assembly) were inscribed, by which outsiders were prohibited from entering the village. It was declared that no central or state laws were applicable in the village. Local administration obviously deemed this act unlawful. Sagar was brought to Khunti police station and, after an interrogation, the police force numbering 35 again went to Kurunga. This time the villagers responded differently and the policemen were taken hostage by the villagers for trespassing into their area. They were however released after the District Collector and Superintendent of Police of the district gave in writing that they would not enter these areas without the permission of the GS. Sagar Munda was brought back and handed over to them the same day.[1] This was not however the solitary instance. Similar incidents had occurred in August 2017 when 300 policemen were taken hostage in Kanki village of Khunti district. These events can be interpreted as responses of the villagers to the supposed denial of the traditional as well as constitutional right of the Adivasis by the state government.

There was another aspect to the story. This was to lodge a protest against the lack of development of the region by the state. Geeta Samad, the Mukhiya (headmen) of Kurunga village, gave vent to popular frustration:

> *Gaon mein ab bhi vikas ki kiran nahi pahunchi hai. Log chahte hain ki gaon mein vikas ho. Abhi bhi gaon ke log payjal ke liye karunga nadi ke pani par nirbhar hain. Koi bimar pad jaye to Arki ya Khunti ke svasthya kendra jana padta hai, gaon tak pahunchne ka rasta jarjar hai Gaon ke logon ko malum hi nahi hai ki bahar ki duniya mein kya chal raha hai.*
>
> English translation: Village has not seen the ray of development. People want that village should develop. People of Kurunga village are still

> dependent on Kurunga River for water. If someone gets sick then he has to be taken to either Arki or Khunti health centre. Even the approach road to the village is in a bad shape. People of village are unaware about the developments outside village (Prabhat Khabar, 24 February 2018).

It will be very interesting to apprehend why Pathalgadi (see Figure 10.1) should be invoked as an instrument of resurrecting the traditional form of governance? 'Pathalgadi' is a custom of Adivasis where stone slabs are erected to mark occasions of importance. The records of their pasts are enshrined in their oral tradition and cultural symbols. Pathalgadi acts as not only a parameter of tribal identity but also as something capable of addressing the aspirations and interests of the Adivasis, which the state-sponsored development schemes fail to address. In this context, it is notable that the

Figure 10.1 Traditional stone slab depicting the genealogical table in the Bhandra village of Khunti

development model adopted in India after independence had no place for socio-cultural factors because it did not have avenues for the involvement of local communities. The development model was premised on centralised rational bureaucratic planning and the implementation of industry-led development that did not suit the development requirements of the tribal and more backward regions. The overall consequence of this model was that the local communities became passive beneficiaries of the state's development policy instead of being active partners. Absence of socio-cultural factors and participative local development structures in the state's policy led to the emergence of politics over conflicting ideologies of development in which local communities resorted to agitational politics over meaningful exchange of resources with the state (Prakash 2001: 228–229).

An empiricist will be tempted to address the events as a simple conflict of ideologies that have originated since the passing of the Panchayati Raj (Extension to Scheduled Areas) Act, 1996 (PESA). But a researcher with hindsight will be tempted to argue that it had been shaped by the history of tribal rural governance as it had developed from the pre-colonial and colonial times to the introduction of the Panchayati Raj (local governance system) post-independence. Enriched by a historical and empirical understanding of the evolving system of tribal village administration, the present chapter seeks to unfold the nature and the spectrum of the conflict, the cause of discontent against the present system of governance, the polarisation of the state and people, and the recent modality of tribal protest drawing legitimacy from an official act, yet using it as a tool against the state itself. These issues will be addressed through four sections of the chapter. The first will attempt to understand the Pathalgadi movement in Jharkhand. The second will critically examine the strategy of constructing a counter narrative and the conflict between the modern and the traditional forms of governance. The third will focus on the conflict of ideologies and their manifestations and analyse the rationale behind popular protest and official policy towards it. And the last will seek to discuss the challenges it poses to the governance of the schedule areas.

Understanding the Pathalgadi movement

Pathalgadi movement saw its emergence with the erection of a stone slab on the boundary of village Bhandra of Khunti district of Jharkhand on 9 March 2017(Hindustan, Ranchi, 10 March 2018). Adivasis consider their oral tradition of *Purkha Sahitya* (ancestral literature) and cultural symbols vitally important for them, as they believe that these have been transmitted to them through succeeding generations. For Adivasis, they are embodiments of their living histories that have enclosed the question of their identity rather than creations for entertainment (Tete 2013: 12–13). In the absence of literary traditions, the Adivasi communities normally seek legitimacy from the colonial document, where their customs and traditions are recorded in various papers.

They also draw support from their archaeological evidences as *sasandiri* (sepulchral stone), Pathalgadi, and such related customary symbols.

The immediate reason for the erection of the these stone slabs was the recent propaganda made by the Jharkhand government over the issue of development. The government organised a global investor's summit titled 'Momentum Jharkhand' in Ranchi on 16–17 February 2017. It aimed at making the state a hub for investments in mining and industries and a number of Memorandums of Understanding (MoUs) were signed (Times of India, 19 May 2017).[2] Chief Minister of Jharkhand Raghubar Das claimed that, 'MOUs worth 3 lakh crore was signed during the Momentum Jharkhand meet. Out of which, proposals worth Rs. 700 crore [7,000 million] have already been implemented on the ground'[3] (Times of India, 18 June 2017). Most of the investments were in the mining sector and companies as Usha Martin group, RSB group, Tata Steel Growth Shop (TGS), and others showed interest. In the wake of these announcements, Adivasis were alarmed that they would be victimised and their lands would be taken away to promote these activities.[4] The fear of land alienation mounted when it was announced by the government that the government would create conducive environment for investment in the state. The Adivasi fear of appropriation of land for the government-sponsored scheme triggered the Pathalgadi movement.

Since its inception, the popular protest gradually spread to the Ranchi, Khunti, and Saraikela districts and mineral rich and industrially viable areas as Ghatsila, Ruasol, Maubhandar, and Galudih in East Sinhbhum. In Khunti, the major areas are Ulidih, Bhandara, Konwa, Kurunga, Kochang, and others. The stone crushers of these places supply building materials which are in great demand in the neighbouring city of Ranchi (Hindustan, Ranchi Live, 25 February 2018). The piece of stone slab erected on the boundary of Bhandara village mentions the provisions of the constitution namely Article 13(3)(a),[5] Article 19(5)(6),[6] Article 244(1)part(b)Para (5)(1)[7] of the Fifth Schedule. Apparently, they were conflating Adivasi custom, symbolised by the erection of a vertical piece of stone as done in *sasandiri*, with the Fifth Schedule of the Indian constitution inscribed on it. However, in reality it was pregnant with deeper meaning. To understand its significance, I would like to quote the contents of the stone inscription and the relevant provisions of the constitution. Here, instead of a verbatim reproduction of the constitution, we notice that the words are differently presented. This change of words may be explained as a counter strategy evolved by the socially marginalised and dominated groups as against the dominant trend of the distortion of the 'historiography of class struggle . . . in a state-centric way' by the state and ruling class (Scott and Kerkvliet 1990: 5) (Figure 10.2).

English translation of the declaration on the slab

1 By Article 13 (3)(a) of Constitution of India, custom or tradition is the force of law (i.e., power of constitution).

Figure 10.2 Pathalgadi movement stone slabs erected on the boundary of the village

2 By Article 19(5) prohibition is imposed on entry of outsider or non-custom individuals to freely, roam, reside, stay or settle in fifth schedule district or area.
3 By the constitution of India Article 19(6) prohibition is laid on outsiders to carry trade, business and seek employment in this area.
4 Under the fifth schedule area or districts according to Article 244(1) part (b) para (5)(1) no general law of centre or state is applicable.

By Orders
Gram Sabha – Bhandra

The Pathalgadi movement appears to be a well-planned movement as conceptualised and spearheaded by Adivasi Mahasabha. Their objective is to mobilise the Adivasis on one platform around a customary practise common among many tribal communities[8] in the state (Hindustan, Ranchi, 14 March 2018). Contrary to this version, media reports claims that the entire programme of creating Adivasi leadership was designed in the training camps of Adivasi Mahasabha and its detail plan was prepared by Benjamin Bara who is a faculty in the Xavier Institute of Social Science (XISS), Ranchi, the leading management institute of the state(Hindustan, Ranchi, 14 March 2018). Apparently, since all of them are Christian by faith, the Bharatiya Janata Party, the ruling party of Jharkhand, allege that the movement is mentored and economically supported by the Church administration of the state. But Bishop Telesphore Bilung brushes aside this allegation as fanciful (Dainik Bhaskar, Ranchi, 5 March 2018). Adivasi Mahasabha, a political outfit, was built on the initiative of Ignace Beck, the *Chota Nagpur Unnati Samaj*, *Chota Nagpur Catholic Sabha*, and the *Hor Malto Marang Sabha* in 1938. In 1939, *Marang Gomke* (Supreme Leader) Jaipal Singh joined this party and took the leadership in its own hands. From its inception, Adivasi Mahasabha had twin objectives, the first being statehood of Jharkhand and the second being the protection of the Adivasis against the exploitation by outsiders and colonial state (Tirkey 2002: 62–73). Since the formation of the state on 15 November 2000, the party has been relegated to the background in electoral politics. Presently, its leadership is in the hands of educated Adivasis as Joseph Purty alias professor, who is a faculty in St. Joseph College, Torpa, Vijay Kujur, the Deputy General Manager in Shipping Corporation of India, Krishna Hansda, Babita Kacchap and Powell Tuti (Dainik Bhaskar, Ranchi, 22 February 2018; Hindustan, 19 March 2018, Hindustan 20 March 2018).

The movement has varying demands of a generic and specific nature. Adivasi Mahasabha and its leaders avow that the salient purpose of the movement is to diffuse consciousness among the Adivasis about their rights. It is crucial to know how they define the source of their rights. First, instead of drawing legitimacy from the Indian Constitution, the legal basis of rights accruing to an Indian citizen, they refer to an unspecified contract with the British. They also invoke colonial legacies such as the land revenue rule 1921, Gandhi-Irwin pact 1931, and Government of India Act 1935(ibid.). Leaders indulge in spreading the idea amongst the Adivasis that the SAs of Jharkhand are not a part of the government of India but that of the British Empire, which had allowed the Adivasis free existence. Through the strategy of the misrepresentation of history, they further contend that the rules framed by the constitution of India are not applicable in the SA as they have not been approved by either the Privy Council of Britain or the Parliament of Britain (ibid.). They couple this by superimposing natural laws, explained later, which they put above state and central laws (ibid. 12 March 2018).

After defining the source, protagonists specify their inventory of rights. The spell of demands is premised on the claim that they are the owners of Jharkhand (Hindustan, 8 March 2018). The following question arises: How does this ownership accrue to the Adivasis? We can draw on Asoka Sen

(2018: Chap III, 76–83) to understand the basis of their argument. Territorial control is established by two processes, 'rights of occupation' and 'rights of conquest.' Here the referents are nature and British rule. Accordingly, rights of occupation are derived from the historical occupation of the unoccupied forested tracts of Jharkhand by the Munda tribe since the 6th century AD as a matter of natural right. They reinforce this claim by their imagery of a creation myth, according to which the land is *Singbonga*'s creation, and their right of occupation accrues as a divine gift. Accordingly, the Mundas became the *khuntkattidars* (clearers of primeval forest) over large swathes of Chotanagpur plateau region. The other, the right of conquest, refers to the British conquest of the tribal region of Jharkhand. The territory the British conquered devolved on them, by virtue of transfer of power referred to earlier. Since they are the real owners, GS has the right to issue currency notes, open schools, issue identity cards as *Aadhar* card and caste, income, and residential certificates. What this inventory of demands foregrounds is the prized position of the GS. This problematises the very concept of GS. This will be disentangled in the next section.

Juxtaposition of the traditional and modern forms of village governance

The protagonists of the movement juxtapose traditional and modern forms of village governance. Therefore, information empirically derived need to be replenished by an engagement with memory and history, the two principal sources for adducing an indigenous tradition. But there is a problem. Pierre Nora (1989: 8) writes, 'Memory and history, far from being synonymous, appear to be now in fundamental opposition.' In reconstructing the institutional framework of village governance, one is handicapped by paucity of information about the origin and growth of an indigenous form of self-rule. Adivasis of Jharkhand formed a pre-literate community having no written records of how the village administration functioned. Even the colonial records, which form the main source of information about the ethnic groups, fall short of our expectations. This was so because these had been written mainly by the British officials and Christian missionaries either for ethnographic or administrative use (Ranendra 2008: 12). However, we are aware that village old men had been the socially accepted custodians of Adivasi village tradition and history, which survived as a kind of social memory (Sen 2015: 27). But the reality is that the surviving memories of the customary and traditional rights of the Adivasi are not relied upon by local officials. In practise they are completely ignored when tribal villagers claim rights on the basis of their traditions. Michel Foucault (1974: 11) cautions us against the failure to preserve and honour 'the living, fragile, pulsating "history" of the pre-literate group of people.'

S. C. Roy's famous book on the Mundas published in 1912 (Roy 1970) presents a dependable and more or less detailed account of the system of village governance in Chotanagpur plateau during pre-colonial times. Understandably, his sources were the memory of the old system as related by the village old men and the author's personal observation of the institution in function. The ideology of the traditional form of village governance was laid down after the Mundas reclaimed the virgin forests of Jharkhand and founded their *hatu* (village) and later *Khuntkatti Hatu* (village of the family of original settlers) (Hallett 1917: 22–23; Roy 1970: Chapter III). The dominant idea of Adivasi polity was of pre-state village republics (Sen 2018: 83). The whole village acknowledged the chiefship of the Munda in matters temporal as well as spiritual (Tirkey 2002: 39). They grouped themselves in wider brotherhood of villages termed *Parha* or *Patti* and laid the foundation of a supra-village pre-state tribal polity headed by the Manki. The village was governed by the traditional panchayat which was composed of the Munda and the *Pahan*(religious head) among others. (Hallett 1917: 22–24; Tirkey 2002: 40–41). Originally, Adivasi settlements were autonomous and the Parha Panchayat governed their life and resources. It was observed during fieldwork that some stone slabs mentioned about the *Rurhi Pratha Prakritik Gram Sabha* (traditional natural village assembly) of the village which had issued the rules stated previously.[9] This means that the Adivasis hold that they derive their power and authority from the nature and customary social institution. But the remarkable fact is that instead of the traditional parha-panchayat, Adivasis mention the GS. This is the juxtaposition of the tradition (i.e., the former) and the modern (i.e., the latter) rather the custom and constitution. But to know why the GS became relevant for Adivasis, it is important to understand the reinvention of the institution of village governance on timeline.

The original *Parha Panchayat* system underwent several changes after the advent of the feudal rule of the Chota Nagpur rajas in the plateau region (Sen 2018: 114). The *patti* or *parha panchayat* were still there but had become subservient to the new structure (Tirkey 2002: 44). In the colonial period, whatever survived was amalgamated within the Raj administrative framework in which the villages lost their existing autonomy. But as a unit of colonial bureaucracy, it wielded the power to collect revenue, administer justice, and maintain law and order (Sen 2018: 118–123).

After independence, the state (Bihar) and the central government introduced the Panchayati Raj System to govern Indian villages, including those of the SAs. The most historic step in this direction was the passing of the separate Act for the SAs, titled PESA (Panchayats Extension to Scheduled Areas) Act by the Parliament on 24 December 1996. The PESA provides for the formation of elected GS (or panchayat at the appropriate level). The GS has been vested with the command over natural resources in the village including the minor minerals, water bodies, the minor forest produce and the power to control money lending. No mining lease can be granted without prior consultation with the GS (Sundar 2005: 4432). The act stipulates that the legislation on the Panchayats in the Fifth Schedule area shall be in conformity with the customary laws, social and religious practices, and traditional management practice of the community resources. It also makes prior consultation with the GS mandatory before any acquisition of land in the village and resettlement and rehabilitation of the project affected persons in the village.[10] On the basis of these provisions, Jharkhand passed the Jharkhand Panchayati Raj Act (JPRA) 2001. The government amended the Act three times in 2003, 2005, and 2010[11] to surmount the legal challenge and social discontent. Accordingly, Panchayat elections were held in 2010 and 2015. Thus, the Parha-Panchayat system has been relegated in the background and the GS has been constitutionally recognised as the legitimate agency of regulating and overseeing village governance in SAs.

During a recent tribal protest, through the juxtaposition of the tradition and modernity, agitators drew legitimacy from an officially created agency, yet used it as a tool against the state itself. The strategy is to deploy it as a parallel institution of village governance armed with new powers and jurisdictions which the aforementioned inventory of demands claim. The counter ideology of development detailed in the next section.

Pathalgadi movement: the conflict of ideologies

In the midst of the Pathalgadi movement my fieldwork[12]revealed that it was basically anchored on alternative ideologies of village governance[13] and development. It is shaped by their perception of the prevailing system of governance and the endemic backwardness of the region and people mainly because of its dysfunction. The main objective of the agitators was to highlight the issue of non/mal-development through the official agencies. The fulcrum of the movement was therefore to focus on the salience of development through the invented indigenous institution of rural governance. But before detailing their development-related demands, it is imperative to apprehend the Adivasi notion of development and change.

The Adivasis had their parallel discourse of development as adduced from the statement made by Sambit Topno, a Gram Pradhan (elected representative) in Ranchi on 4 April 2018 in a meeting convened by Draupadi Murmu, the Governor of Jharkhand. He averred: '*vikas ki bahari vichardhara hum par kyun thopi ja rahi hai. Sarkar Gram sabhaon se puchkar vikas kyun nahi karti hai* (Why is outsider ideology of development being imposed on us. Why doesn't government ask Gram Sabhas for the development).' This highlights that the ongoing scheme of development is extraneous and that Adiviasi's have their own notion of development which the state should adhere (Hindustan, Ranchi, 4 April 2018). During conversations with the villagers, I observed that they are averse to *Diku* (outsider) ideology and gave more importance to their traditional Panchayats, which are more sensitive to the ideas and aspirations of the people.

Two recent studies reveal how the concept of development has evolved over time. Adivasis imagine that the development schemes should originate at the local level as a social initiative, and that the social cost of development should be minimal (Sen 2018: 188–190). Furthermore, their voice should be heard while policies are framed and implemented at the local level. Adivasi perception has been that if the funds for the development of village are given to traditional Panchayats then real development would take place at the grass root level. If these institutions are strengthened and proper education is imparted for strengthening of these traditional institutions, then the Adivasi society would feel safe and realise that its traditions and customs are given respect by the ruling sections of the country (Sinku 2008: 128–129).

One should reason why Adivasis are opposed to the existing idea of development. The principal reason is that state-sponsored development has a strong bias towards mining, industrialisation, and urbanisation. This has rendered them victims rather than beneficiaries of development projects. Consequently, the percentage of their population is on constant decline in Jharkhand, as mining and industrialisation have attracted large number of outsiders to the state who have gained increasing control over the levers of political power and resources. The population of the Adivasis that was around 50 percent in 1901[14] came down to 26.3 percent by the 2001 Census (Corbridge 2003:156) and then to 26.2 percent according to 2011 census. This has whetted up a sense of fear that is channelled into anti-government feelings amongst Adivasis. Even during the course of the Jharkhand movement, which aimed at the creation of a separate state, the region was projected more as a cultural region than a mere political entity with a distinct identity (Adivasi), language form, cultural traits, elements of material culture, and historical development (Tirkey 2002: 243). These aspirations remained unfulfilled years after the formation of a separate state and the crisis accentuated by the problem of land alienation cited earlier.

Selective attributes like identity and self-determination have been articulated through various popular movements (Xaxa 1999), which revolve around the specificity of their landscape, against their non-development and marginalisation (Ibid. 2010; Sen 2018: Chap 10). In fact, this has been the principal reason why most of the movements in the SAs of Gujarat, Madhya Pradesh, Orissa, and others are for the safeguard of their landscape to which Adivasis are materially and morally linked. At the pan-Indian level, they worked on a more ambitious programme of building Adivasi solidarity and developed into a larger movement of the creation of Adivasi sub-nationalism.[15] A situation has therefore emerged which has rather posed a challenge before Adivasi society either to find a way towards re-structuring itself in accordance with the 'modern' ethos of democracy or strive to sustain the 'tradition' at the cost of its own peril. While several attributes from 'tradition' are worth preserving, changing society (and the discriminatory practices in customary system) entails the need to adopt democratic institutions (Kumar 2014: 64). A similar conflict of ideologies in the Pathalgadi movement is visible.

The key geographic locations of the Pathalgadi movement had been those where Naxalism[16]was very strong earlier, as reported by a newspaper

(Hindustan, Ranchi, 26 Feb 2018). In fact, the entire Adivasi-dominated regions in Jharkhand saw the emergence of Maoism. Adivasis had no idea of Maoism or its basic ideology, but a favourable response to it was seemingly a way to vent their anger and protest against the failure of the state to remove their backwardness and systematic marginalisation. Adivasi disenchantment with the nationalist discourse of development is visible in the formation of what has been identified as 'Red Corridor.'[17] Gudavarthy argues that the Maoist movement has, through the use of counter-violence, stalled the entry of multi-national companies and has succeeded in stopping any mining activity that involves the displacement of tribal people from proceeding ahead. In beginning with this rather condensed political question, the Maoist movement opened up spaces for political mobilisation and kept the state and capital at bay. It had questioned the legitimacy of the state in monopolising the use of violence to control, govern, and maintain order (2013:70).

However, the Naxal movement began to lose its sheen slowly in tribal regions because it could not give an answer to their problems in the first place and second, instead stopping mining and industrialisation, the Naxal groups started collecting 'Levy' (extortion of money) from the contractors working in the areas and nurtured their political ambitions at the cost of Adivasi sentiments. After the weakening of this movement, Adivasis therefore chose the platform of the GS and social organisations to carry out their struggle (Dungdung 2016: 183–186) for empowerment and challenging the state-sponsored policy of development. Adivasi discourse of development in this way merged into the reinvented institution of village governance symbolised by the GS.

The principal programme of the protagonists of the movement was to put restrictions on the entry of outsiders in the village without the permission of GS,[18] as the latter have been the cause and consequence of the ongoing process of development. This explicates that the protagonists consider Adivasi villages to be autonomous domains; the right of entry is restricted and to be controlled by the GS. Significantly, while choosing the source of legitimacy they deployed the provision of the constitution and not the PESA Act which alone reinforced the concept of *Gram Ganarajya* (Village Republic). But one should ask whether the constitution really accords autonomy to the Fifth Scheduled Areas and puts a blanket ban on the entry of outsiders? The digression seems to be rooted in pre-colonial past when some parts of the Adivasi homeland was *terra incognito* for the outsiders. More so, an outsider could enter and settle in the village founded by the Adivasis on the invitation of the village community headed by the Munda.

Another message is loud and clear. The movement practically seeks to assign the role of the state to the GS in the Pathalgadi villages. But this ignores the fact that drawing power from the Constitution of India and refusing to acknowledge the existence of government is contradictory. In fact, the supporters have tried to challenge the presence of the state. Weekly meetings are organised by the GS at a fixed place between 7.00 and 8.00

a.m. and those matters which have normally gone to courts and police stations since British rule are taken up here. After hearing the matter, a decision is arrived at the GS, and if a person defies its order he/she is ostracised from the village (Dainik Bhaskar, Ranchi, 20 February 2018). They have not only taken judicial role in their hand but GS have also appropriated the works of the administration and are issuing character certificates, caste, income, birth, and death certificates (ibid.). The challenge to the state machinery borders on violence, as mentioned in earlier, by taking police and district officers' hostage and organising *Gheraos* (seige) of police stations (Hindustan, Ranchi, 14 March 2018).

In a recent essay, it has been argued (Kumar 2016) that the grassroot Adivasi movements, in their defiance of the authority of the state and subsequent assumption of the role of governance of the village, are trying to be a bargaining instrument with the state where the community intends to gain the maximum advantage. The movements signal their acceptance of the state by subscribing to an 'accepted' means of protest. Displaying their knowledge of the edifice upon which the modern state is built, they draw on the Constitution to legitimise their demands such as the implementation of laws like Schedule V, Article 244, and so on. Cultural symbols and identity issues are highlighted at the same time to bond the society, as society is, more often than not, reluctant to accept change that may be caused due to the impending effects of commodification of land.

Opposition to the state-sponsored scheme of development was the other prominent agenda. Geeta Samad's statement noted earlier articulates the popular resentment and anguish against the ongoing discourse of development. Two more recent instances are the statements of Gram Pradhans made before the Governor of Jharkhand. In one, Sameer Munda said, '*Gaon mein yojna ke naam par sirf dalali ho rahi hai* (In the name of plan only brokerage is done in the village).' In the other, Damu Munda said, '*Tribal sub plan ka paisa dusre madd mein kharch kiya jaa raha hai* (The funds for tribal sub plan is spend for other purposes).'[19] Announcements are made at the village level by GS, which refuses to take help from such government schemes as *Swachh Bharat Abhiyan* (Clean India Campaign), *Indira Awas Yojna* (Indira Housing Scheme), *Rajiv Gandhi Gram Sadak Yojna* (Rajiv Gandhi Village Road Construction Scheme), and others. Claiming the right of the management of educational institutions by the village is the other important step.[20] Villagers are dissuaded from sending their children to the government schools. Announcements are also made in the villages to abstain from the participation in national festivals and approaching government agencies. Attempts have been made to vandalise the foundation stones laid down by the government for different schemes in the village that have remained incomplete in these areas even after long years (Prabhat Khabar, Ranchi, 24 February 2018; Dainik Bhaskar, Ranchi, 24 February 2018; ibid., 10 March 2018). Initially, only the Fifth Schedule of the Constitution and its favourable provisions for the GS used to be written on one side of the stone slabs painted in green, keeping the other side blank. Now-a-days, on the other side of the stone, the decisions of the GS are being written where voter identity cards and Aadhar cards are declared to be anti-Adivasi documents. It is declared that the Adivasis are not the citizens of India and the lease of non-Adivasi *Diku* government ended in 1969 (Hindustan, Ranchi, 26 February 2018).

These forms of protest definitely go beyond the urge of sub-nationalism. Challenge to the mainstream, rather Hindu mainstream, is manifest in the imposition of fines to the tune of Rs. 500 from the villagers for visiting a Durga Puja Mela. With this intention, a meeting was organised at Ulidih (birthplace of Birsa Munda, famous leader of the Mundas who gave violent resistance to British rule) in South Arki, which was reportedly attended by thousands. The incidence of 21 February 2018, cited in the introduction, has become a morale booster for the Adivasis (ibid.). In this background, Adivasi Mahasabha's declaration to practise Pathalgadi in their respective villages has emerged as a strong wave of resentment against the state, which is absent from all aspects of people-friendly governance and omnipresent in dispossession and exploitation.

The Pathalgadi movement is not however a uniform and encompassing movement. The ideological contradictions in the movement are visible in almost every step taken by the protagonists of the movement. They dismiss the Constitution of India as an alien construct; contrarily they display that GS derives authority from the Fifth Schedule of the Constitution.[21] They arrogate the role of government and yet demand 100percent reservations for Adivasis in government employment, railways, and airways. They put restrictions on the entry of outsiders in their area and passing of even a Ram-navmi procession (Celebration of Lord Rama's birthday) from the village without the permission of GS, but they refuse to accept that their movement outside the village can be restricted on similar logic (Hindustan, Ranchi, 26 March 2018). This apparent contradiction is explained by Gladson Dundung, a protagonist of the movement, who bases the logical premise of this action on the argument that, as the entry of Adivasis in certain restricted areas in cities is prohibited for the safety of certain government installations, so the entry of 'outsiders' is restricted in the villages for the safety of *Jal, Jungle, Jameen* (water, forest, and land).[22]

To assume that the entire agenda of the movement is supported by all the Adivasis of the area is also a misinterpretation of facts.[23] In fact, the present nature of Pathalgadi assuming the garb of tradition is questioned by the educated and conscious Adivasi leaders and people. They are not opposed to the development schemes of the government. The Mankis and Mundas of Adivasi villages of other districts of Jharkhand except Khunti are also not in conformity with the present nature of the movement. There is non-acceptance of the demands in some villages of Khunti as well (Hindustan, 12 March 2018; Hindustan, 14 March 2018; Dainik Bhaskar, 27 February 2018). Presumably, the issue has flared up in a very short span of time because all the political parties are trying to take over the leadership of the Adivasis before the next Parliamentary elections. They therefore resort to interpreting history and institutions, and they seek to look at the immediate problem often overlooking the larger issue of poverty and backwardness of the region from the historical perspective.

Responses of the mainstream[24]

The response of the mainstream to the Pathalgadi movement has been ambivalent. NGOs working in these areas, and run particularly by the ideologue activists like Sanjay Bosu Mullick, have been favourable. Pathalgadi, according to Bosu Mullick, is practised only in Mundari Khuntkatti (land that was cleared by primeval settlers) villages of the Khunti district. According to him, in the entire Ranchi and Khunti districts, there are only 156 villages where the communal ownership of land prevails (Hindustan, Ranchi, 25 February 2018). He argues that the movement does not target outsiders per se. Rather it is directed against the entry of those outsiders who come to measure the land without the permission of the GS. Measuring land is symbolic of the government's interest in the Adivasi land for putting up projects against the will of the people.

There is yet a section of intellectuals who try to defend the movement. They believe that it is the state that is immune to both the real and perceived 'crisis of legitimacy.' In fact, the crisis of legitimacy understood in terms of democratic practice is seen as a modality, a precondition, through which state absolutism is actualised. This is somewhat akin to capitalism today, which expands in growth and development, not bereft of crisis but precisely because of crisis (Gudavarthy 2013: 71). The movements that are local, autonomous, non-violent, and open define the way we understand democracy today. All this is happening amidst the fact that Adivasi societies are heterogeneous and the entire Adivasi community does not perceive the state similarly. Their action ranges from complete alienation and armed resistance to the strategic use of non-violent methods and customary practices for accruing political benefits.

On the other hand, the newspapers, social media, and regional television, who have given wide publicity to the movement through regular reporting, are more or less critical. They criticise it for conspiring to create a parallel government in the village under the garb of tradition and misrepresentation of the Constitution. The movement, in their perception, is therefore retrograde and anti-development.[25]

The state government has completely brushed aside the professed ideology of the Adivasis and critiqued the Pathalgadi movement for blatant misrepresentation and 'mis'using of the customary laws and traditional practices of Adivasis. No wonder, therefore, has the Jharkhand government dismissed the movement as insignificant, labelled it as anti-development, and resorted to giving advertisements in dailies and billboards, declaring the acts of Pathalgadi illegal and anti-government. As the movement grew and people in the villages of Khunti joined the movement, government agencies imputed that the real motive of the leaders of the movement is more the lure of economic benefits rather than the welfare of Adivasis. In support, the state administration points to the vast stretches of land in the Pathalgadi area used for opium cultivation.[26] It is estimated that opium is cultivated in 2,700 acres of land in Jharkhand, of which 1,500 acres (i.e., almost 58 percent of total area) is in the Khunti district alone.[27] The opium produced is allegedly transported to Punjab, Chennai, Uttar Pradesh, and other parts of India. The administration argues that this has been the main reason is why the leaders are invoking tradition as a shield and propagating the idea of complete autonomy to the villages. No wonder the movement is castigated as a law and order issue. Therefore, the leaders have been charged of secession and their arrests made. In the recent past, Krishna Hansda, Vijay Kujur, Jyoti Lal Besera, and Shaktapado Hansda have been arrested and charged of treason (Hindustan, 19 March 2018).

The pressure of the democratic politics however forced the state government and the ruling party to soften their attitude. The Governor of Jharkhand, Draupadi Murmu, called a special meeting of the Gram Pradhans, Manki Munda, and Parha Rajas on 3 April 2018 to discuss the issues of contention in the Scheduled Areas (ibid.; Ranchi, 3 April 2018). She honoured them by giving shawls and *Pugries* (turban) and tried to be associated with them by saying that she herself is the daughter and granddaughter of Gram Pradhan and that she therefore understands the social set up of the Adivasis (Hindustan, Ranchi, 4 April 2018). However, at the same time, a caution was extended to them to situate their demands within the framework of the constitution. Clearly, the government is conscious of the sensitiveness of the issue of the governance of the Scheduled Areas, the customary rights of the Adivasis, and the perceptible difference in the ideology of development that has been reflected in the course of the movement.

Concluding remarks

Thus, it becomes clear that the Pathalgadi movement has developed as a popular form of Adivasi protest in the Scheduled Areas of Jharkhand where they have more or less lost hope of development through the state. This puts forth two claims of the villagers, the right to be governed by their historically developed distinct form of village governance and the right to be developed as per other developed regions of the country. Undoubtedly, the movement lays bare Adivasi resistance against land expropriation, displacement, and environmental degradation. The movement also underlines the need to formulate and implement a pro-Adivasi and a participatory form of development in which village mechanisms will have a decisive role. In support, historical symbols, tradition, and moments of pride are appropriated. The glorious past of Adivasi heroism and defiance of the authority is referred to create a sense of solidarity amongst the Adivasis. Interestingly, in tandem, the protagonists invoke the Indian Constitution but manipulate it to suit their activism. Clearly, the movement responds to the widespread dissensions within the Adivasi community. But its aggressive and anti-state/nation programme does not receive wide support. In the context of the present movement, the urgent need is the dispassionate reappraisal of the mode of village governance in function after the Panchayat elections so that this may become meaningful and is able to serve the people for which this is meant.

Notes

1 Dainik Bhaskar, Ranchi, 22 February 2018.
2 Visit, www.timesofindia.com, accessed on 9 April 2018.
3 By May 2017 projects worth 30.5 crore were opened in Bokaro, Gumla and Ranchi. Textile, footwear and apparel park worth 200 crores was opened in Ranchi, Visit, www.timesofindia.com, Accessed on 9 April 2018. By August 2017, 74 projects were started in the state which were expected to bring Rs. 2100 crores and generate over 10,000 jobs (Daily Pioneer, 5 October 2017). Visit www.dailypioneer.com, accessed on 13 April 2018.
4 My research is based on field study conducted in Bhandra, PhutkalToli, Zillinga, Belahathi, and Kochang villages in November 2017 and February 2018. During personal interviews with the residents of the village, many villagers were refraining from providing information or interacting with the author and they viewed every outsider with suspicion. One of the respondents accused the researcher having personal agenda, i.e. spying for the government and being paid for the job. What was palpable was that the fear of land alienation that was visible in November 2017 had transformed into anger and distrust for outsiders by February 2018.
5 In this chapter, unless the context otherwise requires, 'Law' includes any ordinance, order, by law, rule, regulation, notification, custom, or usage having in the territory of India the force of law.
6 Article 19 (5) of Indian Constitution, 'Nothing in sub clause (d) and (e) of the said clause shall affect the operation of any existing law in so far as it imposes or prevent the state from making any law imposing, reasonable restrictions on the exercise of any of the rights conferred by the said sub clause either in the interest of any scheduled tribe.' Article 19 (6) says, 'Nothing in the sub clause (g) of the said clause shall affect the operation of any existing law in so far as it imposes or prevents the state from making any law imposing in the interest of the general public, reasonable restrictions on the exercise of the rights conferred by the said sub clause shall affect the operation of any existing law in so far as it relates to and prevent the state from making any law.'
7 The provision of the Fifth Schedule shall apply to the administration and control of the Scheduled Areas and Scheduled Tribes in any state other than state of Assam and Meghalaya.
8 There are 32 tribal communities that reside in the state and Pathalgadi movement is strong in Munda Khuntkatti areas of Ranchi and Khunti districts and among the Oraons.
9 Such words as *Rurhi Pratha Prakritik Panchayat* are used on stone slabs of Kochang, Belahathi, Kurunga, and other villages of Khunti. But this is missing

from the stone slab of Bhandra village, the place of origin and centre of the movement, shown earlier.

10 The Provisions of The Panchayats (Extension to the Scheduled Areas) Act, 1996, No.40 of 1996(24 December 1996).

11 Bill No. 93-F of 2010, Original. The Jharkhand Panchayat Raj (Amendment) Bill, 2010. (As Passed by the Houses of Parliament – Lok Sabha on 17 August, 2010, Rajya Sabha on 25 August, 2010).

12 My conversations, group meetings, and personal interviews were carried mostly in the affected areas of Khunti district of South Arki, namely Bhandra, Phutkal Toli, Zillinga, Belahathi, and Kochang between November 2017 and February 2018.

13 The idea of village governance is vague and although researchers and scholars are trying to study the institution of Parha Panchayat, there is no clear idea amongst the Adivasis themselves about the original form and structure of the institution.

14 Jharkhand was a part of Bihar till year 2000 and by 1900 it was part of Bengal Presidency.

15 Sati-Pati movement is a movement to create Adivasi nationalism in India. This organisation has its headquarters in Kathsavana village of Tapi district in Gujarat. It was built by Dada Kunwar Keshari Singh in 1930 and the organisations that adhere to its principles believe that it is the Government of India. Adivasi Mahasabha adheres to it and is active in Jharkhand, Gujarat, Chhattisgarh, Madhya Pradesh, and Rajasthan. The organisations that are also a part of it are 'Adivasi Pariwar Rajasthan,' 'Bhil Autonomous Council,' 'Birsa Brigade, Madhya Pradesh,' 'Sarv Adivasi Samaj, Chhattisgarh,' 'Manjhi Pargana Mahal, East Singhbhum,' and others.

16 An agrarian movement was started from a village called Naxalbari in West Bengal in 1970s.

17 The Naxal-affected states of India which are deeply forested terrain and are primarily inhabited by the Adivasis are known as *red corridor*. The red colour of the flag of Maoists is generally referred to indicate the presence of Naxals in the area.

18 Villagers were interviewed on 15 November 2017 in Bhandra and Zillinga Village; also reported in a newspaper Dainik Bhaskar, 10 March 2018, Ranchi.

19 Hindustan, 4 April 2018.

20 There are videos on the internet and news in the local and regional dailies that the Adivasis have taken their education into their own hands and teaching the basic idea of protest to their children in these school in Hindi. This blatant overlooking of the indigenous language, which is a store house of the ancestral knowledge and is deeply connected to their ethnic identity, indicates that the motive of the protagonist of the government is to create a semblance of defiance than actually intending to revive their age-old institutions.

21 The speakers of 25 February 2018 meeting of the Adivasis at Kochang village in Khunti expressed these sentiments that were repeated by many in the following days. Dainik Bhaskar, Ranchi, 26 February 2018.

22 Gladson Dungdung, 'Pathalgadi aur Pravesh Nisedh', http://saathijohaar.com/2018/04/08/paththargari.html. (accessed on 8 April 2018).

23 Ibid. 15 March 2018. It was reported that to counter the present movement, a programme was organised in the native village of Jaipal Singh Munda, Takra in Khunti, which was supported by the government. In this programme the heroes of tribal movements of Jharkhand as Birsa Munda were remembered, and their contributions and sacrifices were cited to depict that the present movement negates their contribution, which helped India in gaining independence, by saying that India is not a free state.

24 Mainstream in the present context refers to the non-Adivasis residing in the state, government, media agencies, and NGOs.
25 See Newspapers of Ranchi esp., Prabhat Khabar, Dainik Bhaskar, Hindustan, 20 February; 22 February; 25 February; 26 February; 9 March; 10 March 2018.
26 As reported by Dainik Bhaskar, Ranchi on 6 March 2018, Adivasi Mahasabha and its supporters countered this attack by claiming that the illegal opium trade in the state has been practised for a decade, when Naxalism was a strong force in the area, but the movement has started in the last year. Dainik Bhaskar, Ranchi, 16 March 2018.
27 *Ibid.* it is estimated that almost 30 to 40 kilogram of opium is produced from an acre of land. Each kilo of opium is sold on the international market for Rs. 1,040,000.

References

Bill No. 93-F of 2010, Original. The Jharkhand Panchayat Raj (Amendment) Bill, 2010. (As Passed by the Houses of Parliament – Lok Sabha on 17 August, 2010, Rajya Sabha on 25 August, 2010).

Corbridge, S. 2003. 'The Ideology of Tribal Economy and Society: Politics in the Jharkhand 1950–1980.' In R. Dayal Munda and S. Bosu Mullick (Eds.), *The Jharkhand Movement: Indigenous People's Struggle for Autonomy in India* (pp. 131–170). Copenhagen: IWGIA Document No 108, International Work Group For Indigenous Affair.

Dungdung, G.2016. *Adivasi Aur Vanadhikar: Jharkhand Mein Van Adhikar Ka Jamini Haqueqat*. New Delhi: Prithvi Prakashan.

Foucault, M. 1974. *Archaeology of Knowledge*. London: Tavistock Publications.

Gudavarthy, A.2013, 'Democracy Against Maoism, Maoism Against Itself.' *Economic and Political Weekly*, xlviiI(7), February 16: 69–76.

Hallett, M.G. 1917. *Bihar and Orissa District Gazetteers: Ranchi*. Patna: Superintendent, Government Printing, Bihar and Orissa.

Hunter, W.W. 1975. *Annals of Rural Bengal*. New Delhi: Cosmo Publication.

Interview with the villagers of Bhandra on 15 November 2017.

Interview with the villagers of Kochang on 17 February 2018.

Interview with the villagers of Zillinga on 16 November 2017.

Kumar, S. 2014. 'Interrogating "Integration" in Adivasi Discourse: Customary vs. Democratic Institutions in West Singhbhum, Jharkhand.' *Journal of Adivasi and Indigenous Studies*, I(1), August. ISSN 2394–5524.

Kumar, S. 2016. *Revisiting Anti-Dispossession Resistance Movements*. Available at: www.india-seminar.com/2016/682/682_sujit_kumar.htm (accessed on 13 April 2018).

Nora, P. Spring 1989. 'Between Memory and History: Les Lieux de Memoire.' *Representations*, 26:7–25.

Prakash, A.2001. *Jharkhand: Politics of Development and Identity*. New Delhi: Orient Longman.

The Provisions of the Panchayats (Extension to the Scheduled Areas) ACT, 1996 No. 40 of 1996 (24 December 1996).

Ranendra. 2008. 'Bhumika: Jharkhandi Itihas Ke Bare Mein.' In Ranendra and S. Pal (Eds.), *Jharkhand Encyclopaedia*, Vol. I (pp. 11–17). New Delhi: Vani Prakshan.

Roy, S.C. 1970. *The Mundas and Their Country*. Calcutta: Asia Publishing House.

Scott, J. 1990. 'Everyday Forms of Peasant Resistance.' In J.C. Scott and B.J.T. Kerkvliet (Eds.), *Everyday Forms of Peasant Resistance in South-East Asia* (pp. 5–35). London: Frank Cass.

Sen, A.K. 2015. 'Reconstructing Adivasi Village History: Problems and Possibilities.' *Journal of Adivasi and Indigenous Studies*, 3(2), August: 16–37.

Sen, A.K. 2018. *Indigeneity, Landscape and History: Adivasi Self Fashioning in India*. New York: Routledge.

Sinku, V. 2008. 'Parampara Ki Svasasi Vyavastha.' In S. Pal (Ed.), *Jharkhand Encyclopaedia*, Vol. III. New Delhi: Vani Prakashan.

Sundar, N. 2005. '"Custom" and "Democracy" in Jharkhand.' *Economic and Political Weekly*, 40(41), October8–14: 4430–4434.

Tete, V. 2013. *Adivasi Sahitya: Parampara Aur Prayojana*. Ranchi: Pyara Kerketta Foundation.

Tirkey, A. 2002. *Jharkhand Movement*. New Delhi: All India Coordinating Forum of the Adivasi/ Indigenous People.

Xaxa, V. 1999. 'Transformation of Tribes in India: Terms of Discourse.' *Economic and Political Weekly*, 34(24): 1519–1524.

Xaxa, V. 2010. '"Tribes, Tradition and State", 18, The Focus: "Indigenous" India.' *The Newsletter*, No. 53, Spring 2010.

List of newspapers

Daily pioneer (digital edition).
Dainik Bhaskar.
Hindustan.
Prabhat Khabar.
Times of India (digital edition).

Index

Note: Page numbers followed by 'n' refer to notes.

For Product Safety Concerns and Information please contact our EU representative GPSR@taylorandfrancis.com
Taylor & Francis Verlag GmbH, Kaufingerstraße 24, 80331 München, Germany

www.ingramcontent.com/pod-product-compliance
Ingram Content Group UK Ltd.
Pitfield, Milton Keynes, MK11 3LW, UK
UKHW011006180926
475701UK00004B/600
* 9 7 8 0 3 6 7 7 8 5 1 1 6 *